THE

INTERPRETATION OF NATURE

IN ENGLISH POETRY

AMS PRESS
NEW YORK

THE

INTERPRETATION OF NATURE

IN ENGLISH POETRY

FROM *BEOWULF* TO SHAKESPEARE

BY

FREDERIC W. MOORMAN

OF THE UNIVERSITY OF LEEDS.

> ... and a' babbled of green fields.
> *Henry V.*, ii, 3.

STRASSBURG.

KARL J. TRÜBNER.

1905.

Library of Congress Cataloging in Publication Data

Moorman, Frederic William, 1872-1919.
    The interpretation of nature in English poetry from
Beowulf to Shakespeare.

    Original ed. issued as v. 95 of Quellen und
Forschungen zur Sprach- und Culturgeschichte der
germanischen Völker.
    1. Nature in poetry. 2. English poetry--History
and criticism. I. Title. II. Series: Quellen und
Forschungen zur Sprach- und Culturgeschichte der
germanischen Völker, v. 95.
PR508.N3M6 1972   821'.009'36   78-172741
ISBN 0-404-04398-4

Reprinted from the edition of 1905, Strasburg
First AMS edition published in 1972
Manufactured in the United States of America

AMS PRESS INC.
NEW YORK,N.Y. 10003

PREFACE.

The poetic interpretation of Nature is a province of æsthetics and literary criticism which has attracted to itself many exploring minds since Alexander von Humboldt first marked out its territories in the second volume of his *Kosmos*. In Germany the subject has, within the last twenty five years, received masterly and comprehensive treatment at the hands of Alfred Biese, who, in his two works, *Die Entwickelung des Naturgefühls bei den Griechen und den Römern* (1884), and *Die Entwickelung des Naturgefühls im Mittelalter und in der Neuzeit* (1887), has followed the main course of his theme from the Homeric poems to the romantic school of the nineteenth century. In England, at the very time when Humboldt, "in the late evening of an active life", was analysing the feelings which the contemplation of Nature has awakened in the hearts of the world's poets and painters, John Ruskin, newly come from student life at Oxford, found himself, while at work upon the Fourth Part of *Modern Painters*, engaged in the similar task of interpreting to his readers the nature of landscape art in classical, mediæval, and modern times.

The determination on the part of Humboldt, Ruskin and Biese, and more recently of Francis Turner Palgrave[1]), to regard the ancient and modern world, when looked at from the standpoint of the poetic interpretation of Nature, as "one great confederation" is of immense value to the student of

---

[1]) *Landscape in Poetry from Homer to Tennyson;* London, 1897.

poetry. But such a comprehensive view does not render useless the more limited and more specialised study of the poetry of a single people or literature. The work of the late Professor Veitch, *The Feeling for Nature in Scottish Poetry*, has shown that the subject can be made interesting when looked at from the point of view of a single literature; while numerous essays and dissertations, dealing with the Nature-poetry of individual poets, have also been of value in extending the bounds of knowledge, and enabling us to get nearer to the heart of poetry.

The aim of the present volume is to trace the development of the interpretation of Nature in English poetry from its beginning onwards to the Elizabethan age and the works of Shakespeare. I have endeavoured, as far as the compass of my theme permitted, to secure a certain unity of treatment, and to indicate the influence of one poet upon another, and of one period of poetry upon succeeding periods. At the same time I have recognised that Nature is an open book, from the pages of which every poet who will may read, and I have accordingly been unwilling to ascribe to literary influence whatever may have been sought and found in a poet's direct contemplation of the world around him.

It remains for me only to offer my grateful thanks to a former teacher and present friend and colleague, Professor C. H. Herford, who has furthered the work by valuable advice and suggestions, and has read a considerable portion of it in manuscript.

F. W. M.

Leeds, March, 1905.

CONTENTS.

Chapter I.

BEOWULF.

The poetic interpretation of Nature, like its interpretation at the hands of landscape painters, has, during the last century and a half, made so rapid and far-reaching a progress in England that an attempt to trace the growth of this interpretation may be regarded as a fitting subject of literary criticism. Our English poets, from Old English times onwards, have lived nearer to Nature than those of any other nation of modern Europe. In our earliest poetry, as the following pages will show, the external universe is rarely absent from the thought of the wandering gleeman, and though epochs occur in which an interest in man and in society becomes paramount, Nature rarely disappears entirely from view. Finally, in those periods of reaction when a return to Nature becomes the aim of poetry, it is found that England assumes the lead and directs the movement in the first stages of its progress. The important position which Nature has held in English poetry since the times of James Thomson has encouraged the belief that the poetic interpretation of Nature began in the eighteenth century, and that the earlier poets either neglected the natural world entirely, or found interest in it only in as far as it supplied them with a modest stage-scenery of green fields, smiling gardens and purling streams. One main object of the present enquiry is to show that this is not the case. The following chapters are concerned with English poetry from its first beginnings in the epic lay down to the age of Skakespeare, and the writer's purpose is to show that within this period there is such a thing as Nature-poetry, and that the poetic interpretation of Nature passes through certain well-marked stages.

For the clearer understanding of what is to follow, it is advisable, at the outset, to define, as exactly as possible, what is here meant, first of all, by Nature, and, secondly, by the poetic interpretation of Nature. The word Nature has been used in preference to landscape, because of its wider connotation. For landscape, even when understood so as to include what painters call seascape, as well as the aerial world above us, is too much concerned with contour, colour and grouping to take cognisance of those underlying modes of poetic interpretation wherein the natural world is conceived in its relation to man, or in its relation to God, or, finally, as an independent being endowed with a life and consciousness of its own. These are all subjects which call for consideration in such a study as the present, and for this reason the more comprehensive word Nature has been adopted.

By Nature, then, is here understood all that belongs to the outer world of sense-perception which is not man or the immediate work of man. The line of cleavage between external Nature on the one hand, and man and human enterprise on the other, is easily recognisable in spite of the fact that it is sometimes difficult to distinguish between the works of man and the works of Nature. Man, as the planter of trees, the hewer of wood and stone and the drawer of water, has the power of changing to a certain extent the face of Nature: yet, even where his work in this direction seems most important, achievement is possible only in so far as he can assist the forces of Nature. Thus even where he seems to frustrate natural design, he does so only by enabling other natural powers to come into play, and therefore we may say that the planted forest and the so-called artificial lake are to a far greater degree the work of Nature than of man. A reference to this interaction of Nature and man is in place here because of the fact that at certain stages in the growth of the poetic interpretation of Nature, and in certain poets in all stages, the chief appreciation of Nature has been directed especially to those objects of the natural world — the garden, the park etc. — in which human workmanship is detected.

Defining Nature, therefore, as the outer world of sense-perception which lies apart from man, it remains to be seen what is meant by the *poetic* interpretation of Nature. The poet's interest in the natural world is neither that of the agriculturist nor that of the scientist. A farmerly interest in Nature appears, it is true, in early poetry, and, as has been abundantly shown by Ruskin and others, is very pronounced in the *Odyssey*. Yet, inasmuch as such an attitude implies that the contemplation of Nature is not an end in itself, and that the utility rather than the beauty or sublimity of the universe is in view, it cannot rightly be called a poetic interpretation. For the poet's appreciation of Nature is æsthetic and not utilitarian : he loves Nature for its own sake and for the thoughts which the contemplation of it evokes, nor is he in any way concerned with the marketable value of a forest of oak-trees, or the water-dues of a mountain stream. Again, the poet's interpretation of Nature is not that of the scientist. Cause and effect, which are the concern of science, interest the poet, if at all, only indirectly. The poet is interested in natural form and colour, yet concerns himself but little with morphology; he takes note of the life and growth of things, but does not enter into their physiology. The scientist is engaged in the search after truth, the poet in the search after beauty : and in this instance the true and the beautiful are not one. At the same time, the poet finds himself at liberty to make the fullest use of scientific discovery, and to find therein manifestations of beauty which have escaped the notice of the scientist. That he has up to the present held himself somewhat aloof from science, and at times maintained that the scientist murders to dissect, is no argument to prove that such will always be the case, or to deny the existence of the raw material of poetry in the fruits of scientific research. Surely from out of the brazen world of the scientist the poet will one day deliver a gólden.

Further, while the poet is primarily concerned with

beauty, the poetic interpretation of Nature is often a great deal more than the quest of the sensuously beautiful. Those who have lived nearest to Nature, for example, the poets of the Vedic Hymns and the Sanscrit epics, or in modern times Wordsworth, Goethe and Shelley, have not been content to remain mere descriptive poets, expressing in rhythmic language the outward forms of things. They have sought to probe the arcana of Nature, and to enter into spiritual communion with the universe. At such times Nature has not been conceived merely as a congeries of physical objects — mountain, stream, wood and sea — but as an indivisible whole which is not material but spiritual; which is not the tree, but is in the tree; which is not the flood, but is in the flood. Thus conceived, the poetic interpretation acquires a metaphysical interest which lies beyond the region of æsthetics. The poet's philosophy, whether concerned with Nature or with any other field of thought, is, of course, mainly of an intuitional order. There is no place for the syllogism in poetry, and the conceptions which the poet would have us accept as truths are the result, not of logical reasoning, but of the working of the intuition. Intuitional, therefore, is the poet's conception of pantheism, and intuitional, again, is Wordsworth's idea of the marriage of Nature und humanity.

There is no need to devote here any attention to the psychological analysis of a poet's feeling for natural beauty, or to show how it is that a curved line seems more beautiful than a straight one, or that what the eye takes special delight in is that rich variety of form and colour in Nature which is at the same time subservient to a certain unity of design. This is a topic which has been fully dealt with by Ruskin, Veitch and others, and needs therefore no consideration here. Something, however, must be said in reference to the attempts which have been made to trace the poetic interpretation of Nature through a number of clearly marked stages of development. It has been said[1]) that the earliest

---

[1]) See especially Veitch, *The Feeling for Nature in Scottish Poetry,* Chap. I.

stage in the appreciation of Nature by man is that of a
simple organic feeling of pleasure called forth by genial
sunshine and refreshing shower, corresponding with which
is an equally simple organic feeling of pain in the presence of
chilling wind and driving snow. Next to this, it is argued,
comes, in an ascending scale, the appreciation of the physic-
ally beneficent forces in Nature, and again of those which
are recognised as conducive to utility. Still higher in the
scale, a place is found for the naïve appreciation of certain
aspects of Nature for their own sakes; and this, we may
assume, would be the point at which the poetic interest
would first appear. At last, with advancing civilisation and
the growth of man's faculty for appreciation, a point is
reached where the sympathetic interpretation of Nature comes
into view, when Nature is brought into relationship with
man, and is also regarded as furnishing symbols and analogies to human conduct and human aspiration.

Now it is no doubt possible to trace such a development of the
feeling for Nature in the literature of the Romance peoples,
such as the French or Italians, with whom literary expression begins at a time when a comparatively high state of
civilisation has been reached; but it is impossible to do
this in the case of the Teutonic nations, whose literature,
whether older or not than that of the Romance nations,
reveals conditions of life and attitudes of the human mind
towards Nature which are of a much more primitive character.
The supposition that the starting-point of man's appreciation
of Nature is to be found in his recognition of certain
natural forces as organically pleasurable, useful, or beneficent, may or may not be true: but what is certainly true
is that Nature appealed to something higher in primitive
man than the mere feelings of pleasure and pain. Nature
with its strange and silent changes from night to day, and
from winter to summer; or Nature in its wild moods of
tempest and thunderstorm, awakened in him a sentiment
of wonder and awe. These in their turn begot worship, and
worship led directly to the personifying of the forces of
Nature and the creation of a theogony. Most myths are in

their origin nature-myths, and the establishment of nature-myths presupposes the worship of the forces of Nature. At a later period mythical personifications assume an ethical character, but this is not original: the ethical conception has grown out of the physical. Woden is the personification of the sky and of aerial phenomena before he becomes the dispenser of justice; Freyja is the personification of Nature's fruitfulness before she becomes the goddess of love.

It is, therefore, manifest that at a very early period in a nation's history the natural forces which surrounded man, and which influenced his life in so marked a manner, became the objects first of wonder, and then of worship. In the case of the English nation it is impossible to determine the period at which the worship of these natural forces first attained to literary expression and found a place in poetry. The oldest English poetry now extant, which is also the oldest poetry of the Teutonic race, reveals an age when the mythical conception of Nature was rapidly passing away. Yet the peculiar mental attitude towards the natural world which the primitive myths called into being lived on after the myths themselves had disappeared, and must always be taken into account in any study of Old English literature.

Moreover, it is to be borne in mind that not only a worship but also a philosophy of Nature belongs to a very early period in a nation's life. It would seem indeed that the one is the natural result of the other. The creation of a theogony in a mythopœic age is followed in due course by the construction of a cosmogony. Having deified the forces of Nature, primitive man proceeds next of all to render an account of the origin and development of the world which he sees around him.

The Vedic Hymns bring us face to face with a system of pantheistic thought of the most abstract and elaborate character, in which the early Hindoo discovers a meaning in life and in the world, and traces these backwards to their ultimate source. In like manner, but with less abstraction of thought, the early Teuton sought to interpret the forms and

forces of the natural world, and to unravel the origin of
these as well as of himself. In the Younger Edda of Snorri
Sturluson we are told that the beginning of all animated
life was the cow Authumla, from whom sprang the giant
Ymir. The cow, under the figure of which we are to understand the clouds which give moisture and fruitfulness to
the earth, licked the blocks of ice which lay in the vast
chaotic abyss of Ginnungagap, and from the warmth thus
produced sprang Buri, the father of Borr, and the grand-
father of Odin, Wili and We. These sons of Borr then slew
the giant Ymir, and from his dead body sprang the physical
world. His blood formed the sea and streams, his flesh the
land, his bones the mountains, his hair the woods, his skull
the heavens, and his brain the clouds.[1]) Another, and probably later, version of the creation-story, current among the
early Teutonic peoples, and set forth in the Voluspa-saga,
conceives of the beginning of all things as a mighty tree,
the ash-tree Yggdrasil, in the branches of which dwell the
goat, the stag, the hawk, the eagle, the dragon, and the
squirrel. Such conceptions of a cosmogony as the above cannot
be wholly ignored in such a study as the present one, for
they show that in the remotest periods of Teutonic life of
which we have any cognisance, men were not content
simply to take the world as they found it, but in conceiving
of a mythical theogony and a cosmogony, endeavoured to
establish both Nature-worship and a philosophy of Nature.

The unique position which the poem of *Beowulf* occupies
in the history of English literature makes a study of its
Nature-poetry peculiarly interesting. The pictures of land and
sea which are found in it are limited in range, but they are
characterised by great vividness and imaginative power. As
in the Homeric poems and epic poetry generally, the scenery

---

[1]) See E. Mogk, Mythologie, in Pauls *Grundriß der germanischen
Philologie.* I. 1112.

is introduced as a background to human action and not for
its own sake; but at the same time the interpretation of
Nature is not wholly objective in character. The intimate
relationship which the primitive Teuton recognised as
existing between Nature and man finds frequent expression
in _Beowulf_; there is no spiritless literalism in the outlining
of a landscape, but everything is touched with imagination.
Moreover, if the poem shows no direct trace of a pantheistic
conception of Nature, the attitude of the poet is nevertheless
that of one who recognises in the natural world the hiding-
places of vast Titanic powers. The mythopœic age of the
Teutonic race had not wholly vanished when this epic was
fashioned into its present form.

For the most part, the forces of Nature are represented
in _Beowulf_ as standing in hostility to human endeavour —
a representation which is fully in keeping with the ceaseless
struggle with the elements which the dwellers by northern
seas were ever waging. The poem tells us little of sunshine
or summer calm; instead of these, we meet with wintry
cold, darkness and raging storm. The element which is introduced most frequently into these descriptions of Nature
is the sea. The sea is near at hand in each of Beowulf's
three undertakings, and also plays an important part in many
of the episodes introduced into the main story. In all these
sea-pictures the tempestuousness of the sea is the prevailing
theme; what the poet loves best of all to depict is the sea
beating against "the wind-swept cliffs" and lashing the nesses
with its wintry surge. If its wild fury is restrained at all,
it is only when the bitter winter chains the waves with
fetters of ice:

> holm storme weol,
> won wiþ winde; winter yþe beleac
> is-gebinde.　　　　　　　_Beowulf,_ 1132—1134.

The sea is made to appear yet more terrible by the
frequent reference to the monsters which lurk in its depths
and wage deadly feud with mankind. We hear on more
than one occasion of nickors, sea-dragons and sea-beasts.
When Beowulf tells the story of his swimming-match with

Breca, we are informed that besides the welter of the waves, the icy cold and the darkness, there were sea-monsters to encounter. "The anger of the sea-fish was roused" are his words as he narrates his hand-to-hand conflict with one of these "hateful robbers":

> Þa wit ætsomne on sæ wæron
> fif nihta fyrst, oþ þæt unc flod todraf,
> wado weallende, wedera cealdost,
> nipende niht ond norþan wind
> heaþo-grim andhwearf; hreo wæron yþa.
> Wæs mere-fixa mod onhrered:
> þær me wiþ laþum lic-syrce min,
> heard hond-locen, helpe gefremede;
> beado-hrægl broden on breostum læg,
> golde gegyrwed. Me to grunde teah
> fah feond-scaþa, fæste hæfde
> grim on grape: hwæþre me gyfeþe wearþ,
> þæt ic aglæcan orde geræhte,
> hilde-bille; heaþo-ræs fornam
> mihtig mere-deor þurh mine hand.   544—558.

The terrors of the sea are further enhanced by the gloomy mists which enshroud the billows and threaten the bold voyager who, in his foamy-necked ship, seeks to win his way across the waters and overcome the battling of the waves. But while these pictures of the sea are fraught with whatever is wild and destructive, it would be wrong to suppose that the poet shrank from the sea in cowering fear; the close intimacy with sea-life which is everywhere disclosed, and the imaginative power revealed in these descriptions are in themselves proofs of the contrary. The prevailing mood of the poet — and, indeed, of the people whose spokesman he is — is one of grim exultation awakened by the sense of man's victory over this unwearying foe, combined with which there is also manifest an æsthetic feeling called forth by the poet's sense of the grandeur and sublimity of an ocean storm. The mood of the Viking seizes upon the gleeman, and he lingers fondly over the details of his pictures. The keen interest and delight of the *Beowulf*-poet, and of Old-English poets generally, in the ever-changing face of the ocean is revealed in the rich

profusion of imagery which he lavishes upon his descriptions
of it. The metaphorical *kennings* employed by the Beowulf-
poet in his sea-pictures,[1]) while they serve to indicate the
strain of rhetorical fancifulness already present in the
earliest English poetry, also betoken the closest observation.
The sea is the whale-road *(hronrad)*, the swan-road *(swanrad)*,
or the gannet's bath *(ganotes bæþ)*, while the ship is the
swimming-wood *(sundwudu)* or the foamy-necked floater *(flota
famigheals)*. Lastly, it must be borne in mind that there is a
dramatic fitness in this background of sea-storm. The theme
of *Beowulf*, even beyond that of most epics, is one of conflict.
The hero's fight with Grendel is at once followed by that
with Grendel's mother; then the fifty years of peace are passed
over without comment, and we are straightway brought to the
dragon-encounter with which the poem ends. To have placed
such an epic of struggle against a background of peaceful seas
and summer sunshine would have been strangely incongruous:
as it is, the animation of the work is in part sustained by
this accompaniment of sea-tempest and wintry weather.

It is a noticeable feature in the poet's seascapes that
we are never far from land: the open sea with no land in
sight is, in fact, never painted by him. Accordingly, we
find that the shore and the stretch of country behind the
shore is almost as fully described as the sea itself. The
coast-scenery of *Beowulf*, whether the occasion be the fight
with Grendel's mother in the land of the Hring-Danes, or
the later fight with the dragon in Geatland, is formed of
clear-shining cliffs with beetling nesses, while behind these
are the moor-fastnesses, covered with treacherous swamps.
Some discussion has arisen with regard to the character of
the spot at which the fight with Grendel's mother takes
place, the determination of which decides whether we are
to regard Beowulf's adversaries as monsters of the sea or
of the inland fen. There can be little doubt, as Mr. Stopford
Brooke has pointed out,[2]) that they are sea-monsters, and

---

[1]) See Heinzel, *Über den Stil der altgermanischen Poesie* (Quellen
und Forschungen, X.)

[2]) *History of Early English Literature*, Vol. I. p. 51.

that the conflict takes place by the sea-shore and in a tide-washed cave. But to Grendel's realm belong also the fens and swamps, together with the marchland bordering on the dwellings of men:

> wæs se grimma gæst Grendel haten,
> mære mearc-stapa, se þe moras heold,
> fen ond fæsten.   102—104.

We are therefore to picture to ourselves as the scene of this section of the story a steep and rocky coast, where the sea-currents, dashing in fury against the cliffs, have hollowed out gloomy caves: this coast-line is backed by moorlands, wholly uncultivated, and rendered treacherous by reason of countless swamps, —

> profound as that Serbonian bog
> Betwixt Damiata and Mount Casius old,
> Where armies whole have sunk.

The poet never introduces meadows or river scenery into his work, while the occasional references to woodlands and to trees covering the hillsides point to the fact that such scenery called forth only a sense of terror:

> oþ þæt he færinga fyrgen-beamas
> ofer harne stan hleonian funde,
> wynleasne wudu.   1415—1418.

Most of the descriptions of scenery in *Beowulf* are brief, drawn with a few bold and suggestive strokes; those who listened to the recital of the story had to fill in the details for themselves. But on one occasion the contrary is the case. Before Beowulf starts out on his second expedition — the slaughter of Grendel's mother who in the preceding night has borne away Æschere, the trusted counsellor of Hrothgar, — he hears from the aged king's lips a description of the monsters who have wrought such woe in Heorot.

> Hie dygel lond
> warigeaþ, wulf-hleoþu, windige næssas,
> frecne fen-gelad, þær fyrgen-stream
> under næssa genipu niþer gewiteþ,
> flod under foldan; nis þæt feor heonon,
> mil-gemearces, þæt se mere standeþ,
> ofer þæm hongiaþ hrimge bearwas,
> wudu wyrtum fæst, wæter oferhelmaþ.

> Þær mæg nihta gehwæm niþ-wundor seon,
> fyr on flode; no þæs frod leofaþ
> gumena bearna, þæt þone grund wite;
> þeah þe hæd-stapa hundum geswenced,
> heorot hornum trum holt-wudu sece,
> feorran geflymed, ær he feorh seleþ,
> aldor on ofre, ær he in wille,
> hafelan hydan. Nis þæt heoru stow:
> þonon yþ-geblond up astigeþ
> won to wolcnum, þonne wind styreþ
> laþ gewidru, oþ þæt lyft drysmaþ,
> roderas reotaþ.   1358—1377.

The passage has been quoted in full because of its unique character. It is an inland scene of awesome grandeur, and we scarcely need the poet's assurance — "It is no pleasant place" — to make us realise its gloominess. He has taken care, too, to place the scene in an atmosphere of storm and wintry cold. But the poet's art appears most strikingly in the sense of unity which knits the various elements in the landscape together. The lonely mere with the mountain-streams rushing down into it, the steep hillsides covered with trees which instead of leaves bear a covering of hoar-frost, above these the wolf-haunted crags, and above all a storm-swept sky — all these go to make up a scene of strictest harmony. No human figure is introduced into the picture, but the reference to the hart, "the heath-stepper", which, refusing to enter the dreary forest, lays down its life on the shore of the mere, introduces an element of pathos that tends to soften the savagery of the landscape.

It is in keeping with the lurid intensity of the *Beowulf* landscapes that they are generally represented as they appear in winter and by night. Almost the only reference to summer sunshine and the leafage of the trees occurs in one of the Christian interpolations of a later date. The gleeman has taken his harp, and is singing of the creation of the world:

> cwæþ þæt se ælmihtiga eorþan worhte,
> wlite-beorhtne wang, swa wæter bebugeþ,
> gesette sige-hreþig sunnan ond monan,
> leoman to leohte land-buendum,
> ond gefrætwade folda sceatas
> leomum ond leafum.   92—97.

Yet while the poet's landscapes are mainly those of winter, there is frequent expression of his delight in the radiance of the sun. The sun is "the bright beacon of God", "the joy of heaven", "the candle of the firmament", which, "robed in ether" (*swegl-wered*) dispels the mists and the darkness, and gladdens the heart of man. In the Finn-episode, sung by the *scop* to the warriors as they sit in Hrothgar's hall, there is a brief description of the passing of winter and the coming of spring:

> winter yþe beleac
> is-gebinde, oþ þæt oþer com
> gear in geardas, swa nu gyt deþ,
> þa þe syngales sele bewitiaþ,
> wuldor-torhtan weder. Þa wæs winter scacen,
> fæger foldan bearm. 1133—1138.

The poet has nothing to tell of flowers, which would be strangely out of place in this landscape of storm and ice, while the chief references to animals — not including the strange sea-monsters which lurk bodefully in the depths of the sea— are to the horse, the dog, the wolf and the hart. The eagle is mentioned once, but references to the raven, the sacred bird of Woden, are more frequent. It is represented as a bird of prey and also of ill-omen. Very impressive is its introduction, in company with the eagle and the wolf, in Wiglaf's speech to the Geat warriors over the bier of Beowulf.

> Forþon sceall gar wesan
> monig morgen-ceald mundum bewunden,
> hæfen on handa, nalles hearpan sweg
> wigend weccean, ac se wonna hrefn
> fus ofer fægum fela reordian,
> earne secgan hu him æt æte speow,
> þenden he wiþ wulf wæl reafode. 3022—3028.

On one occasion the raven appears as the herald of the dawn:

> gæst inne swæf,
> oþ þæt hrefn blaca heofones wynne
> bliþ-heort bodode. Þa com beorht sunne
> scacan ofer grundas. 1801—1804.

In *Beowulf*, as in the Homeric poems, the colour-sense is primitive and lacking in discrimination. The poet is very

sensitive to the effects of light and shade, and refers frequently to the brightness or dimness of objects, but he
rarely notices their colours. The adjective *blac*, 'glittering',
occurs again and again, both singly and joined to some other
word, while *hwit* is found only once, and then in the sense
not of 'white', but of 'bright', 'glittering' — *se hwita helm.*
In the same way the adjective *blæc*, 'black', appears only
once — *hrefn blaca* — whereas *wonn*, 'dark', is very common;
it is used of the night, the raven, and even of the flame
— *wonna leg.* Although the sea occupies so important a place
in *Beowulf*, its colour is very rarely referred to; it is never
described as green or blue, — the latter being an adjective
which, in spite of its Teutonic origin, never occurs in Old
English poetry. The only colour-attribute which is applied
to it is fallow *(fealu)*, which is suggestive of the sea near
the shore and in time of storm, when the waves have washed up
the yellow sand from the bottom. The frequent occurrence of
the adjective *fealu* is in itself an indication of the vagueness
of the colour-sense in *Beowulf*: not only is it used to denote
the colour of the sea, but also of a horse and a stone-paved
path, while on one occasion the compound 'apple-fallow' is
found — *æppelfealuwe mearas.* The only other colour-adjec-
tive which is at all common is 'grey' *(græg)* which is chiefly
used to denote the colour of armour.

To appreciate the interpretation of Nature in *Beowulf* aright,
it is necessary to compare it with that found in the epic
poetry of other literatures. The epic which most readily claims
comparison with it in this respect is the Odyssey. Both
poems have a framework of natural description formed by
the sea; both are deficient in the exact discrimination of
colours, and in both there is a clear representation of the
strife which man has ever to wage with the forces of Nature.
But the points of contrast exceed those of comparison.
Homer's heart was set upon what was fruitful and placidly
beautiful in the Greek landscape, and though he possessed
the gift of portraying its sterner and sublimer aspects, he
did not exult in sea-storm and wind-swept crag as did the
Beowulf-poet. To find a parallel to the scenery of the northern

epic we must turn from those scenes of rich cultivation in which Homer so greatly delighted to his description of the misty Cimmerian land or the sheer rocks of Scylla. The rare beauty of the landscape-scenes of the Odyssey is largely due to their fidelity, to the felicitous choice of words which the poet uses in impressing that beauty upon us, and, above all, to the artistic selection of that feature in the landscape which brings the whole scene before the reader's mind. The *Beowulf*-poet, though in his picture of the inland mere he attains a mastery of art worthy of Homer, does not show anything like the same power of simple and succinct expression: like all Old English poets, he is prone to redundancy. Moreover, the poetic force of his descriptions of Nature lies not so much in accuracy of delineation as in imaginative suggestiveness. The difference between the two poets is accordingly the difference between the classic and the romantic.

But it is when we compare the *Beowulf* with such modern epics as the *Chanson de Roland* and the *Nibelungenlied* that its masterly interpretation of Nature impresses us most. The *Roland* is far superior to *Beowulf* in unity of design, regularity of structure, and in most of the highest qualities of epic poetry, but in its landscape painting it is strikingly inferior. Its descriptions of scenery are curt, commonplace and unsympathetic. Scarcely any attempt is made to harmonise the natural surroundings with the action, and the poet, while describing the armour and equipment of the various combatants with considerable detail, furnishes very little information as to the nature of the country through which they pass, or in which the great fight of Roncesvaux takes place. The rocky defiles of the Pyrenees where the Saracen hosts surround the little band of Christian warriors are often referred to, but only once described, and then the description is chiefly negative:

> Soleilz n'i luist, ne blez n'i poet pas creistre,
> Pluie n'i chiet, rusée n'i adeiset,
> Pierre n'i ad que tute ne seit neire.
> Dient alquant que li diable i meignent.
>
> *Chanson de Roland,* 980—983.

Elsewhere the descriptions of Nature are confined to one, or at most two, verses. Instead of the clouds and mists of the English epic, we find throughout the *Roland* an atmosphere of clear sunshine or moonlight:

> Clers fut li jurz, e bels fut li soleilz.   1002.
> Clers fut li jurz e li soleilz luisant.   3345.
> Clere est la noit e la lune luisant.   2512.

The change from day to night, or from night to day, is described with similar brevity:

> Tresvait la noit, e apert la clere albe.   737.
> Passet li jurz, la noit est aserie,
> Clere est la lune, les esteiles flambient.   3658—9.

When the poet attempts a description of the natural features of the country in which the scenes are laid, he still keeps within the region of the general and commonplace:

> Halt sunt li pui e tenebrus e grant,
> Li val parfunt, e les ewes curanz.   1830—31.
> Halt sunt li pui e li val tenebrus,
> Les roches bises, li destreit merveillus.   814—15.

In all this there is very little to show that the author of the *Roland* had a discerning eye for Nature, still less, a sense of the grandeur of the natural world such as we find throughout the *Beowulf*. The *Nibelungen Lied* is in this respect almost as primitive as the *Roland*. The transition from day to night, or from winter to summer, is noticed in the same curt manner:

> Der tac der hete an ende und nâhet in diu naht
>   Aventiure XXX., 1.
> Vor âbende nâhen, do diu sunne nieder gie,
> unt ez begonde kuolen, niht langer man daz lie,
> sich huoben gegen der bürge manic man unde wîp.
>   Aventiure X., 601—3.

In Middle English poetry contemporaneous with the *Nibelungen Lied* there is generally a good deal of description of forest scenery introduced in connection with a hunting episode, but in the German epic the famous hunt which precedes the murder of Siegfried is described with only the barest reference to the character of the country in which it takes place:

> Dô riten si von dannen in einen tiefen walt
>
> XVI., 926.
>
> Der brunne was küele, lûter unde guot   XVI., 979.
>
> Die bluomen allenthalben von bluote wâren naz.
>
> XVI., 998.

Thus the Nature-poetry of the Old English epic, so far from suffering by comparison with the epics of France and Germany, reveals its high originality only when such comparison is made.

Chapter II.

CHRISTIAN NARRATIVE POETRY.

The evangelisation of the Anglo-Saxon races, which, through the instrumentality of Augustine and Paulinus, Aidan and Chad, was effected in the course of the seventh and eighth centuries, was destined to produce a change in men's conceptions both of human life and of external Nature. The higher civilisation which followed in the wake of the evangelising movement made the austere delight in the pageantry of storm gradually yield place to a more subdued pleasure in the beauty of such idyllic scenes as are furnished by richly cultivated fields and pleasant woodlands. The conquest of Britain by Saxon and Angle led, moreover, to a change in the tenor of men's lives. The Viking became the farmer, and from being a rover on the high seas, settled down to the less adventurous pursuits of agriculture and commerce. But these changes in manner of life and in religious belief were not effected suddenly; while new ideas were assimilated and new conditions of life came into vogue, there was everywhere a tenacious clinging to much that was old. Bede's story of the evangelisation of England furnishes numerous instances of this attempt to pour new wine into old wine-skins, and, wherever possible, to bring about a compromise between Christianity and the worship of Woden and Thor. The festival of Eostre, the goddess of spring, became the Christian Easter, while the East Anglian prince, Rædwald, set up a Christian and a pagan altar within the same temple.

This union of Christian and pagan ideas confronts us also in the earliest Christian narrative poetry. Cynewulf, the greatest of these Christian poets, and the one in whose works the personal note rings clearest, had been converted to the new faith in the course of his bardic career. While searching for new themes in sacred lore to replace those which Christianity had ostracised, he at the same time contrived to introduce into his Christian poems as many of the old poetic traditions as were capable of transference. The primitive delight in the shock of arms and in voyaging could not be given up, and Cynewulf accordingly chose for poetic treatment those stories which told of battle or of the sea. The Old Testament appealed to the early poets much more than the New, and in addition tho the Bible, there was at hand the Latin compilation of the *Lives of the Saints* — a mine which, both before and after the Norman Conquest, yielded Christian poets an almost inexhaustible supply of raw material, capable of being purified of its grosser elements and consecrated to the service of poetry.

It would be difficult to find a more fitting subject for poetic treatment at the hands of "these convertites" than that of the crossing of the Red Sea by the children of Israel and the overthrow of Pharaoh amid the waves. The Old English poem which sets forth this splendid theme is, of course, the *Exodus*. The Bible narrative is expanded to five hundred verses, and though the poet adheres to the main outline of the story, he enriches it with so much detailed description, that it has all the merits of an original work. The poem is also of considerable importance in connection with our present study of the interpretation of Nature: with fine imagination, the poet represents the play of the great forces of Nature, and lingers fondly over pictures of the warring elements. First of all, he describes the pillar of cloud and the pillar of fire:[1])

> Þær halig god
> wiþ færbryne folc gescylde,
> bælce oferbrædde byrnendne heofon,
> halgan nette hatwendne lyft.

---

[1]) All the quotations from Old English poems in this and the following chapter are taken from Professor Wülcker's edition of Grein's *Bibliothek der Angelsächsischen Poesie* (Kassel, 1883).

> Hæfte wederwolcen widum fæþmum
> eorþan ond uprodor efne gedæled,
> lædde leodwerod.   71—77.

Then, with a zest which the new evangel of peace and goodwill could not quench, he represents the Israelites and Egyptians as two armies awaiting the order of battle, introduces the raven and the wolf as attendants upon the fray, and even pictures the carnage which should accompany the fight :

> On hwæl hreopon herefugolas,
> hildegrædige ; . . . . . .
> deawigfeþere ofer drihtneum,
> wonn wælceasega. Wulfas sungon
> atol æfenleoþ ætes on wenan,
> carleasan deor.   161—166.

A little later follows Moses' description of the parting of the waves of the Red Sea :

> Yþ up fareþ, ofstum wyrceþ
> wæter ond wealfæsten. Wegas syndon dryge,
> haswe herestræta, holm gerymed,
> ealde staþolas, þa ic ær ne gefrægn
> ofer. middangeard men geferan,
> fage feldas, þa forþ heonon
> iu ece yþe þeahton,
> sælde sægrundas : suþwind fornam
> bæþweges blæst, brim is areafod,
> sand sæcir spau.   282—291.

Boldly original as is the working of the poet's imagination in this passage, his picture of the return of the waters to their old abodes, and of the engulfing of the Egyptian hosts, is yet more forcible : there gathers round it a lurid intensity which transcends even the descriptions of sea-storm in *Beowulf* :

> Folc wæs afæred : flodegsa becwom
> gastas geomre, geofon deaþe hweop.
> Wæron beorhhliþu blode bestemed,
> holm heolfre spaw, hream wæs on yþum,
> wæter wæpna ful, wælmist astah.

*   *   *

Streamas stodon, storm up gewat
heah to heofonum, herewopa mæst;
laþe cyrmdon; lyft up geswearc:
fægum stæfnum flod blod gewod.

* * *

Wide wæþde, wælfæþmum sweop,
flod famgode, fæge crungon,
lagu land gefeol, lyft wæs onhrercd,
wicon weallfæsten, wægas burston,
multon meretorras, þa se mihtiga sloh
mid halige hand, heofonrices weard
werbeamas, wlance þeode.   446—496.

Though this description may in places seem crude, it is impossible to overlook the barbaric vigour of the whole scene. The poet's imagination carries him away, and the wild exultation which the theme calls forth leads to inartistic repetitions. But it is this constant return to the main features of the picture, and this lavish accumulation of striking images, which reveal how strong was this passion for the sea in time of storm among the early English poets. It would be easy to criticise in the above extracts the prolixity of the description, the over-charged epithets, and the sacrifice of syntactical coherence to rude parallelism of clauses; yet while architecturally weak, the poem betrays at every point an appreciation of the sublimest aspects of the natural world, and shows clearly that this appreciation was not wholly lost amid the changes in manners and in ideas which were brought about by the settlement and the conversion to the Christian faith.

With the *Exodus* are usually grouped the two poems known as the *Genesis* and the *Daniel*; all three works, in spite of many points of dissimilarity, having been formerly attributed to Cædmon. The *Genesis*, which is not a homogeneous work, first tells of the fall of the angels, and then proceeds with the Bible narrative as far as the offering-up of Isaac. Full of vigour and beauty as the poem is, it demands in this place a much briefer notice than the *Exodus*. The authors of the work keep fairly closely to the material which had been handed down to them from the Bible and old Rabbinical writings, and it is significant of the deep interest of Old English poets in the manifestations of external Nature, that the chief freedom of treatment is to be detected in the account of the six days' work of Creation, and in the story of the Flood. In the representation of the latter, we realise the changes which were taking place in the minds of Englishmen towards the forces of the natural world. It is easy to conceive of the delight which the authors of the *Beowulf*, the *Exodus*, or the *Riddles* would have experienced in the representation of this scene. With what gladness of heart they would have painted the engulfing of the land beneath the waters! How they would have revelled in the scene of devastation, pressing into their service all the wealth of epithet which an over-opulent poetic diction afforded, and returning again und again to the scene, lest some aspect of it should have been overlooked! But such is not the manner of the Genesis-poet. He gives us an orderly and vigorously outlined picture which brings the scene effectively before us: he describes the rise and subsequent fall of the waters, and devotes some thirty verses to the account of the threefold despatch of the dove from the ark. What we miss is the passion, the breathlessness, the fine frenzy of the more primitive poetry.

This change in the poetic attitude towards external Nature is still more pronounced in the *Daniel*. The poem brings into view a fair summer landscape, sparkling with dew and rich in leafage. The author makes little attempt to describe the raging fury of the fire into which the three youths are cast, but prefers to dwell upon the transcendent faith of the heroes, and, under the guidance of the apocryphal *Song of the Three Holy Children*, to depict the fiery furnace after Christ has entered it and cooled its heat: —

> Him þær owiht ne derede,
> ac wæs þær inne ealles gelicost
> efne þonne on sumera sunne scineþ
> ond deawdrias on dæge weorþeþ,
> winde geondsawen.

The comparison is one of great beauty, and the poet show his delight in such a summer landscape by returning to it a little later (verses 346—350).

As illustrating the manner in which the *Daniel*-poet handles his subject, it will be instructive to quote from the Apocrypha the passage on which this description is based. It is in keeping with the sympathies of Old English poets that the chief expansion of the original is found in the landscape painting:

"But the angel of the Lord came down into the furnace together with Azarias and his fellows, and he smote the flame of the fire out of the furnace; and made the midst of the furnace as it had been a moist whistling wind, so that the fire touched them not at all, neither hurt nor troubled them."

Passing by the *Judith* and the poem entitled *Christ and Satan*, neither of which calls for notice here, we have next to consider the works of Cynewulf. Of the four poems which bear his acrostic signature, only two — the *Elene* and the *Christ* — have a special bearing upon our subject. The descriptions of landscape found in the *Elene* recall in many ways those of *Beowulf*, and show how the poetic traditions of an heroic age were retained at a time when that age had passed away. There is first of all the reference to the wolf, the raven, and the eagle as the attendants upon the fight waged between Constantine and the Huns; —

> fyrdleoþ agol
> wulf on wealde, wælrune ne maþ;
> urigfeþera earn sang ahof
> laþum on laste.
>
>   *   *   *
>
>   hrefen uppe gol,
> wan and wælfel.   27—53.

A little later Cynewulf introduces the sea. Helena and her followers are sailing across the Mediterranean, bound for the Holy Land, where the quest of the cross of Christ is to be made, and the poet describes their voyage: —

> Leton þa ofer fifelwæg famige scriþan,
> bronte brimþisan: bord oft onfeng
> ofer earhgeblond yþa swengas,
> sæ swinsade.
>
>   *   *   *

Þær meahte gesion, se þone siþ beheold,
brecan ofer bæþweg, brimwudu snyrgan
under swellingum, sæmearh plegean,
wadan wægflotan.   237—246.

No Old English poem is so completely permeated with
Christian ideas as the *Christ*, the longest and most important
of Cynewulf's works. It illustrates more fully than any other
work the change which the new faith was producing upon
the life of the nation, and upon men's thoughts and aspirations.
Lyric praise is blended with didactic moralising, and both
with dramatic dialogue, when Mary converses with the
angel and with her husband Joseph. In its interpretation
of Nature, much of the lurid imagery of the earlier poetry
is surrendered, and in the place of this there appears a keen
appreciation of the beauty of the stars, the rain and the
dew, and of all the fair things of earth. Near the beginning
of the poem Christ is invoked as the morning-star *(earendel)*
and as the soothfast sunny radiance *(soþfæsta sunnan leoma)*,
brighter than all stars, who out of his own brightness gives
light to mankind. Figurative language is also used in describing
Satan: he appears as the accursed wolf *(se awyrgda wulf)*,
the beast whose deeds are done in darkness, and whom
Christ has utterly destroyed. Then, in an outburst of lyric
rapture, Cynewulf sings of the goodness of Christ as made
manifest in the world around. The terrors of the natural
world are forgotten, and the picture is one of sunshine and
fruitfulness:

He us æt giefeþ and æhta sped,
welan ofer widlond and weder liþe
under swegles hleo. Sunne and mona
æþelast tungla eallum scinaþ
heofoncondelle hæleþum on eorþan.
Dreoseþ deaw and ren, duguþe weccaþ
to feorhnere fira cynne,
iecaþ eorþwelan,   604—611.

Cynewulf's use of natural description in simile, a striking
instance of which occurs in the *Elene*, is found in a much
more elaborate degree in the *Christ*, where the life of man on
earth is poetically compared with a voyage across the ocean:

Nu is þon gelicost, swa we on laguflode
ofer ceald wæter ceolum liþan,
geond sidne sæ sundhengestum
flodwudu fergen: is þæt frecne stream,
yþa ofermæta, þe we her on lacaþ
geond þas wacan woruld, windge holmas;
ofer deop gelad wæs se drohtaþ strong,
ær þon we to londe geliden hæfdon
ofer hreone hrycg.   851—59.

In the latter part of the work there occurs an extremely
vivid description of the Judgment Day. Much of this. is
founded upon biblical authorities, but there are also reminiscences throughout of those stories of old Teutonic
mythology which told of the Twilight of the Gods, and of
the final overthrow of the dwellers in Asgard by Loki and
the spirits of darkness. Cynewulf puts all his strength into
this picture, and paints with rare effect the extinction of
sun, moon and stars, and the raging of the winds on seven
sides, whereby the plains of earth are filled with fire. The
earth with its mountains, the sea with its fishes, the heaven
with its stars, all are consumed by the devouring flames.
From this scene of annihilation, the poet, somewhat neglectful
of the order of things, passes to the crucifixion, and finds
there an occasion for giving utterance to the sympathy felt
by Nature with the great tragedy which centres in the cross
of Calvary. Cynewulf tells us how the silent creation, the
green earth and the heaven above, felt and bemoaned the
sorrows of their Prince:

                          Scire burstan
    muras and stanas monge æfter foldan,
    and seo eorþe eac egsan myrde,
    beofode on bearhtme, and se brada sæ
    cyþde cræftes meaht and of clomme bræc
    up yrringa on eorþan fæþm.
    Ge on stede scynum steorran forleton
    hyra swæsne wlite on þa sylfan tid.
    Heofon hluttre ongeat, hwa hine healice
    torhtne getremede tungolgimmum.   1142—1151

The representation of the whole creation groaning and
travailing in sympathy with the death of Christ marks a
distinct advance in the poetic interpretation of Nature. It

is akin to, and yet in some measure the reverse of, the attitude of the *Beowulf* epic. Both poems bring humanity and the natural forces of the universe into close association with each other, but in the *Beowulf* their relationship to each other is one of feud, whereas in the *Christ* it is one of sympathy. In Beowulf's swimming match with Breca, in his fight with Grendel's mother, and in almost all his other adventures, the powers of Nature are in arms against him, and seek to rob him of victory: but here in the *Christ*, the bursting asunder of the rocks, the inrush of the sea, the failing light of the stars, all serve to indicate the sympathy of Nature with the sufferer on the cross. Striking as the difference is, it is nevertheless to be remembered that a similar conception of the sympathy of Nature is to be found in the later versions of the Baldur-myth, where the sorrow of Nature at the death of the young and beautiful god is brought into prominence. It is extremely probable that this myth was familiar enough to Englishmen of Cynewulf's time, inasmuch as it seems to have taken its rise among the Geats and Danes who occupy the foreground of the *Beowulf*, and it is therefore not impossible that Cynewulf had the Baldur-myth in view in depicting the consternation of Nature at the death of Christ. At the same time it is open to question whether this conception of the sympathy of Nature, as revealed in the story of Baldur, is, after all, the birthright of the Teutonic races. Bugge, in criticising this myth, has claimed to discover in it traces of Celtic suggestion, more especially of the Irish legends of the life and death of Christ, and it is possible that Cynewulf's conception of this scene is ultimately referable to a Celtic source. Yet speculation in this matter is extremely hazardous, and it may be that the vivid picture quoted above is nothing more than a poetic enlargement of the statement of St Matthew: "The earth did quake, and the rocks rent".

Among other poems which have been attributed, in part or altogether, to Cynewulf, but which lack his acrostic-signature, are the *Andreas*, the *Guthlac*, and the *Dream of the Rood*. The *Andreas*, which narrates the story of the journey of St Matthew to the Myrmedonians, is largely the description of a marvellous sea-voyage, made in a boat manned by Christ and two angels. The sea is described in much the same way as in the *Beowulf* or the *Elene*. There is the same bold painting of the lashing of the waves, while the animated character of the description is further enhanced by the introduction of the whale, the sword-fish, and the grey sea-mew:

> Þa gedrefed wearþ,
> onhrered hwælmere: hornfisc plegode,
> glad geond garsecg and se græga mæw
> wælgifre wand; wedercandel swearc,
> windas weoxon, wægas grundon,
> streamas styredon, strengas gurron,
> wædo gewætte, wæteregsa stod
> þreata þryþum. 369—376.

The concrete imagery is here wonderfully moving: every stroke tells, and our interest is raised in a steady *crescendo* movement, till at last the concrete gives place to the abstract, as the poet tells of the "water-terror", which, by reason of its very indefiniteness, enhances the sense of awe.

The poet of the *Andreas* is interested in such natural phenomena as the succession of the seasons, or the change from night to day. Almost at the outset of the poem there occurs a description of daybreak which is almost Homeric in its directness:

> Nihthelm toglad,
> lungre leorde: leoht æfter com,
> dægredwoma. 123—125.

The advent of winter is described with fuller detail, and the imaginative faculties of the poet are called into full play in the production of a picture at once comprehensive and intense.

> Snaw eorþan band
> wintergeworpum; weder coledon
> heardum hægelscurum, swilce hrim and forst,
> hare hildstapan hæleþa eþel
> lucon, leoda gesetu; land wæron freorig
> cealdum cylegicelum; clang wæteres þrym
> ofer eastreamas, is brycgade
> blæce brimrade. 255—62.

In such a picture as this there appears much of the
sublimity of the descriptions found in the *Beowulf,* to which
the *Andreas*, in spite of its Christian theme, has a certain
affinity.

Of a totally different character is the scenery of the
Guthlac, a poem describing the life of an English hermit-
saint who died in the year 714. Here the sterner aspects
of Nature are almost entirely absent, and in their stead there
appears the soft, rich beauty of an English upland which
fitly harmonises with the gentle life of the recluse. St Guthlac, like St Francis of Assisi at a later date, has tamed the
birds of the woodlands, and the poet describes with singular
charm the welcome which the birds accord to the saint when
he returns to his hill-side hermitage after a season of trial
and persecution:

> Sigehreþig cwóm
> bytla to þam beorge: hine bletsadon
> monge mægwlitas meaglum reordum:
> treofugla tuddor tacnum cyþdon
> eadges eftcyme: oft he him æte heold,
> þonne hy him hungrige ymb hond flugon
> grædum gifre, geoce gefegon.
> Swa þæt milde mod wiþ moncynnes
> dreamum gedælde, dryhtne þeowde,
> genom him to wildeorum wynne, siþþan he þas
> [woruld forhogde.
> Smolt wæs se sigewong and sele niwe
> fæger fugla reord, folde geblowen,
> geacas gear budon.   704—716.

In these verses we meet with the utterance of a sincere
delight in the beauty of a spring landscape, in the return
of the migrant birds, and the blossoming of the flowers. The
terms of the description are for the most part somewhat
general, but this only serves to bring into bolder relief the
one particularising trait — the reference to the cuckoo as
the bird which heralds the incoming spring. Are we not at
once reminded of Wordsworth, to whom the cuckoo was also
the "darling of the Spring", and the "blithe-New-comer"?

Chapter III.

OLD ENGLISH LYRIC AND ALLEGORIC POETRY.

1. The Lyric Poems.

Ten Brink has well said that "the Old English lyrical feeling knows in reality but one art-form, that of the elegy".[1] The Anglo-Saxon temperament was prone to melancholy, a melancholy which casts its chequered light upon much of the poetry of the time and makes it responsive to human sentiment. Even in moments of exultation the Old English poet is not wholly free from wistful regret: only too often he turns aside from the high emprise to which he has dedicated himself in order to reflect upon the transitoriness of human life and mortal possessions.

> Feoh æghwæn biþ
> læne under lyfte, landes frætwe
> gewitaþ under wolcnum winde geliccost
> þonne he for hæleþum hlud astigeþ,
> wæþeþ be wolcnum, wedende færeþ
> and eft semninga swige gewyrþeþ
> in nedcleofan nearwe geheaþrod,
> þream forþrycced.   *Elene*, 1269—1276.

Among the earliest of these secular lyrics written in an elegiac mood is *The Wanderer*. The introduction and close of the poem are Christian in spirit, but the central portion is distinctly pagan, and there can be little doubt that the verses which breathe the spirit of Christianity were additions of a later date. Throughout the poem the reader feels himself in the presence of the great powers of Nature: the sea is always in the foreground, and the contemplation of it

---

[1] *Early English Literature*, vol. I. p. 61.

enhances the poet's prevailing mood of melancholy. The sense of grim pleasure which is manifested in *Beowulf* in regard to the wilder aspects of the ocean in time of storm, and which was the outcome of man's sense of victory over the fury of the elements, passes in *The Wanderer* into a feeling of dread. The sea is terrible and lonely, a dreary place of exile for those bereft of home. The wanderer relates how, after weary voyagings, he falls asleep, and dreams that he is at home with his lord in full enjoyment of the bounty of the throne. Then he awakes, the vision is rudely snatched from him, and the desolation of his surroundings "makes his heart-wounds the heavier":

> Þonne onwæcneþ eft wineleas guma,
> gesihþ him biforan fealwe wegas,
> baþian brimfuglas, brædan feþra,
> hreosan hrim and snaw hagle gemenged.
>
> 45—48.

This picture of a winter seascape is followed by one of a winter landscape, and the sense of desolation becomes yet further accentuated:

> And þas stanhleoþu stormas cnyssaþ;
> hriþ hreosende, hruse bindeþ
> wintres woma, þonne won cymeþ,
> nipeþ nihtscua, norþan onsendeþ
> hreo hæglfare hæleþum on andan.   101—105.

The sea holds a yet more prominent place in *The Seafarer*, the tone of which is less elegiac than that of *The Wanderer*. The dangers of the sea are held up to view, together with the hardships of a sea-faring life, but the poet knows something of the irresistible fascination of the ocean and of the spell which it casts upon all who have shared in its dangers. Modern criticism, following the suggestion of Rieger, has generally resolved the first sixty-two verses of the poem into a dialogue between an old sailor and a young man eager for the sea. The former paints the voyager's life as follows:

> Þæt se mon ne wat,
> þe him on foldan fægrost limpeþ,
> hu ic earmcearig iscealdne sæ
> winter wunade wræccan lastum,

wynnum͜ biloren, winemægum bidroren,
bihongen hrimgicelum : hægl scurum fleag.
Þær ic ne gehyrde butan hlimman sæ,
iscaldne wæg, hwilum ylfete song :
dyde ic me to gomene ganetes hleoþor
and huilpan sweg fore hleahtor wera,
mæw singende fore medodrince.
Stormas þær stanclifu beotan, þær him stearn oncwæþ
isigfeþera : ful oft þæt earn bigeal
urigfeþera.   14—25.

The author of this poem was evidently one who knew
from personal experience the sights and the sounds of the
ocean. The picture which he brings before us has not a
merely conventional significance : it is not simply a part of
the stock-in-trade of the professional gleeman, but the outcome
of direct observation ; to this is chiefly due the realism which
gives such a force to the whole description. This picture
is painted by the old mariner to warn the youth of the
hardships which he must expect if he adopts a sea-faring
life. But with fine dramatic art, the poet makes the old
mariner express how, in spite of its hardships, the sea still
appeals to him with irresistible force. The harp, the bestowal
of rings, the joys of wedded life, are powerless to break
the spell : nothing can satisfy him except the roar of the
waves. This the youth appreciates, and continues in the
same strain :

Bearwas blostmum nimaþ, byrig fægriaþ,
wongas wlitigaþ, woruld onetteþ :
ealle þa gemoniaþ modes fusne
sefan to siþe, þam þe swa þenceþ
on flodwegas feor gewitan.   48—51.

This fascination of a sea-faring life is felt in Old English
poetry whenever the sea is introduced, even when the
uppermost feeling is one of shrinking dread. The poet expresses in masterly fashion what other poets had vaguely
felt, but had not known how to set forth in words. No poem
is truer to the Anglo-Saxon spirit of the seventh and eighth
centuries.

Two other elegies, which have been named *The Husband's
Message*, and *The Wife's Lament*, call for briefer notice. In

both we find Nature made to reflect the mood of the characters introduced. Thus in the former there is a reference to the song of the cuckoo. In the *Guthlac*, as we have seen, this bird is introduced as the herald of spring, and forms part of a picture which is full of gladness; in *The Husband's Message*, the cuckoo is still the bird of spring, but its song is felt to be mournful. The husband, in his loneliness, addresses his absent wife and bids her come to him, —

> siþþan þu gehyrde on hliþes oran
> galan geomorne geac on bearwe.

In *The Wife's Lament* the sorrow is deeper, and draws nearer to despair. The wife has been separated from her husband and banished to a cave situated in the dreary forest, beneath the roots of an oak-tree. This is how she describes the place of her abode:

> Heht mec mon wunian on wuda bearwe
> under actreo in þam eorþscræfe :
> eald is þes eorþsele, eal ic eom oflongad :
> sindon dena dimme, duna uphea,
> bitre burgtunas, brerum beweaxne,
> wic wynna leas.   27—32.

2. The Riddles.

Riddle-writing was a form of poetic literature which reached a high state of perfection in England before the Norman Conquest, the riddles, like the sonnets of the Elizabethan Renascence, being ranged in cycles. The cycle of English riddles preserved for us in the Exeter Book contains some ninety in all, and the authorship of them has, not altogether conclusively, been assigned to Cynewulf. These riddles fall, in respect of their themes, into two main classes: there are first of all the riddles which unfold the life of the outer world of Nature, and secondly, those which treat of the domestic life of a settled and home-loving people. It is with the first class alone that we need concern ourselves here. Although, thanks to the labours of Prehn and others, it is possible to discover, in almost every case, the sources of these Old English riddles among the Latin riddle-poems of

Symphosius, Eusebius and Aldhelm, their originality is thereby in no sense impaired. On the contrary, a comparison of these riddles with their Latin models only serves to show how keen was the Old English poet's appreciation of natural phenomena, and how greatly he excelled in descriptive power. The Latin riddles are, for the most part, didactic and moralising: the English are free from any such prosaic purpose, and are content with a vivid presentment of the actual picture.

It has already been remarked that the early English settlers were prone, long after a strictly mythological representation of Nature had disappeared, to regard such elemental forces as the sea and the wind as conscious beings, instinct with life. In minds so constituted, the animation of inanimate things which the riddle-poem demanded, and the endowment of these with speech, were attained without any great mental effort. Nowhere was this process of animation so simple as in the case of the wind, the spiritual nature of which had been recognised by poets from earliest times. It is, therefore, not surprising to find that some of the most detailed and imaginative riddles treat of the wind in time of storm. These are the second, third and fourth riddles of the Exeter Book. The first two, which describe the storm on land and the storm on sea respectively, serve as preludes to the third, in which the storm-wind, personified as a being of gigantic stature and irresistible power, sweeps over land and sea, and through the welkin, leaving misery, panic and devastation in its wake. This poem, which Mr. Stopford Brooke has well compared with Shelley's *Ode to the West Wind*, extends over seventy four verses, and only a portion of the whole can be given here. The poet describes first of all the course of the wind over the sea: —

> Hwilum ic sceal ufan yþa wregan,
> streamas styrgan and to staþe þywan
> flintgrægne flod: famig winneþ
> wæg wiþ wealle, wonn ariseþ
> dun ofer dype, hyre deorc on last
> eare geblonden oþer fereþ,
> þæt hy gemittaþ mearclonde neah

hea hlincas. Þær biþ hlud wudu,
brimgiesta breahtm; bidaþ stille
stealc stanhleoþu streamgewinnes,
hopgehnastes, þonne heah geþring
on cleofu crydeþ.　　　　　　　Riddle IV., 17—28.

Then the scene changes from the sea to the air, and the storm-wind tells how it cleaves its way among the clouds:

Hwilum ic þurhræse þæt me on bæce rideþ,
won wægfatu, wide toþringe
lagustreama full, hwilum læte eft
slupan tosomne. Se biþ swega mæst
breahtma ofer burgum and gebreca hludast,
þonne scearp cymeþ sceo wiþ oþrum,
ecg wiþ ecge: eorpan gesceafte
fus ofer folcum fyre swætaþ,
blacan lige and gebrecu feraþ
deorc ofer dreontum gedyne micle,
faraþ feohtende, feallan lætaþ
sweart sumsendu seaw of bosme,
wætan of wombe.

＊　　　＊　　　＊

Swa ic þrymful þeow þragum winne
hwilum under eorþan, hwilum yþa sceal
hean underhnigan, hwilum holm ufan
streamas styrge, hwilum stige up
wolcnfare wrege, wide fere ı.
swift and swiþfeorm. Saga, hwæt ic hatte,
oþþe hwa mec rære, þonne ic restan ne mot,
oþþe hwa mec stæþde, þonne ic stille beom!

36—74.

This riddle of the storm-wind may fitly be regarded as the most imaginative piece of Nature-poetry in Old English literature. The conception is extremely bold, and the picture is elaborated with fulness of detail and with rare imaginativeness. It seems as though everything which earlier poets had sung of the storm were compressed into this one poem, and reproduced in a manner entirely original. The sweep of the poem is throughout grandiose: the poet never allows the tension to be relaxed, and with all the wealth of incident, there is no repetition. At every point, too, it is manifest that he delights in the scene which he is so vividly portraying.

He is able to step out of himself, and, though he feels that
the storm-wind is the deadly foe of man, he can sympathise
with its sense of delight in the plenitude of its power. In
effecting this, the poet's imagination is stretched to its utmost
limit: losing sight of self, he merges his own personality in
that of the hurricane. It is also to be borne in mind that,
though the storm-wind is represented as a being endowed
with life and consciousness, it is not a self-dependent, self-
constituted power, but absolutely dependent on its lord, its
wielder (*wealdend*), who alone is able to arouse it or lull it
to silence. More than once in the course of the riddle the
poet reminds us of this fact, and assures us that behind the
forces of Nature, and governing them in his supreme control,
is one to whom they all owe subjection. Who is this lord
of the storm-wind, this wielder of the powers of Nature?
It may be that the poet is thinking of Woden, for the riddles
are full of pagan conceptions, but it may also be the Christian
God who is thus introduced, the one, whom the Hebrew
poets regarded as the supreme lord of the natural world, the
Jehovah Jirah, who "commandeth and raiseth the stormy
wind, which lifteth up the waves of the sea".

Other objects and phenomena of Nature are made the
subjects of the poet's riddles. One is devoted to the sun,
another to the moon, and a third to the sun and the moon
together. The last of these (Riddle XXX.) is full of beauty,
but to a modern reader it seems somewhat fanciful, though
it is possible that early mythological conceptions of the
relations of sun and moon to each other are imbedded
in it: —

> Ic wiht geseah wundorlice
> hornum bitweonum huþe lædan,
> lyftfæt leohtlic listum gegierwed,
> huþe to þam ham of þam heresiþe,
> wolde hyre on þære byrig bur atimbran,
> searwum asettan, gif hit swa meahte.
> Þa cwom wundorlicu wiht ofer wealles hrof,
> seo is eallum cuþ eorþbuendum,
> ahredde þa þa huþe and to ham bedraf
> wreccan ofer willan, gewat hyre west þonan

fæhþum feran, forþ onette :
dust stonc to heofonum, deaw feol on eorþan,
niht forþ gewat. Nænig siþþan
wera gewiste þære wihte siþ.   Riddle XXX.

The central idea of the riddle — the overthrow of the
moon by the sun, and the westward journey of the latter —
is finely imagined; what seems a little fanciful and precious
is the reference to the moon's booty which she bears to her
homestead. This is, as the second verse of the riddle clearly
shows, the ring of the old moon, and the idea is closely
allied to that set forth in the Scottish ballad of *Sir Patrick
Spens:*

> Yestreen I saw the new moon
> With the auld moon in her arms,

The forty-first riddle, though only a fragment, is by
far the longest of the cycle, and the idea which it sets forth
is again taken up in the sixty-seventh. The answer which
Prehn and others have given to this riddle is 'the Creation',
but I prefer to substitute for this the reading 'Nature', which
seems to correspond more exactly to the description. Nature,
the poet tells us, is the handiwork of God, and is in all,
and through all, the works of God in creation. The poem
reads like a string of paradoxes, each one quaintly imagined,
and revealing an intimate acquaintance with the life of
flower, bird and beast. Nature, we read, is colder than the
frost, yet hotter than the flames of Vulcan, sweeter to the
taste than honey from the honey-comb, yet bitterer far than
the grey wormwood which grows in the copses: heavier
than stone or lead, yet lighter than the little water-fly which
walks dry of foot on the stream :

Ic eom on stence strengre micle
þonne ricels oþþe rose sy,
þe swa anlice on eorþan tyrf
wynlic weaxeþ : ic eom wræstre þonne heo ;
þeah þe lilie sy leof moncynne
beorht on blostman, ic eom betre þonne heo ;
swlyce ic nardes stenc nyde oferswiþe
mid minre swetnesse symle æghwær :
and ic fulre eom þonne þis fen swearte,
þæt her yfle adelan stinceþ.   XLI., 23—32.

Nature is higher than heaven, and sees the hidden secrets of God; deeper also than hell, where she beholds the accursed spirits. She is swifter in flight than eagle or hawk, or the wind which blows from the west; yet is she slower than the snail, the rain-worm, or the fen-frog.

This riddle reveals a close intimacy with the weak and unassuming objects of the natural world : the poet has noted the life of the water-fly and the fen-frog, and has not even overlooked the sea-weed, which lies as an evil thing rejected by man. He has observed not only the forms of animal or plant-life, but also their strength or weakness, their sweetness or bitterness; and in them all he has discovered that there dwells a predominant force — Nature. This savours of pantheism, yet the poet's outlook upon the world is not pantheistic but monotheistic. Nature as a whole is no more self-constituted than the individual storm-wind introduced in Riddle IV.; both obey the mandate of God, the eternal 'shaper' of the world. As in the riddle of the storm, so here, and with closer reference to Christian doctrine, the poet makes Nature declare her dependence upon God:

He mec wrætlice worhte æt frymþe,
þa he þisne ymbhwyrft ærest sette.   6—7.

And again in verses 33 and 34: —

Eal ic under heofones hwearfte recce,
swa me leof fæder lærde æt frymþe.

Amongst other riddles dealing with the objects and phenomena of the natural world is that describing night with its grey-hued dress, decked with red and sparkling adornments (Riddle XII.), and that of the sun which, rising over ocean's billows, gladdens the heart of man (Riddle VII.). Nor are the terrible and destructive aspects of the natural world lost sight of in these poems. Water is described as an element which brings blessing and fruitfulness to men, and is the mother of many noble things; yet at other times it is wild and stormy, the greediest and most devouring of all things which human eye has ever seen (Riddle LXXXI.).

Of the riddles devoted to the animal kingdom, mention may be made of those which describe the badger (XVI.), the swan (VIII.), the heifer (XXXIX.), the dog (LI.), the falcon (LXXVIII.), the jackdaw (LVIII.), the cuckoo (X.), and the oyster (LXXXVI.). There is much homely fancy in these descriptions; at times even a touch of quaint humour. Thus the oyster describes itself as opening its mouth to meet the tide, and then adds —

> Nu wile monna sum
> min flæsc fretan, felles ne receþ,
> siþþan he me of sidan seaxes orde
> hyd arypeþ, ...
> þe siþþan iteþ unsodene.

Riddle LXXVII.

The tenth riddle is devoted to the cuckoo, and the bird gives a faithful and humorous account of its strange upbringing, and its cruelty towards its foster-parent's young ones:

> Mec on þissum dagum deadne ofgeafun
> fæder ond modor: ne wæs me feorh þa gen,
> ealdor in innan. Þa mec an ongon
> wel heold me gewedum þeccan,
> heold ond freoþode, hleosceorpe wrah
> swa arlice swa hire agen bearn,
> oþþæt ic under sceate, swa min gesceapu wæron,
> ungesibbum wearþ eacen gæste.
> Mec seo friþemæg fedde siþþan,
> oþþæt ic aweox, widor meahte
> siþas asettan: heo hæfde swæsra þy læs
> suna ond dohtra, þy heo swa dyde.

But all the riddles dealing with animal life are excelled in graphic portrayal, as they are exceeded in length, by that which describes the badger (Riddle XVI.): —

> Hals is min hwit ond heafod fealo,
> sidan swa some; swift ic eom on feþe,
> beadowæpen bere; me on bæce standaþ
> her swylce sue: on hleorum hlifiaþ
> tu earan ofer eagum; ordum ic steppe
> in grene græs.

Then the badger recounts how he is hunted by man, and forced to flee with his young, scratching a way with his feet through the steep hill in order to save the lives of his dear ones.

Ready as the riddle-poet was to appreciate animal-life under all its forms, it is only natural that he should take delight in the song of birds. Two riddles — the ninth and the twenty-fifth — are given up to this subject. The ninth runs as follows:

> Ic þurh muþ sprece mongum reordum,
> wrencum singe, wrixle geneahhe
> heafodwoþe, hlude cirme,
> healde mine wisan, hleoþre ne miþe,
> eald æfensceop, eorlum bringe
> blisse in burgum, þonne ic bugendre
> stefne styrme: stille on wicum
> sittaþ nigende. Saga, hwæt ic hatte,
> þe swa scirenige sceawendwisan
> hlude onhyrge, hæleþum bodige
> wilcumena fela woþe minre!

The bird is a little difficult to identify, but Mr Stopford Brooke's suggestion of the nightingale is, perhaps, in closest touch with the description, though the last verses seem to point to the owl. The powers of a bird in mimicking other sounds is again referred to in Riddle XXV., where the bird, as the runes indicate, is the jay.

Only one other riddle calls for special comment here, namely that which describes the ice-floe (XXXIV.). The appearances of winter were at all times calculated to quicken the imagination of the Old English poets, and in this riddle of the ice-floe the reader is presented with a picture of a wintry scene as vivid and imaginative as anything in Old English poetry:

> Wiht cwom æfter wæge wrætlicu liþan,
> cymlic from ceole cleopode to londe,
> hlimsade hlude: hleahtor wæs gryrelic
> egesful on earde, ecge wæron scearpe.
> Wæs his hete grim hilde to sæne,
> biter beadoweorca; bordweallas grof
> heard ond hiþende, heterune bond,
> sægde searocræftig ymb hyre sylfre gesceaft:
> "Is min moder mægþa cynnes
> þæs deorestan, þæt is dohtor min
> eacen up liden, swa þæt is ældum cuþ
> firum on folce, þæt seo on foldan sceal
> on ealra londa gehwam lissum stondan".

The high interest of the Old English riddle-poems
justifies the somewhat detailed treatment in the foregoing
pages of some of the riddles based upon natural life. Whatever
be their origin, they are clearly of later date than Aldhelm
(✝ 709), inasmuch as many of these English riddles are based
ōn those which he had written in Latin. Such being the
case, they furnish the student of Old English poetry with
abundant evidence that the primitive attitude of the Teutonic
mind towards the external world, above all the sense of
exultation felt at contemplating the stormier forces of Nature,
did not die out with the Settlement.

3. The Allegoric Poems.

Reference has already been made to the changes which
the introduction of Christianity into England produced in
the attitude of men towards the natural world. We have seen
how in the place of the keen interest of the primitive age
in the wild sublimity of Nature, and especially of the sea
in time of wintry storm, there gradually grew up a quiet
delight in idyllic inland scenery — a garden or meadow
decked with spring flowers — which is the common possession of mediæval Christendom, and which characterises
most English poetry written after the Norman Conquest. If
something was gained by this exchange, much was lost: how
much only a careful study of Old English poetry will fully
reveal. The introduction of Christianity influenced the
attitude of the poet towards Nature in yet another way. The
direct observation of Nature for its own sake was now
largely replaced by the symbolic interpretation of certain
individual objects of the natural world. The Middle Age was
the age of symbolism and allegory. Nature was studied in
order to furnish illustrations of spiritual truths; the natural
world was ransacked for 'evidences' of things spiritual. This
symbolic treatment of Nature probably found its model in
the parabolic teaching of the Gospels, and gradually became
diffused through all forms of didactic Christian literature.
Only too frequently this search for symbols of spiritual truths
assumed a far-fetched and highly fanciful character.

This love of symbolising certain natural forms, especially certain animals, called forth a peculiar class of poetry to which the name 'Physiologus' — *anglice* 'Bestiary' — was given. The earliest of these Physiologi was in Greek, and written in early Christian times in the city of Alexandria.[1]) Nothing is known of its author, but so widespread was its influence that, in the succeeding centuries, Physiologi appeared among most of the nations of Christendom, and in countries so far removed from each other as England and Armenia. The Old English Physiologus is but a fragment, furnishing a symbolic treatment of only three members of the animal kingdom — the panther, the whale, and the partridge. The poem entitled *The Phœnix* is, however, in reality an expanded Physiologus-poem, while the influence of the Physiologi is also traceable in the Latin riddles of Aldhelm.

The ancient Oriental legend of the Phœnix was first pressed into the service of Christianity, and made a symbol of the resurrection and of immortality, at the time of Clement of Rome; the English version of the fabulous story is directly based on the Latin poem, *De Phœnice*, which has been ascribed to the Ante-Nicene father, Lactantius. The one hundred and seventy hexameter verses of the Latin poem are expanded in the English rendering to six hundred and seventy-seven, much of the expansion being due to a greater fulness in the descriptions of natural scenery. The poem opens with a detailed description of the land where the phœnix has its abode, and beautiful as this description is, it is wholly un-English in character. It is an ideal landscape, a paradisaic land, wherein is much which has never been revealed to the eye of sense, but which poets have at all times loved to imagine. Most of the main features of this landscape are taken from the Latin original, but the English poet has warmed to his subject, and has added many new details at the cost of a certain redundancy of expression. Contrasted with the landscapes of *Beowulf*, or indeed with the general tenor of the interpretation of Nature

---

[1]) Lauchert, *Die Geschichte des Physiologus*.

in Old English poetry, the picture afforded by the *Phœnix*
is most striking. All the sublimer features, including the
exultant delight in storm by land or water, have been
removed, and the *Phœnix* landscape, beautiful as it is, is
largely made up of negative features. The bird dwells in
a winsome plain, where falls neither rain nor snow, where
there is neither breath of frost nor blast of fire, where the
sun does not scorch nor the cold freeze, and where no
harmful influence is felt:

> Is þæt æþele lond
> blostmum geblowen. Beorgas þær ne muntas
> steape ne stondaþ; ne stanclifu
> heah hlifiaþ, swa her mid us,
> ne dene ne dalu ne dunscrafu,
> hlæwas ne hlincas, ne þær hleonaþ oo
> unsmeþes wiht.   20—26.

In this land of smoothness are sunny groves and pleasant
holts, with flowers and fruits which abide for ever. There
is no need of rain, for wells of water bubble up every month
from the ground, and irrigate the fields and groves. These
groves with their flower- and fruit-laden boughs are without
breach; a holy fragrance is breathed over the land, and
neither change nor decay enters into it. Thus through the
compass of eighty-four alliterative verses the wonderful
country is described.

From the land, the poet passes next to the bird that
inhabits it, and depicts its wondrous beauty, the sweetness
of its song, the character of its life, and its lordship over
other birds. Next comes the story of its nest-building, in
effecting which the bird leaves its own fair abode and visits
Syria. The arrival of the bird in Syria means the cessation
of all storms:

> Þonne wind ligeþ, weder biþ fæger,
> hluttor heofones gim halig scineþ,
> beoþ wolcen towegen, wætra þryþe
> stille stondaþ, biþ storma gehwylc
> aswefed under swegle, suþan bliceþ
> wedercondel wearm, weorodum lyhteþ:
> þonne on þam telgum timbran onginneþ,
> nest gearwian.   182—189.

There follows a description of the fire which consumes the phœnix, and of the apple which is found lying in the ashes: the apple changes to a worm, and the worm passes gradually into a new phœnix. In the picture of the bird after its resurrection, there occurs a colour-passage, the fine discrimination of which is especially noticeable when it is remembered how obtuse is the colour-sense of the earliest Old English poets: —

> Is se fugel fæger forweard hiwe,
> bleobrygdum fag ymb þa breost foran;
> is him þæt heafod hindan grene,
> wrællice wrixleþ wurman geblonden.
> Þonne is se finta fægre gedæled,
> sum brun, sum basu, sum blacum splottum
> searolice beseted. Sindon þa fiþru
> hwit hindanweard ond se hals grene
> nioþoweard ond ufeweard, ond þæt nebb lixeþ,
> swa glæs oþþe gim, geaflas scyne
> innan ond utan. 291—301.

With all its splendour of colour and gorgeous landscapes, the *Phœnix* cannot be placed, in respect of its interpretation of Nature, on a level with such works as *Beowulf* and the Riddles. Its descriptions are· rarely original, and are certainly never based on actual observation. We trace here, far more than in any other Old English poem, the conventional landscape which was borrowed from classical poetry, and which came so much into vogue in later times. In this respect the poem marks the decadence of the descriptive powers of pre-conquest poetry. The poet turns his back upon the landscape of the country in which he lives, and ignoring native tradition, substitutes for it one which is wholly exotic, if not wholly imaginary, and the main features of which he has garnered from books, and not drawn from the sources of his own experience.

The symbolic poems entitled *The Panther, The Whale,* and *The Partridge,* probably form, as stated before, a portion of a larger Physiologus, similar in character to the many Latin Physiologi, to one or more of which they owe their origin. *The Partridge* is only a brief fragment of sixteen verses, but *The Panther* and *The Whale* are longer, and, keeping closely to the conventional symbolism of the Physiologus, are made to adumbrate the characters of Christ and Satan respectively. The panther is a wonderful animal who is kind to all creatures on earth, save only the poisonous dragon. When he has fed, he seeks a resting-place under the mountain hollows, and there he sleeps three nights. On the third morning he awakes, and from his mouth come winsome music and sweet fragrance, which draw all men and all animals after him.

The Whale presents a direct contrast to all this. It fixes itself near the shore, so that men, sailing in their boats, mistake it for an island, and cast anchor upon it. They light a fire and make merry, when suddenly the whale, the teller of falsehoods, dives beneath the waves and overwhelms the men with their boat, fettering the lost ones in its death-hall at the bottom of the sea. The whale has yet another plan of seduction: when hungry, it opens its mouth, and from it proceed pleasant odours which entice the fish to enter. When the mouth is full of fish, the whale shuts its gaping jaws, and the fish are swallowed up. It is beside our purpose to attempt to discover in such symbolism as this any very deep observation of the natural world. Animal life is studied, not as it is in reality, but in its fanciful relation to things spiritual. Yet inasmuch as such symbolic poems as these kept before men's minds the points of contact which subsist between the world of Nature and the world of spirit they deserve a passing notice.

Chapter IV.

THE AGE OF TRANSITION.

The century which succeeded the Norman Conquest might almost be described, as far as English literature is concerned, as the century of silence. During this period poetry was wholly at a standstill, while in prose the only monuments were the Chronicles kept by the monks of Winchester, Abingdon and Peterborough. In the year 1154, the last of these — the Peterborough Chronicle — terminated, and with its termination the writing of Old English — the West-Saxon dialect out of which the strenuous efforts of Alfred had formed a King's English — also ceased. Meanwhile, however, there was springing up in England an Anglo-French literature, both sacred and secular, which, though at first checking the development of the vernacular, was destined to give birth in the near future to a vigorous growth of Middle English poetry and prose. Towards the close of the twelfth century the silence was at last broken, and, a new era of song, fitful and faltering at first, but gathering strength as it advanced, began in England.

At the threshold of the middle English period of our literature stand the two figures of Layamon and Orm or Ormin. Both were clerics and both wrote in the vernacular; but beyond this they have very little in common. Orm, who was a monk living in the north-eastern part of what had once been the Mercian kingdom, where the Danish influence was most widely felt, has left us in his *Ormulum* a work as full of philological pedantry as of homiletic piety, but without much poetic feeling, and quite devoid of interest in the outer world of Nature. Far more interesting, and for our

present purpose, far more important, is Layamon, the author
of the *Brut* [1]).

Layamon's home was at Arley Regis, in the marchland by the Severn, a district where the traditions of Old
English poetry were longest preserved, and where Englishmen
came into contact with the rich romanticism of the Celt.
Nor was Layamon in his Worcestershire home outside of
the influence of Norman and Anglo-French poetry, so that
the possibility of discovering French, Celtic and English
elements in the *Brut* gives an added interest to the poem and
to its author. As Ten Brink finely says, [2]) "A most significant
figure, Layamon stands upon the dividing line between two
great periods, which he unites in a singular manner. He
once more reproduces for us an age that is forever past.
At the same time he is the first Englishman to draw from
French sources, the first to sing of king Arthur in English
verse ". Layamon is thus, as far at least as English poetry
is concerned, the poet who laid the foundation-stone of that
temple of Arthurian legend, which rose to so high an
eminence in the centuries that followed, and in which the
greatest poets of our own century have made such full and
frequent obeisance.

Deriving most of his material from the metrical *Geste
des Bretons* of the Norman poet Wace, Layamon amplified
his story very considerably, and it is probable that much
of what he added was drawn from oral traditions current in
the Severn valley. In his manner of telling his story,
Layamon keeps fairly closely to the traditions of Old English
verse, building up his sentences by means of parallel clauses,
and introducing frequent, though somewhat irregular, alliteration.

As a painter of natural scenery, too, Layamon falls into
line with the pre-conquest poets. Like them, he delights
in descriptions of sea-storm. How near he approaches in
some of these sea-pictures to the Old English masters will

---

[1]) Ed. Sir Frederick Madden, 1847.
[2]) *Early English Literature,* Vol. I. p. 193.

be seen in the following passage from the *Brut* describing the voyage of Godlac: —

> Æst aras a ladlich weder, þeostrede þa wolcne;
> þe wind com on weþere, and þa sæ he wraþede;
> uþen þer urnen, al þe tunes þer burnen,
> rapes þer braken, balu wes fulle riue.
> Scipen þer sunken . . . .
> þer þreo and fifti scipen feollen to grunde,
> in þa teonfulle sæ torneden sæiles.
>
> > *Brut*, MS. Calig. 4573 *et seq.*

Still closer perhaps is the analogy in the following passage describing the voyage of Ursele, some of the verses of which seem as though taken directly from Cynewulf:

> Inne þere Temese heo teuhten heore seiles;
> wind heo hæfden wunsum, weder mid þan bezsten,
> and heo seileden forþ þæt inne sæ heo comen;
> þa umbe stunde ne sæʒe heo noht of londe.
> Pa aras heom a wind a þere wiþer side,
> swurken under sunnen sweorte weolcnen,
> haʒel and ræin þer aræs, þe hit iseh him agras,
> uþen þer urnen, tunes swulche þer burnen,
> bordes þer breken, wimmen gunnen wepen.
> Pa scipen þa urnen bi-voren, twelve þer weoren for-loren;
> þa oþere weoren al to-driven, and forþ mid þere sæ iliþen.
>
> > 11964 *et seq.*

In addition to these foreground pictures of the sea in time of storm, Layamon gives us in the course of his *Brut* several pictures of a distant and wide-stretching land. As an illustration of this, let us take his description of his own land of Britain, as first seen by its mythical founder Brutus:

> Brutus hine bi-þohte, and þis folc bi-heold,
> bi-heold he þa muntes feire and muchele,
> bi-heold he þa medewan, þat weoren swiþe mære,
> bi-heold he þa wateres and þa wilde deor;
> bi-heold he þa fisches, bi-heold he þa fuʒeles,
> bi-heold he þa leswa and þene leofliche wode;
> bi-heold he þene wode hu he bleou,
> bi-heold he þæt corn hu hit greu;
> all he iseih on leoden, þat him leof was on heorten.
>
> > 2001 *et seq.*

In this simple picture we miss almost entirely the touch of the artist: yet through the baldness of the language it is possible to trace the poet's genuine delight in the beauty of an English landscape. His standpoint is neither wholly topographical nor wholly utilitarian: he has also an eye for the beauty of the land he is describing. He notes the blossoming of the wood and finds it 'lovely', while even the mountains are fair in his eyes.

Towards the close of his long poem, he describes a wonderful mere, and here, thanks to a closer attention to points of detail, he produces a well-ordered picture:

> Þat is a seolcuþ mere, iset a middelærde,
> mit fenne and mid ræode, mid watere swiþe bræde,
> mid fiscen and mid feoȝelen, mit univele þingen.
> Þat water is unimete brade, nikeres þer badieþ inne;
> þer is ælvene ploȝe in atteliche pole.
> Sixti æit-londes beoþ i þam watere longe;
> in ælc of þan æit-londe is a clude hæh and strong,
> þer næstieþ arnes and oþere græte voȝelas.
>
> <div align="right">21740 <i>et seq.</i></div>

Here too the resemblance to Old English poetry is not to be missed. The nickors which Layamon describes as bathing in the mere recall the nickors which haunt the pools and the shore where Grendel's mother has her dwelling, or those which drag Beowulf down to the sea-bottoms in his swimming-match with Breca. Thus do the poetic traditions of Old English poetry live on in the verses of Layamon's *Brut*.

The religious poetry of this age of transition consists mainly of poetical renderings of bible story, and of lives of the saints. To the former class belongs the poem entitled *Genesis and Exodus*[1]), which is, in all probability, the work of a man who lived in the east of England, and wrote in the east-midland dialect. In this poem scarcely any attempt is made to introduce ideas or pictures which are not found in the bible narratives, or in the *Historia scholastica* of Petrus Comestor. Of the vivid sea-pictures of the Old English *Exodus* there is here no trace. In the *Genesis* section, the

---

[1]) Ed. Morris (Early English Text Society VII).

story of the creation is told in clear and succinct language;
there is very little filling in of details, though the poet's
conception of the firmament is curious. He imagines it to
be a wall of ice, raised as a huge vault above the world;
no fire can melt it, and it shall stand unchanged until the
day of doom (verses 95—100). The story of the flood,
which the poet of the earlier *Genesis* had described with
some detail, is here told prosaically enough, though there is
a quaint trace of mysticism in the reference to the rainbow:

> God gat it a token of luven,
> Taunede him in þe walkene a-buven
> Rein-bowe, men cleped reed and blo;
> þe blo tokeneþ þe wateres wo
> þat is wiþ-uten and is gon;
> þe rede wid-innen toknet on
> wreche þat sal get wurþen sent
> wan al þis werld wurþe brent.
>
> *Genesis and Exodus*, 635—642.

In the section of the work which is based on the Book
of Exodus, the poet passes over the story of the crossing
of the Red Sea with but slender comment, but he makes an
attempt to paint Nature in his account of the thunders of
Sinai (verses 3461—3466).

Of greater importance for our present purpose than the
Genesis and Exodus is the Middle English *Physiologus* or
Bestiary,[1]) which belongs to the first half, or, at latest, the
middle, of the thirteenth century. It is a much fuller Bestiary
than that which was written in Old English, and in addition
to the familiar whale and panther stories, reference is
made to the lion, the eagle, the serpent, the ant, the hart,
the fox, the spider, the mermaid, the elephant and the turtle-
dove. This Bestiary is based directly upon the Latin one
of Theobaldus, and the English poet has usually kept closely
to his original. In the parable of the ant, however, he has
allowed himself some amount of expansion.[2]) This parable,
which is a mixture of truth and of Plinian fancifulness, may

---

[1]) Ed. Morris, *An Old Miscellany* (E. E. T. S. XLIX).

[2]) The Latin original is given in Appendix I. of Morris' edition.

be quoted here as illustrating the popular class of literature
to which it belongs: —

> Þe mire is magti, mikel ge swinkeþ
> in sumer and in softe weder, so we oft sen haven.
> In þe hervest hardilike gangeþ
> renneþ rapelike, resteþ hire seldum,
> fecheþ hire fode þer ge it mai finden,
> gaddreþ ilkines sed boþen of wude and of wed,
> of corn and of gres, þat ire to haven es,
> haleþ to hire hole þat siþen hire helpeþ
> þar ge wile ben winter agen;
> cave ge haveþ to crepen in,
> þat winter hire no derie ;
> mete in hire hule þat ge muge biliven.
> Þus ge tileþ þar, wiles ge time haveþ
> so it her telleþ;
> oc finde ge þe wete, corn þat hire qwemeþ,
> al ge.forleteþ þis oþer sed þat ic er seide ;
> ne bit ge nowt þe barlic beren abuten,
> oc suneþ it and sakeþ forþ so it same were.
> Get is wunder of þis wirm more þanne men weneþ,
> þe corn þat ge to cave bereþ al get bit otwinne,
> þat it ne forwurþe, ne waxe hire fro,
> er ge it eten wille.   234 *et seq.*

In this curious parable, in which the ant is made the
type of a well-ordered life, the winter represents death; the
wheat is the new law of the Gospel, the barley the old law
of Moses. Each new law has two applications, the one
directed to things spiritual, the other to things temporal.
Far-fetched as the analogy is, this parable in verse shows
the eagerness with which the mediæval mind brought
the world of Nature into touch with things spiritual. In
modern poetry the sympathy which is felt to exist between
man and Nature finds more artistic utterance in lyric poetry ;
but the mediæval poet, with a mind trained to symbolism,
found expression for this sense of sympathy in the fable,
or, as here, in the parable of a bestiary. Whereas, too, in
modern poetry, this mystic affinity is extended to all manifestations of the natural world, inanimate as well as animate,
it was in mediæval times confined to the animal world, to
which fable and bestiary-parable alike confine their attention.

The beast-epic or animal-saga proper, which grew to such proportions in the Low Countries and in France, seems scarcely to have won favour in England at this period, but the closely allied *debate (desbat)*, in which two birds are made to discuss some moral or theological problem, is represented already in this transition age by *The Owl and the Nightingale*[1]), a poem written in Dorsetshire during the early part of the reign of Henry III. The dispute is between youth with its beauty and joyance, and 'crabbed age' with its leanings towards asceticism. The poet reveals at every step how closely he is in touch with the life of birds: in this respect the poem is, in fact, no mean forerunner of Chaucer's famous *Parlement of Foules.* It begins as follows: —

> Ich was in one sumere dale,
> In one swiþe diȝele hale,
> I-herde ich holde grete tale
> An ule and one niȝtingale.
> Þat plait was stif and starc and strong,
> Sum wile softe, and lud among;
> And aither aȝen oþer swal.
> And let þat vule mod ut al.
>
>   *   *
>
> Þe niȝtingale bi-gon þe speche,
> In one hurne of one beche;
> And sat up one vaire boȝe.
> Þar were abute blosme i-noȝe
> In ore waste þicke hegge,
> I-meind mid spire and grene segge.
>
>   *   *
>
> Þo stod on old stoc þar bi-side,
> Þar þo ule song hire tide,
> And was mid ivi al bi-growe,
> Hit was þare ule earding-stowe.   1—28.

Then the quarrel begins: the nightingale complains of the foul behaviour of the owl, and the latter retorts with savage threats. The nightingale enrages the owl yet more by taunting him with his ugliness and uncleanness:

> Þu art lodlich to bi-holde,
> And þu þart loþ in monie volde;
> Þi bodi is short, þi sweore is smal,
> Grettere is þin heved þan þu al;
> Þin eȝen beoþ col-blake and brode,
> Riȝt swo heo weren i-peint mid wode;

---

[1]) Edited by T. Wright (Percy Society Publications). 4*

> Þu starest so þu wille abiten
> Al þat þu miȝt mid clivre smiten;
> Þi bile is stif and scharp and hoked,
> Riȝt so an owel þat is croked,
> Þar-mid þu clakest oft and longe,
> And þat is on of þine songe;
> Ac þu þretest to mine fleshe,
> Mid þine clivres woldest me meshe;
> Þe were i-cundur to one frogge,
> Þat sit at mulne under cogge,
> Snailes, mus, and fule wiȝte
> Beoþ þine cunde and þine riȝte.
> Þu sittest adai, and fliȝst aniȝt,
> Þu cuþest þat þu art on un-wiȝt;
> Þu art lodlich and un-clene,
> Bi þine neste ich hit mene,
> And ek bi þine fule brode,
> Þu fedest on heom a wel ful fode.   71—94.

The mocking taunts of the nightingale do not leave the owl unmoved. With downcast eye, she sits "swollen and bulged out as though she had eaten a frog", and as soon as the nightingale has finished, she has her answer ready. She maintains that her song is not harsh but melodious: —

> Mi stefne is bold and noȝt un-orne,
> Heo is i-lich one grene horne,
> And þin is i-lich one pipe
> Of one smale weode un-ripe.
> Ich singe bet þan þu dest:
> Þu chaterest so doþ on Irish prest;
> Ich singe an eve ariȝte time,
> And seoþþe won hit is bed-time,
> Þe þridde siþe at middelniȝte,
> And so ich mine song adiȝte
> Wone ich i-seo arise veorre
> Oþer dai-rim oþer dai-sterre.   317—328.

In reply to this, the nightingale declares that the owl sings only in winter, and that his song is wrathful and gloomy:

> Þu singest so doþ henne a snowe,
> Al þat heo singeþ hit is for wowe.   413—414.

The owl, she declares, behaves like the Evil One who loves to see tears in each man's eye, whereas the nightingale brings hope and bliss.

Þe blostme ginneþ springe and sprede
Beoþe ine treo and ek on mede;
Þe lilie mit hire faire wlite
Wol-cumeþ me, þat þu hit wite,
Bit me mid hire faire bleo
Þat ich schulle to hire fleo;
Þe rose also mid hir rude,
Þat cumeþ ut of þe þorne wude,
Bit me þat ich shulle singe
Vor hire luve one skentinge.   437—446.

The owl in reply dilates on his usefulness and on the
piety of his good works. He cleanses the barns, and even
the house of Christ, of foul mice, and if he desires a less
holy dwelling-pláce, he has the ivy-mantled tree, which is
ever in leaf. Here he dwells warm in winter and cool in
summer. Neither bird will yield to the other's arguments,
though the nightingale claims the victory. Singing her
loudest, she summons to her side the other birds, the
thrush, the woodpecker and the wren among the rest. The
wren proposes that Master Nicholas de Guildford, who lives
at Portisham in Dorsetshire, shall be called in to settle the
quarrel. The disputants agree, and the poem closes with the
picture of all the birds in full flight for the home of Master
Nicholas. Throughout the poem it is easy to recognise the
fact that it was the work of a man who knew the country,
and had an appreciative eye for the life of birds. There is
nothing trite or conventional in his descriptions, and he is
free from the artificiality of many fabulists who, in making
beasts and birds talk like human beings, lose sight altogether
of the true animal nature. Our poet's close attention to the
realities of bird life enables him to steer clear of this
shoal. His observation of Nature is clear-sighted and faithful.
What could be truer than the nightingale's description of the
owl, or the reference to the frog squatting beneath the
cog-wheel of the mill? There is, too, an idyllic beauty in
many of the descriptive passages. The welcome offered to
the nightingale by the lily and the rose is most delicately
conceived, as is also the owl's description of his abode in
the ivy-mantled tree. Nor is humour, an exceedingly rare

gift in English literature before Chaucer's time, entirely absent. The poet is evidently enjoying the fun which he allows the nightingale to create at the expense of his more sombre rival. Taken altogether, this poem is by far the most original of the shorter works of this transition period; and from the present standpoint, by far the most interesting.

The lyrical poems of this period are chiefly religious in character, the finest amongst them being hymns to the Virgin Mary, who, in an age of chivalry and *courteoisie*, called forth from men a homage which was foreign to English life and English poetry before the Conquest. These religious lyrics show little interest in the appearances of Nature, but a passing reference is occasionally made to the outer world by way of comparison, as in that beautiful *Love-Rune*[1]) which begins with the words: "A Mayde Cristes me bit yorne", in which the lyrist comments in the following manner upon those whose love is set upon the things of this life: —

> Þeos þeines þat her weren bolde
> beoþ aglyden so wyndes bles,
> Under molde hi liggeþ colde,
> faleweþ so doþ medewe gres.

Again in the *Song on the Passion*[2]) we trace the true lyric feeling which contrasts the joy which the birds feel at the return of summer with the sadness of the poet's own heart:

> Somer is comen and winter gon,
> þis day biginniz to longe,
> and þis foules everichon
> joye hem wit songe.
> So stronge kare me bint
> al wit joye þat is funde
> in londe
> Al for a child
> þat is so mild
> of honde.

---

[1]) Dr R. Morris, *An Old English Miscellany.*
[2]) *An Old English Miscellany.*

To this period of transition belong, further, some of the earliest Middle English verse-romances, written at the close of the thirteenth or the beginning of the fourteenth century. These belong to no definite cycle of romance, but embody popular native traditions and tell of English or Danish heroes. The most important of them are *Havelok the Dane, King Horn, Sir Beves of Hamton,* and *Guy of Warwick.* These romances are planned in the simplest fashion possible; the story is told rapidly, and with very little rhetorical flourish or brocading; the interest lies solely in the tale and the characters. Accordingly, we look in vain for anything like detailed landscape painting; there is nothing of that concentration of power upon isolated scenes which quickened the poet's imagination in Old English times. The romance-writer, allowing himself no pause, tells his story from beginning to end without break. In both *Havelok* [1]) and *King Horn* [2]), a good deal of the action takes place on, or in the neighbourhood of, the sea, yet scarcely any attempt is made to paint any of those sea-pictures which produce so fine an effect in the poems of Cynewulf. The following is a typical illustration of the Havelok-poet's curt method of procedure: he is describing the passage of Grim and his company over the North Sea:—

> And sone dede he leyn in an ore,
> And drou him to þe heye se,
> Þere he mict alþer-beste fle.
> Fro londe woren he bote a mile,
> Ne were nevere but ane hwile,
> Þat it ne bigan a wind to rise
> Out of þe north, men calleþ 'bise',
> And drof hem intil engelond.   719—725.

Once or twice the poet introduces a homely simile: he tells us, for instance, that at Godrich's assault his adversaries fell down "as doth the grass before the scythe full sharp". This is how he speak of Levive, Grim's daughter, and the bride of Bertram, Earl of Cornwall:

---

[1]) Ed. Skeat (E. E. T. S. Extra Series XIV).
[2]) Ed. Lumby (E. E. T. S. XIV).

> Hir semes curteys forto be,
> For she is fayr so flour on tre;
> Þe heu is swilk in hire ler
> So is the rose in roser,
> Hwan it is fayr sprad ut newe
> Ageyn the sunne, brith and lewe.
>
> 2916—2921.

In *King Horn* still more of the action takes place on the sea, yet even less attempt is made to paint sea-pictures. The only reference to it, or indeed to anything else in the natural world, occurs at the outset, where the voyage of Horn and his fellows is narrated as follows:

> Þe se bigan to flowe
> And horn child to rowe,
> Þe se þat schup so faste drof
> Þe children dradde þerof.
> Hi wenden to-wisse
> Of here lif to misse,
> Al þe day and al þe niȝt,
> Til hit sprang dai liȝt,
> Til Horn saȝ on þe stronde
> Men gon in þe londe.
> "Feren", quaþ he, "ȝonge,
> Ihc telle ȝou tiþinge,
> Ihc here foȝeles singe
> And þat gras him springe.
> Bliþe beo we on lyve,
> Ure schup is on ryve."
>
> 119—134.

In the twelve thousand verses of *Guy of Warwick*[1]) there is lavish description of hand-to-hand encounters, and of adventures in general, but only the barest reference is made to the physical features of the many countries through which Guy wanders during his pilgrimage. Where such references occur, they are extremely meagre, and often, too, of the most conventional character. Of the Old English delight in the sublime manifestations of the natural world there is no trace whatever, but the romance-writer is not wholly devoid of a sense of pleasure at the return of spring. Thus the story of one of Guy's many adventures opens with the following piece of description:

---

[1]) Ed. Zupitza (E. E. T. S., Extra Series XXV, XXVI).

Hyt was in may on a daye,
When every fowle makyth hys laye :
Thorow a foreste as þey dud ryde
(A feyre cyte was besyde),
Wyth grete love Gye badde hys men
Wende unto the cyte then
To take þer innes, þere þey dud knowe ;
For þere he wolde be a þrowe
To here fowles merely synge
And see feyre flowres sprynge..

Cambridge MS., 4254—64.

Almost at the end of the poem, in the part which serves as sequel to the main story, there appears a short but appreciative description of a green meadow by a river:

He sawe a watur depe and brode ;
Thedurward full faste he rode.
Beȝonde þe watur he sawe a grene,
A feyrer had never kynge nor quene.
All maner flowrys grewe there,
That of any vertews were.
Ther was in þat herber grene
All spycys that myght bene.

11389—97.

Within the green stands a fair palace and in front of the palace gates is a tree:

Theryn were fowlys nyght and day
That songyn mony a mery lay.

This landscape is fairly typical of the kind of natural description which is found in most of the romances of the period. It is made up of flowery meadows, trees full of birds, and a broad stretch of smooth-flowing water. In such landscapes we never get far away from palace or castle, or from the busy life of man, and the prevailing mood of the landscape is one of cheerfulness. In all this, as we shall have occasion to notice in a later chapter, it is the forerunner of the Chaucerian landscape.

Chapter V.

THE VERSE-ROMANCE.

The transition from the heroic atmosphere of the English epic to the chivalric atmosphere of the romance is little less than a literary revolution. Instead of the restrained and business-like temper of the epic, which reflects the spirit of a nation rather than of an individual, there arises the self-conscious and sentimental frame of mind of the romance-writer, prone to fantasy, in love with the marvellous, conforming to certain closely determined literary traditions. Love in its varied forms becomes a frequent theme, blended with which is the spirit of exuberant adventurousness which impels the knight to feats of chivalry that a more calculating age is prone to term quixotic. This change of temper, which the twelfth century saw carried into effect, was much more gradual in England than in France. Some four or five hundred years divide the *Beowulf* from the earliest Middle English romances, whereas there is little more than a century lying between the epic *Chanson de Roland* and the works of the first French romance-writers. Moreover, in England, some of the later Old English poems help to bridge over the gulf between the epic and the romance, whereas in France the change is as sudden as it is complete. The love of the marvellous, which forms so striking a feature in the mediæval romance, manifests itself already in the Old English *Phœnix*, while distinctly romantic elements appear in such a work as the *Guthlac*.

The great length of most of the romances gave their authors ample scope for the introduction of passages of description, but these descriptions are not usually concerned with Nature. Whereas detailed pictures are often given of royal pavilions and queenly bowers, tournaments and the garniture of horseman and steed, landscape scenes are passed by unheeded. In some of the romances, it is true, descriptions of scenery are occasionally prefixed to some important section of the story, being introduced in the pauses between one adventure and the next. Their effect in such cases is always pleasing, though, having no connection with the story, they are of the nature of excrescences. The coming of the romance to England means also the introduction into English poetry of the conventional landscape of a May morning in a beautiful garden. The transition from the storm-pictures of Old English poetry to this idyllic springtide scenery is not the least of the changes which came over English narrative verse in its passage from epic to romance, though the landscape painting of the *Guthlac* and the *Phœnix* prepares us for the change. We pass from the wind-swept coast of a northern clime under a wintry sky to the halcyon calm of a May morning in a land where May mornings know nothing of frost or east winds, and where all is sunshine, bird-song and flower-bloom. In the painting of such a landscape convention plays a considerable part, as the close resemblance to one another of these May-morning scenes clearly shows. The pleasure which poets felt in describing such scenes is real enough, yet we see again and again how the free impulses of the heart are brought under the control of accepted canons of taste, and the spontaneous bird-like delight in the spring month checked by conventionalism. There is a trimness in all these landscapes which is poles apart from the lawless freedom of Old English scenic description, and Nature is loved best when it is brought most closely under the hand of man. The rich luxuriance of thicket or forest is exchanged for the cultivated beauty of the garden or park: trees are admired, but not woods; a cool brooklet running through a well-kept meadow, but not the great river or the open sea.

It will be readily recognised that these springtide landscapes in garden or grove are of foreign origin. They entered England with the romance and are thus of French descent. Of their ultimate source it is not easy to speak with certainty; much of their idyllic charm appears in the lyric and epigrammatic verse of the Alexandrian period of Greek literature, and again in the lyrics of the Roman poets, Tibullus and Propertius. But the classical lyric is, in its landscape painting, not so exclusively attached either to garden scenery or to the months of April and May as are the mediæval romances. A close resemblance to the landscape-painting of the latter is, however, furnished by the lyrics of the twelfth century Troubadours of Provence. In the *sirvente*, the *pastorelle* and the *tenson* of such Troubadour poets as Bertran de Born, Aimeric de Belenoi and Bernart de Ventadorn, we find most of the characteristic features of the landscape scenes of the romances; all that is absent from the latter is that personal element which is the distinguishing mark of lyric poetry. We come very near to the feeling for Nature of the romances in the following *sirvente* of Bertran de Born:

> Be·m platz lo gais temps de pascor,
>   que fai fuolhas e flors venir
> e platz me, quan auch la baudor
>   dels auzels, que fan retentir
> lor chan per lo boschatge.

or again in the following lyric of Aimeric de Belenoi:

> Pos lo gai temps de pascor
>   renovel' e ve
> vestit de folh e de flor,
>   cantarai de se;
> qu'atressi s'es mos pessatz
>   de fin joi renovelatz.

The main features of this spring landscape, which appears in English narrative and lyric poetry from the thirteenth century right down to the Elizabethan age, are from time to time subject to modification. In the more popular poetry native prepossessions make their influence felt: thus in the Robin Hood ballads, in many of the folk-songs, and in the half-historical and half-fabulous romance of *Thomas of Ercel-doune* the season is still that of spring, but we pass from

the courtly and half-artificial garden to the freedom of the
English greenwood, where, instead of the nightingale, there
sings the woodpecker. Moreover, with the revival of alliterative
verse in the middle of the fourteenth century, which meant
also a revival of so many of the traditions of Old English
poetry, there came back the primitive love for winter scenes
and for the phenomena of Nature in time of storm, such as
Cynewulf and the Beowulf-poet had painted centuries before.
In romances like *Gawayne and the Green Knight* and *Ralph
the Collier* these replace almost entirely the exotic garden-
landscapes of the courtly school, but in the great *Troy-Book*
we see how that delight in May-morning scenery, to which
French troubadours and *trouvères* had given poetic expression,
is blended with the Teutonic exultation in the savagery of
Nature and the pageantry of storm by land and sea.

In the following pages the romances are arranged
according to their cycles. This method of arrangement will
serve to bring out those features in the interpretation of
Nature which are more or less peculiar to each cycle. The
disadvantage of such an arrangement is that it brings into
juxtaposition works which, in certain instances, are sundered
by centuries. For convenience' sake the works of the Gawayne-
poet are reserved for special treatment in Chapter VII.

1. The Arthurian Cycle.

The well-deserved fame of Malory's later prose-version
of the Arthurian legends has somewhat tended to hide from
view the earlier verse-romances which tell of Arthur and
his Round Table knights. The poetical versions of the
Arthurian legends, together with the saga of the Holy Grail
and the Tristram saga, which were at an early date in-
corporated with them, form a very considerable portion of
our Middle English literature, and their composition extends
over some two hundred years. The earliest of them, *Sir
Tristrem*, dates from the end of the thirteenth century,
whereas others, such as the beautiful *Lancelot of the Lake*,
are as late as the end of the fifteenth.

Setting aside for future consideration what is undoubtedly
the finest of them, *Sir Gawayne and the Green Knight*, we
can review those which remain more or less in the order
of their composition, referring in every case only to those
which claim attention in respect of their interpretation of
Nature. In *Sir Tristrem*[1]) descriptions of scenery are extremely rare. Here, as in *Havelok* and *King Horn*, much
of the action takes place on the sea, and once the hero
suffers shipwreck; but all that the poet tells us of the storm
is contained in the comment, "The waves were so mad with
wind". In the same way, when land is sighted, the description
is of the slenderest:

> A lond thai neighed neighe
> A forest as it ware,
> With hilles that were heighe,
> And holtes that weren hare.   I. 35.

The *Morte Arthur*,[2]) which deserves to be placed in
the front rank of Arthurian romances, is of Scottish origin,
though in its extant form it shows traces of the Midland
dialect. Professor Trautmann has conclusively shown[3]) that
it is the work of the Scottish poet Huchown — Huchown
"of the Awle Ryale" (aula regalis) as he was called — who
lived in the latter portion of the fourteenth century. It is
written in the alliterative long line, and, in company with
many other poems, it belongs to that revival of alliterative verse which set in about the middle of the fourteenth
century in the Severn valley, and became for a while the
powerful rival of the various rhyming measures then in
vogue. In this poem the delineation of landscape is kept
well in the background; yet where it is introduced, it reveals
a keen appreciation on the poet's part of some of the fairest
scenes of Nature. Huchown is no mean word-painter, and
his descriptions of the dragon and black bear, which are
seen by Arthur in his dream, and of the terrible conflict
between them, are given in a singularly telling manner. He

---

[1]) Ed. Sir Walter Scott, 1804.
[2]) Ed. Perry (E. E. T. S. VIII).
[3]) See *Anglia*, Vol. I. p. 109.

paints the dragon as it comes "wandering unworthily over the eddying waves", and the "destroying black bear above in the clouds", and the conflict between the two beasts is symbolic of the encounter shortly to ensue between Arthur and the giant. As Arthur, accompanied by his knights, rides forth in search of this giant, Huchown unfolds a summer landscape, the peaceful beauty of which contrasts very effectively with the scene of terror which follows immediately afterwards:

> Thane they roode by that ryver, that rynnyd so swythe,
> Pare þe ryndez overrechez with realle bowghes ;
> The roo and þe rayne-dere reklesse thare rounene,
> In ranez and in rosers to ryotte þame selvene;
> The frithez ware floreschte with flourez fulle many,
> With fawcouns and fesantez of ferlyche hewez ;
> All the feulez thare fleschez, that flyez with wengez,
> Fore þare galede þe gowke one grewez fulle lowde,
> Wyth alkyne gladchipe þay gladdene þeme selvene :
> Of the nyghtgale notez þe noisez was swette,
> They threpide wyth the throstills thre-hundreth at ones!
> Pat whate swowynge of watyr, and syngynge of byrdez,
> It myghte salve hyme of sore that sounde was nevere.
>
> *Morte Arthur,* 920—932.

Huchown was undoubtedly a poet whose eye and ear were alike open to the beauty of the natural world. There is scarcely anything in this description which is merely conventional or borrowed from books; the brightness and animation of the woodland scene are real, the firstfruits of the poet's own appreciation of such scenery. The fulness of meaning in the closing verse of the description — "It might heal him of sickness that never was sound" — is such as the poet himself might have felt; it rings true to his own inner consciousness.

In *Arthur and Merlin, Golagrus and Gawayne,* and again in the *Aunters (Adventures) of Arthur at the Tarne-wathelan,* occasional descriptions of landscape occur, and in every case the features introduced are based on the actual observation of Nature. In the last-named work the scene is laid amid the rocky hill-country around Carlisle, and the

storm which overtakes the hunting party, and drives them
to the rocks to seek shelter from the sleet and snow, is
realistically depicted. We are reminded in this romance of
the descriptive powers of the Gawayne-poet, and it is
possible that the romance is actually his.

Of the remaining strictly Arthurian romances, *Lancelot
of the Lake*[1]) alone calls for special consideration. This is
one of the latest of the cycle; it is post-Chaucerian, and
its composition has been assigned by Professor Skeat to the
last decade of the fifteenth century. The poem is based on
the French prose-romance, *Lancelot du Lac*, but the prologue
to the English work is entirely new, and many of the
landscape-pictures introduced into the body of the work
will be found, on comparison with the French source, to
be original. The poem was written in the Lowlands of
Scotland, but its authorship is quite unknown. One of the
most noticeable features in the poem is the influence of
Chaucer, which is everywhere strongly marked, and nowhere
more so than in the painting of the landscapes.

The prologue introduces the season of early spring: —

> The soft morow and the lustee aperill,
> The wynter set, the stormys in exill,
> Quhen that the brycht and fresch illumynare
> Uprisith arly in his fyre chare
> His hot cours in to the orient,
> And from his spere his goldine stremis sent
> Upone the grond, in maner of mesag,
> One every thyng to walkyn thar curage,
> That natur haith set under hire mycht,
> Boith gyrs and flour, and every lusty wicht.
>
> *Prologue*, 1—10.

The poet, abandoning himself to his love-melancholy,
enters a garden, the description of which is, verse for verse,
in the orthodox Chaucerian style: —

> Syne to o gardinge that wes weil besen,
> Of quiche the feild was al depaynt with gren.
> The tendyre and the lusty flouris new
> Up throue the gren upon thar stalkis grew

---

[1]) Ed. Skeat (E. E. T. S. VI.).

Aghane the sone, and thare levis spred,
Quharwith that al the gardinge was i-clede;
That pryapus, in to his tyme before,
In o lustear walkith nevir more.

*   *   *

Thar was the flour, thar was the queen alcest
Rycht wering being of the nychtis rest,
Unclosing gane the crownel for the day;
The brycht sone illumynit haith the spray,
The nychtis sobir ande the most schowris,
As cristoll terys withhong upone the flouris,
Haith upwarpith in the lusty aire,
The morowe makith soft, ameyne and faire,
And the byrdis thar mychty voce out-throng
Quhill al the wood resonite of thar songe.

Prologue, 45 *et seq.*

The reference to Priapus, and to the Queen Alceste of the
Legend of Good Women, as well as the delicate outlining
of this picture is quite Chaucerian, and illustrates the influence
of the English poet upon his Scottish successors in the
fifteenth century. The story of Lancelot is ushered in with
another description of the month of April, in almost every
verse of which one is reminded of the opening of the Prologue
to the *Canterbury Tales.* At the outset of the third Book
there occurs yet another spring landscape, and here there
is more originality in the choice of circumstance; yet throughout we feel that the poet's thought runs in a Chaucerian
direction: —

The long dirk pasag of the winter, and the lycht
Of phebus comprochit with his mycht;
The which, ascending in his altitud
Awodith Saturn with his stormys rude;
The soft dew one fra the hewyne doune falis
Apone the erth, one hillis and on valis,
And throw the sobir and the must humouris
Up nurisit ar the erbis and the flouris.
Natur the erth of many divers hew
Our-fret, and cled with the tendir new.

2471—2480.

Originally distinct from, but in Middle English times
absorbed into, the Arthurian cycle, are the romances which

deal with the legend of the Holy Grail. Mysticism, which prevails through the whole cycle of Arthurian romance, becomes especially prominent in those of the Grail, and, by weaving the supernatural around the natural, influences, in some measure, the interpretation of Nature. The chief romances which belong to this section are *Joseph of Arimathea, The Life of Joseph of Arimathea* and *The Holy Grail.* The first of these was written about the middle of the fourteenth century, and belongs to the series of alliterative romances which at that time rose to such distinction. It is almost entirely wanting in descriptions of landscape. Near the beginning there is a reference "to a forest with floures ful feire, that was called Argos", and later on there is an account of the vision of the three trees, on the stems of which are inscribed words written in gold, silver, and blue ink; but such description belong to the region of the marvellous, and not to the world of Nature.

The Life of Joseph of Arimathea[1]), the date of which is about one hundred and fifty years later, illustrates better than the work just noticed the interweaving of the supernatural with the natural. Of this character is the description of the walnut-tree at Glastonbury which "bereth no leaves tyll the day of saynt Barnabe", and still more so the description of the famous Glastonbury hawthorns: —

> Three hawthornes also that groweth in Werall
> Do burge and bere grene leaves at christmas,
> As fresshe as other in May, whan the nightingale
> Wrestes out her notes musycall, as pure as glas;
> Of all wodes and forestes she is the chief chauntres,
> In werall she might have a playne place,
> On those hawthornes to shewe her notes clere.

385—391.

In the romance of the *Holy Grail,* an English rendering of the *Roman du Graal* of the French poet Boron, there is the usual supernatural treatment of Nature, and, in addition, the frequent introduction of symbolism, akin to that found in the early Physiologi. Here, however, the symbolism is not

---

[1]) **Ed.** Skeat (E. E. T. S. XLIV.).

confined to animal life, but pertains also to inanimate objects.
As an instance of the poet's symbolic treatment of Nature,
the following passage may be taken:

> Hym thowhte that in a medewe he was,
> Whiche was large and grene in that plas,
> And in that medewe a fair tree there was tho,
> And many divers flowres owt of it gonnen go,
> That envirowned this tre al abowte,
> And ful of flowres it heng with-owte,
> As it axeth the kende after a tre. XXXII. 219—225.

The picture is here a visionary one, and the meadow
is symbolic of the world in which we live. The tree is man's
person, out of which grows, as a fadeless flower, the Virgin
Mary.

2. The Carlovingian Cycle.

The Carlovingian romances of Middle English literature
are for the most part fairly close translations of French
originals, and belong almost entirely to the fourteenth and
fifteenth centuries. The literary power of these romances is
not great, and they are certainly lacking in the refinement
of manner, the psychological depth, and the spirituality of
the poems which deal with the heroes of the Round Table;
moreover, though many of them owe their theme to the
crusades and to contact with the East, there is scarcely any
attempt made to paint an oriental landscape. The interpretation
of Nature is throughout extremely slight. Thus in *Sir Otuel*[1]),
one of the earliest of the group, the author has no interest in
scenic description, even as background to the main action.
Occasionally he refers to the change from night to day, or
from winter to summer, but confines himself to the most
general terms:

> On morwe tho the dai sprong,
> And the larke bigan hire song,
> King Charles wente to cherche,
> Godes werkes for to werche.
>
> 387—390.

---

[1]) Ed. Herrtage (E. E. T. S. Extra Series, XXXIX.).

5*

Or again, —

> Averil was comen, an winter gon,
> And Charles toke the weie a non.
>
> 677—678.

In *Sir Ferumbras* [1]) the treatment of Nature is equally meagre. There is the same abrupt reference to the coming of morning as in *Sir Otuel*: —

> On the morwe, wan it was day and the larke bygan to synge,
> Thys messegers come in god array alle byfore the kynge.
>
> 1498—1499.

On rare occasions a simile is introduced:

> Als furde thay with that ilke hepe, withoute tales mo,
> As doth wolves among the shepe, wan thay cometh hem to.
>
> 950—951.

The Siege of Melayne (Milan) and *Rowland and Vernagu* may be passed over without comment, but *Duke Rowland and Sir Otuel* [2]) claims a moment's notice, if only because in it some attempt is made to localise the scene where the great duel between Roland and Otuel takes place: —

> Thay broghte tham by-twene two watirs brighte,
> Sayne and Meryn le graunte thay highte,
>   As the bukes gan us saye —
> Into a medowe semely to sighte,
> There als these doghety men solde fighte
>   With-owten more delaye.
>
> 379—384.

The fragmentary *Song of Roland* [3]), which is based on the great French epic of the eleventh century, is superior to its original as far as the delineation of scenery is concerned, as the following description of a spring sunrise clearly shows:

> While the knyghtis roun, risithe the soun;
> The daye was faire, the clowdis be roun,
> Dew diskid adoun and dymmyd the floures,
> And foulis rose and song full amorous.
> Ther did no wind blow, but wedir full still.
>
> 578—582.

---

[1]) Ed. Herrtage (E. E. T. S., Extra Series, XXXIV.).
[2]) Ed. Herrtage (E. E. T. S., Extra Series, XXXV.).
[3]) Ed. Herrtage (E. E. T. S., Extra Series, XXXV.).

Again, in the description of the storm which passes over France on the occasion of the battle of Roncesvaux, the English poet shows a marked superiority to the French; he gives to the picture a greater amplitude, and makes it appear much more animated:

> But while our folk fought togedur,
> There fell in Fraunce a straung wedur.
> A gret derk myst in the mydday-tym,
> Thik, and clowdy, and evyll wedur thene,
> And thiknes of sterres and thonder light:
> The erthe dynnyt doillfully to wet.
> Foulis fled for fere, it was gret wonder:
> Bowes of trees then brestyn asonder.
> Best ran to bankis and cried full sore,
> They durst not abid in the mor:
> Ther was no man but he hid his hed,
> And thought not but to dy in that sted.
> The wekid wedur lastid full long,
> From the mornyng to the evynsong:
> Then rose a clowd evyn in the west,
> As red as blod, withouton rest;
> It shewid doun on the erthe and ther did shyn,
> So many doughty men as died that tym.
>
> 845—863.

What the English poet has to say of the birds, the wild beasts and the trees, and also of the cloud as red as blood, is of his own devising, as a glance at the original will at once make clear. (See *Chanson de Roland*, 1423—1437.)

The Sowdane (Sultan) of Babylone[1]) is of later date than most of the Carlovingian romances, belonging, in fact to the early part of the fifteenth century. It is thus post-Chaucerian, and Chaucer's influence makes itself felt in the painting of the landscapes as in much else. Who, for instance, can fail to recognise in the following picture the direct bearing of the opening verses of the Prologue to the *Canterbury Tales*?

> Hit bifelle by-twyxte March and Maye,
> Whan kynde corage begynneth to pryke,
> Whan firth and felde wexen gaye,
> And every wight desirith his like,

---

[1]) Ed. Hausknecht (E. E. T. S., Extra Series, XXXVIII.).

Whan lovers slepen with opyn yȝe,
As nightyngalis on grene tre,
And sore desire that thai cowde flye,
That thay myghte withe here lovere be.

                                      41—48.

Later on (verses 963—970) there occurs another spring landscape in which Chaucer's influence is equally apparent.

The *Tale of Ralph Collier*[1]) may be said, by reason of its merry, popular theme, to stand somewhat apart from the more formal verse-romances. It differs from them, too, in its painting of scenery. There is less insistence on the conventional spring landscape, and in one place the poet gives us a picture of a storm which resembles the vigorous representations of storm in Old English poetry — a resemblance which the use of alliterative verse does much to increase:

And as that Ryall raid ovir the rude mure,
Him betyde ane tempest that tyme, hard I tell:
The wind blew out of the eist stiflie and sture,
The deip durandlie draif in mony deip dell;
Sa feirslie fra the firmament, sa fellounlie it fure,
Thair micht na folk hold na fute on the heich fell,
In point thay war to parische, thai proudest men and pure.
In thay wickit wedderis thair wist nane to dwell.
Amang the myrk montanis sa madlie thay mer,
        Be it was pryme of the day,
        Sa wonder hard fure thay,
        That ilk ane tuik ane seir way,
        And sperpillit full fer.   14—26.

3. The Romances of Alexander the Great.

The name of the famous king of Macedon was for the mediæval romance-writers a name to conjure with. Several Alexander romances, most of them written in alliterative verse, have come down to us, and in all of them the eastern travels of that king play a considerable part. A love for the marvellous is very marked in them, though the marvels recorded are of a different character from those found in the Arthurian romances. In the latter, the marvellous assumes the more spiritual form of mysticism, whereas in the Alexander

---

[1]) Ed. Herrtage (E. E. T. S., Extra Series, XXXIX.).

romances it centres in the crudely fabulous, the imagination running riot in its endeavour to body forth the forms of things unheard of in Christendom, but with which the magic East was supposed to teem.

This craving for whatever is mysterious affects in many ways the interpretation of Nature; what is merely natural is set aside for the supernatural and fabulous. Such is eminently the case with the longest of these romances, *The Wars of Alexander* [1]). In this work there is a description of the sun and moon trees which have the power of speech, and address Alexander in the languages of India and Greece. The actual description of these trees is, for the present purpose, less interesting than that of the wood in which they are growing. Here the poet descends from the region of the marvellous, and bases his description on actual observation:

Then metis he doun of the mounte into a mirk vale,
A drere dale and a depe, a dym and a thestir;
Miȝt thare na saule undire son see to anothire;
Thai ware umbe-thonrid in that thede with slike a thike cloude,
That thai miȝt fele it with thaire fiste as flabband webbis,
With all the bothom full of bournes, briȝt as the silvire,
And bery-bobis on the braes, brethand as mirre.   4803—4809.

A good deal of imaginative detail gathers round the description of the high hill which was "loken all in lange lindis like to the cedres" (verse 537), while that of the storm which rages at the time of Alexander's birth is conceived in accordance with the exalted native traditions of tempest scenery which foreign models, delighting in spring sunshine and halcyon days, could not wholly eradicate:

The liȝt, lemand late, laschis fra the hevyn,
Thonere thrastis ware thra thristid the welkyn,
Cloudis clenely to-clefe clatird unfaire,
All blakenid aboute and boris the son.
Wild wedirs up werpe, and the wynd ryse,
And all flames the flode, as it fire were,
Nowe briȝt, nowe blaa, nowe on blase efter,
And than over-quelmys in a quirre and quatis ever e-like.
                                            553—560.

---

[1]) Ed. Skeat (E. E. T. S., Extra Series, XLVII.).

Towards the end of the poem there is a reference to Alexander's visit to Dindimus, king of the Brahmins, which forms the main theme of the romance entitled *Alexander and Dindimus*[1]). In this work there is a reappearance of the fabulous. The poet writes of wonderful trees which bear fruit when the sun shines, but disappear entirely when it grows dark; on each tree sits a bird which spits fire whenever anyone approaches.

In some respects the life of the Brahmins under their wise ruler, Dindimus, is pictured as an ideal golden age of simplicity. In Dindimus's letter to Alexander, the idyllic charm of that life lived in accordance with Nature is set forth with fine appreciation:

> We han mirthe ful miche in medus and feldus,
> There faire places and plain han plente of flourus,
> That sote savouron til us; and with the siht clene
> We ben as fulsom ifounde, as tho3 we fed were.
> Us is likful and lef in laundus to walke,
> There won walleth of watur in the welle-springus.
> Miche wilne we wende in the wodus thikke,
> For to rome undur ris that rif is of levus;
> That we mowe graspen on the grene and gret joie here
> Of brem briddene song in the braunchus a-lofte.
>
> 494—503.

The poet had not quite a free hand in this description, but a comparison with the Latin original will bring to notice the fact that many of the features introduced are the poet's own invention. The Latin prose version of this passage reads as follows: "Delectamur etiam videre florigeros campos, ex quibus in nostros nares suavissimus odor intrat. Delectamur etiam in optimis locis silvarum et fontium, in quibus iocundissimas avium audimus cantilenas". The English poet has not merely enlarged the picture; he has added new ideas, and of these not the least striking is that which tells how the joy of the Brahmins in the sight of the flowers is so great that it is as food to their bodies.

The last of the three alliterative Alexander romances, known simply by the name *Alisaunder*, is quite fragmentary,

---

[1]) Ed. Skeat (E. E. T. S., Extra Series, XXXI.).

and does not call for special notice. It is by the same hand
as the *Alexander and Dindimus*, both being fragments of a
larger *Life of Alexander* which in its entirety is no longer
extant. There is, however, a romance which bears the same
name [1]), written in rhyming verse, and somewhat older than
the alliterative romances which have just been considered.
In this poem the custom of introducing descriptions of natural
scenery in the pauses of the main action is in force, and
the poet accordingly furnishes on these occasions several
short sketches of the spring or autumn season. In the following
summer morning scene there is, over and above the pure
description, a trace of elegiac sentiment which is somewhat
rare in Middle English poetry:

> Clere and faire the somerys day spryng,
> And makith mony departyng
> Bytweone knyght and his swetyng.
> Theo sunne ariseth, and fallith the dewyng;
> Theo nesche clay hit makith clyng.
> Moni is jolif in the mornyng,
> And tholeth deth or the evenyng.   911—917.

Full of simple charm is the poet's picture of the autumn
season with its ripening fruits and corn:

> In tyme of hervest mery it is ynough;
> Peres and apples hongeth on bough.
> The hayward bloweth mery his horne;
> In everyche felde ripe is corne;
> The grapes hongen on the vyne:
> Swete is trewe love and fyne.
>   5754—5759.

The ingenuousness and fidelity of such a picture as this
appeals to the modern reader with more force than the record
of gross marvels which in the Alexander romances frequently
serve as natural description. It shows, moreover, that even
where the scene is laid in a far-off, and, to a large extent,
imaginary land, the prominent features in the familiar English
landscape still appeal strongly to the poet's sense of beauty.

---

[1]) Ed. Weber, *Metrical Romances,* Vol. I.

4. The Non-Cyclical Romances.

In addition to the romances which group themselves naturally into cycles, others were written in Middle English times which are without any such cyclic character. Of these only two demand special attention here — *William of Palerne* and *The Gest Hystoriale of the Destruction of Troy,* or, more briefly, *The Troy-Book.* Both of these poems are in alliterative verse, and both were probably written in the second half of the fourteenth century: beyond this, however, they have nothing in common. *William of Palerne*[1]) is a pure *roman d'aventure.* It has a peculiar interest in the fact that it introduces the mediæval tradition of the werwolf, the werwolf of the romance playing the part of good genius to the hero and heroine amid their varied adventures. A good deal of the action of the poem takes place in the forests of Italy, yet, in spite of this, there is very little description of forest scenery. We read on one occasion of a "fayr forest floriched ful thik", but further details are not given. The work contains only two detailed descriptions of landscape, and in either case the time of year is the month of May; the one brings us to the outskirts of a forest, the other to a beautiful garden. In the former, the poet tells how the child William is found by the cowherd: —

> Lovely lay it a-long in his lonely denne,
> and buskede him out of þe buschys þat were blowed grene.
> and briddes ful bremely on the bowes singe.
> What for melodye þat þei made in þe mey sesoun,
> þat litel child listely lorked out of his cave,
> faire floures forto fecche þat he bi-fore him seye,
> and to gadere of þe grases þat grene were and fayre.
> And whan it was out went, so wel hit him liked
> þe savor of þe swete sesoun and song of þe briddes,
> þat he ferde fast aboute floures to gadere,
> and layked him long while to lesten that merthe.
>
> 20—31.

The other occasion on which the poet halts in the course of his story to introduce a piece of natural description is when the heroine, Melior, finds William of Palerne asleep in

---

[1]) Ed. Skeat (E. E. T. S. Extra Series, I.).

her father's garden. The garden, as will be seen more fully
in the chapter dealing with Chaucer's work, is the centre-piece of
the courtly landscape in mediaeval poetry. It appealed to the
quiet interest in a cultivated landscape which was characteristic
of the time, and afforded pleasure where the wild grandeur
of mountain or forest scenery would have only repelled:

> And whan þe gaye gerles were into þe gardin come,
> faire floures þei found of fele maner hewes,
> þat swete were of savor and to þe siȝt gode;
> and eche busch full of briddes þat bliþeliche song,
> boþe þe þrusch and þe þrustele bi þritti of boþe,
> meleden ful merye, in maner of here kinde.
> And alle freliche foules þat on þat friþ songe,
> for merþe of þat may time þei made moche noyce,
> to glade wiþ uch gome þat here gle herde.

816—824.

Such descriptions as the above are extremely simple and
also extremely limited in their scope. The horizon is bounded
by the four walls of the king's garden, and the poet's appreciation does not extend beyond the song of the birds and
the gay colours and fragrance of the flowers.

Very different is the interpretation of Nature in the
Troy-Book[1]), a poem extending over fourteen thousand verses,
and holding a very importance place in the history of the
English verse-romance. In the present study the work is
worthy of special attention, in that it unites, in a manner
almost unknown to the other romances of the time, the Old
English attitude towards Nature with that which was introduced from France and Provence in the centuries which
followed the Conquest. In other words, it assimilates the
Old English appreciation of ocean storms and wintry winds
with the Troubadour delight in May morning sunshine and
the beauty of bird-song and flower-bloom. The wild sublimity
of the tempest is here displayed side by side with the idyllic
repose of a flowery meadow. The poet loves to fill his
landscapes with a mass of details, which, being harmoniously
combined, give to the whole picture a pleasing fulness and
breadth. As an illustration of this, and also of the poet's

---

[1]) Ed. Panton and Donaldson (E. E. T. S., XXXIX. and LVI.).

delight in the spring season, the following passage may be
quoted: —

> Þe cloudes wax clere, clensit þe ayre;
> Wynter away, watris were calme;
> Stormes were still, þe sternes full clere,
> Zephorus softe windys soberly blew;
> Bowes in bright holtes buriont ful faire;
> Grevys wex grene and þe ground swete;
> Swoghyng of swete ayre, swalyng of briddes;
> Medowes and mounteyns myngit with floures,
> Colord by course as þaire kynd askit.   1055—63.

The scene here is an extensive one. We are not shut
up in a high-walled garden, but a broad expanse of Nature
is before us. The picture embraces heaven and earth: the
firmament with its stars, the winds and clouds, the forest,
the meadow, the grove, and even the mountain are all included. Through it all, too, there is a freedom from conventionality, a breath of freshness like the poet's "soughing of
sweet air".

Nor is spring the only season which stirs his imagination.
In verses 10630 *et seq.* these is a description of the summer
solstice, and a little later a masterly picture of autumn and
the approach of winter:

> Hyt fell thus by fortune, þe fairest of þe yere
> Was past to the point of the pale wintur:
> Hervest, with the heite and the high sun,
> Was comyn into colde with a course low;
> Trees, thurgh tempestes, tynde hade þere leves;
> And briddes abatid of hor brem songe;
> The wynde of the west wackenet above,
> Blowyng full bremly o the brode ythes;
> The clere aire overcast with cloudys full thicke,
> With mystes full merke mynget with showres;
> Flodes were felle thurgh fallyng of rayne,
> And wintur up wacknet with his wete aire.
>   12463—12474.

In contrast to this picture of the approach of winter,
is another in which its departure is described (see verses
4029 *et seq.*).

In addition to these pictures of inland scenery at all
seasons of the year, the author of the *Troy-Book* has painted

the sea — the sea in time of storm. In this he makes full use of the great inheritance bequeathed by Old English poets, and though there is no suggestion of direct imitation, it is difficult to believe that he was unfamiliar with those descriptions of tempests by sea and land which occupy so important a place in the poems of Cynewulf and his contemporaries. In the course of his romance the poet furnishes no less than four descriptions of a sea-storm, and two others of a storm on land. As is only natural, there is a good deal of repetition in these attempts to paint some of the most sublime aspects of the natural world. Thunder and lightning, which are rarely referred to in Old English poetry, appear here in five out of the six storm-pictures. The description of the storm which destroys Ajax' fleet in Book XXI. may be singled out as a good illustration of the poet's manner:

> Sodonly the softe winde unsoberly blew;
> A myste and a merkenes myngit to-gedur;
> A thoner and a thicke rayne þrublet in the skewes,
> With an ugsom noise, noy for to here;
> All flasshet in a fire the firmament over;
> Was no light but a laite, þat launchit above;
> Hit skirmyt in the skewes with a skyre low,
> Thurgh the claterand clowdes clos to the hevyn,
> As the welkyn shuld walt for wodenes of hete.
> With blastes full bigge of the breme wyndes,
> Walt up the waghes upon wan hilles;
> Stith was the storme, stird all the shippes,
> Hoppit on hegh with heste of the flodes.

12494—12506.

The stringing together of parallel clauses in the above passage, added to the animation and boldness of the imagery, furnishes yet another illustration of the resemblance between the author of the *Troy-Book* and the pre-conquest poets. It is, of course, difficult to determine exactly to what extent Middle English poets were familiar with Old English poetry. Direct influence is in every case uncertain, but the revival of alliterative verse in the west of England and in Scotland during the latter half of the fourteenth century was in all probability based not merely on vague traditions of what Old English poetry was like, but on actual acquaintance with the poetry itself.

Chapter VI.

MIDDLE ENGLISH HISTORICAL AND LYRICAL POETRY.

1. Historical Poems.

The line of demarcation between the verse-chronicle and the metrical romance is never very clearly marked in Middle English times, for the most sober historian was usually ready to introduce into his chronicle legends of as fanciful a character as anything to be found in the pure romances. Especially is this the case with such historical poems as *Richard Cœur de Lion,* and *Thomas of Erceldoune*; and, to a less degree, with Barbour's *Bruce* and Henry the Minstrel's *Wallace.* In consequence of the greater freedom which these chroniclers permitted themselves in the handling of their historical themes, a place is occasionally found for pure description of landscape. Such is the case with *Richard Cœur de Lion*[1]), in which the poet commences the second part of his work by describing the month of May:

> Merye is in the tyme off May
> Whenne foulis synge in her lay:
> Floures on appyl trees and perye;
> Smale foules synge merye.
> Ladyes strowe here boures
> With rede roses and lylye floures.
> Gret joye is in frith and lake;
> Best and byrd playes with his make.

This is simplicity itself, though the picture admits of somewhat greater individualisation than is to be found in many of the spring landscapes of the time. What is of chief interest, however, is the insertion of such a picture in an historical poem.

---

[1]) Weber's *Metrical Romances*, Vol. II.

The mixture of history and romance, as found in *Richard Cœur de Lion,* is much more pronounced in the northern poem, *Thomas of Erceldoune* [1]). Here again references to external Nature are found, and the poem opens with a picture of the birds singing on a morning in May, which has a good deal in common with the scenes of spring which are found in the opening verses of some of the Robin Hood Ballads:

> Als i me wente þis Endres daye,
> Full faste in mynd makand my mone,
> In a mery mornynge of Maye
> By huntle bankkes my selfe allone,
> I herde þe jaye, and be throstyll cokke,
> The Mawys menyde hir of hir songe,
> Þe wodewale beryde als a belle
> That alle þe wode a-bowte me ronge.
>
> Thortnon Ms. 25—32.

The value of the *Bruce* [2]) of archdeacon Barbour (1316?— 1395) is, of course, far higher than that of the historical poems referred to above. Barbour, as he tells us at the outset of his poem, was resolved "to put in wryt a suthfast story"; at the same time, his account of the wanderings and struggles of Scotland's hero has, over and above its historical value, all the interest and adventurousness of a pure romance. The animation of the poem — perhaps its most noticeable feature — is maintained throughout, and Barbour rarely allows himself a pause in the action in which to introduce passages of natural description. Like the romance-writers, however, he is anxious to keep clearly before the minds of his readers the season at which the various events take place; while, when he comes to write of the month of May, and of the spring season generally, he cannot withhold an expression of his delight that the winter is over, and that Nature is awaking to new life. In Book XVI., for instance, he introduces the following passage of description:

> This wes in the moneth of may,
> Quhen byrdis syngis on the spray,
> Melland thair notys with syndry sowne,

[1]) Ed. Murray (E. E. T. S., LXI.).
[2]) Ed. Skeat (E. E. T. S. Extra Series, XI., XXI., XXIX., and LV.).

> For softnes of that sweit sesoune;
> And lewis on the branchis spredis,
> And blomys bricht besyd thame bredis,
> And feldis florist ar with flowris,
> Weill savourit, of seir colowris,
> And all thing worthis blith and gay.

63—71.

In this picture of the May season, there is little attempt at individualisation, but the impression which it leaves behind is that of a naïve and unalloyed delight in the return of spring, such as is met with again and again in the course of Middle English poetry. At the commencement of Book V., another picture of spring is introduced, and the poet seeks this time to descend to details. The result is on the whole satisfactory, but, as Professor Veitch has already pointed out[1]), it leads him to introduce into a Scottish landscape such a bird as the nightingale, which, at least in modern times, does not pursue its northern migration beyond Yorkshire.

Barbour makes but little attempt to describe in detail the various localities which his hero visits in the course of his wanderings: an interesting exception, however, occurs in the case of the mountain Ben Cruachan and the Pass of Brander, which he describes in Book X.: —

> And that wes in ane evill place,
> That so strat and so narrow was,
> That twa men sammyn mycht nocht ryde
> In sum place of the hyllis syde.
> The nether half wes perelous;
> For a schoir crag, hye and hydvous,
> Raucht till the se doun fra the pas.
> On the owthir half ane montane was
> So cumrous, and ek so stay,
> That it wes hard to pas that way.
> Crechanben hecht that montane.

Brus, X. 17—27.

One feels in reading this description that the mountain was regarded as something repellent: yet the clearness and fidelity of the picture emphasize the deep impression which the spot had made upon the poet.

---

[1]) *The Feeling for Nature in Scottish Poetry*, Vol. I., p. 167.

Barbour's descriptions of landscape are, moreover, not confined to inland scenery. Perhaps his most vivid piece of natural description is found in Book III., where he relates the voyage of Bruce and his fellows off the west coast of Scotland : —

> Quhen thai war boune, to saile thai went:
> The wynd wes wele to thar talent.
> Thai raysyt saile and furth thai far,
> And by the mole thai passyt ʒar,
> And entryt sone in-to the rase,
> Quhar that the strem sa sturdy was,
> That wawys wyd that brekand war
> Weltryt as hillys her and thar.
> The schippys our the wawys slayd,
> For wynd at poynt blawand thai had.
> Bot nocht-for-thi quha had thar bene,
> A gret stertling he mycht haiff seyne
> Off schyppys; for quhilum sum wald be
> Rycht on the wawys summite;
> And sum wald slyd fra heycht to law,
> Rycht as thai doune till hell wald draw;
> Syne on the waw stert sodanly.
>
>   Book III., 693—709.

The picture of the boats rising and falling with the waves is most graphically drawn. Barbour's sense of restraint prevents him from dilating at length upon the scene, yet the directness of the presentation certainly enhances its value. Except where he paints the spring season, the poet of the *Bruce* never introduces landscape scenes for the sake of their poetic effect. He has, indeed, very little interest in the picturesque, and where he describes natural scenery, there is always an ulterior end in view. For Barbour landscape painting was of value, only in as far as it helped to make the human interest clearer and more realistic.

In somewhat close connection with Barbour's *Bruce* standst he *Wallace*[1]) of Henry the Minstrel (*fl.* 1470—1492), separated from it, though it be, by nearly a hundred years. The similarity, however, is to be found rather in the subject than in the setting. The later poem is far less naïve and

---

[1]) Ed. Moir (Scottish Text Society Publications).

artless than that of the archdeacon of Aberdeen; Henry the
Minstrel's descriptions of Nature teem with classical conventions, which are due to the study of Virgil and other
Latin poets, together with their mediæval imitators.   His
landscape-scenes are almost entirely confined to the description
of the seasons and months of the year, and are usually to
be found at the beginning of the various Books into which
his poem is divided.   There is frequent reference on these
occasions to Titan, Phœbus, Zephyrus, and, in imitation
perhaps of Chaucer, to the march of the sun through the
various chambers of the zodiac.   In describing the seasons
and months of the year, he shows the customary fondness
for the spring months, but has also a ready appreciation
for other seasons.   September he describes as —

> the humyll moneth suette,
> Quhen passyt by the hicht was off the hete.   IV. 1.

July is painted with much fuller detail in the opening
passage of the third Book.

> In joyows Julii, quhen the flouris suete,
> Degesteable, engenered throu the hete,
> Baith erbe and froyte, busk and bewis, braid
> Haboundandlye in every slonk and slaid;
> Als bestiall, thar rycht cours till endur,
> Weyle helpyt ar be wyrkyn off natur,
> On fute and weynge ascendand to the hycht,
> Conserved weill be the Makar of mycht;
> Fyscheis in flude refeckit rialye
> Till mannys fude, the warld suld occupye.

This is rather humdrum verse, but in thus drawing
attention to the appearance of Nature in the different months
of the year, Wallace shares with Henryson the honour of
inaugurating a form of landscape poetry which subsequently
became very fashionable in Scotland.   The famous May, June,
and mid-winter landscapes which Gawin Douglas introduced
somewhat later into the Prologues to his *Æneid* are a direct
development of these earlier landscapes of Wallace the Minstrel.

*   *   *

If the interpretation of Nature is of rare occurrence in
Middle English historical poems, it may be said to be almost

entirely absent from those which are of a religious and didactic character. Such works as Richard of Hampole's *Cursor Mundi,* the shorter religious poems of Shoreham, and the great mass of cyclical legends of the saints, present absolutely nothing of interest. In the course of Richard of Hampole's long-winded review of sacred history occasional attempts are made to describe the various places of which mention is made; but such descriptions are merely topographical. Scarcely a trace is to be found, either in this work or elsewhere, of any delineation of a landscape for its own sake.

2. Lyrical Poetry.

Middle English lyrical poetry, though extending in range from the end of the twelfth century — the date of the *Poema Morale* — onwards to the Revival of Learning, is unequal, both in bulk and in quality, to the lyrics produced during the same period in France and Germany. England had, in fact, no singers to compare with the best of the Provençal *Troubadours,* or the German *Minnesinger.*

At first it was the religious lyric which was chiefly in vogue. This takes as its usual form a song in honour of the Virgin Mary, the adoration of whom in an age of chivalrous *courteoisie* is characterised by intense fervour. These religious lyrics call for no special notice here, inasmuch as the interpretation of Nature can hardly be said to enter into them : yet at times the singer seeks to find points of comparison for the beauty of the Queen of Heaven among the fair things of earth, and occasionally he addresses the Virgin in the language of metaphor drawn from external Nature. Such is the tenor of the Hymn, entitled *A Salutation to our Lady*[1]), in which the Virgin is addressed by such terms as the "rose hiȝest of hyde and hewe", as the "borgun brihtest of alle bounte, trewore þan þe wode-bynde", and as the "schadewe in uch a schour schene".

In the fourteenth century the religious lyric was to a

---

[1]) *Minor Poems of the Vernon MS.,* ed. Horstmann (E. E. T. S. XCVIII.).

large extent replaced by the secular, and this, under the stress of political and social changes, acquired an increasingly political and social character. This form of lyric, which in the political songs of Lawrence Minot rose to a certain eminence, is, for the most part, as far removed from all attempt to interpret Nature as the religious hymns of the earlier age. There are, however, in addition to the political songs a number of love-songs, in which external Nature is occasionally introduced, together with a few lyrics which tell of the season of spring, and the awakening of the birds to song. The most famous of these is the *Cuckoo-Song*[1]), which probably dates from the latter half of the thirteenth century. This folk-song, the music of which has come down to us together with the words, gives utterance to the simple yet heart-felt delight of the countryman in the return of spring, of which the cuckoo, here as in Old English poetry, is felt to be the true herald:

> Sumer is icumen in,
>   Lhude sing cuccu;
> Groweth sed, and bloweth med,
>   And springeth the wde nu;
>   Sing cuccu!
>
> Awe bleteth after lomb
>   Lhouth after calve cu;
> Bulluc sterteth, bucke verteth,
>   Murie sing cuccu.
>
> Cuccu, cuccu, well singes thu, cuccu,
>   Ne swik thu naver nu.
> Sing, cuccu, nu, sing, cuccu,
>   Sing cuccu, sing, cuccu, nu.

The *Spring-Song* beginning with the words "Lenten ys come with love to toune"[2]) is more comprehensive and more ambitious than the *Cuckoo-Song.* The singer shows a keen appreciation of natural beauty, and brings into his picture not only the birds, but all forms of animal life. He observes, too, the blossoming of the different flowers, the fall of the dew upon the downs, and the brightness of the sun and

---

[1]) Ritson's *Ancient Songs and Ballads,* Vol I.
[2]) Ritson's *Ancient Songs and Ballads*, Vol. I.

moon. Nor is the personal note wanting: at the close of the
second and third stanzas the poet turns bis gaze inwards,
and tells of his own love-longings:

Lenten ys come with love to toune,
With blosmen ant with briddes roune,
   That al this blisse bryngeth;
Dayesyes in this dales,
Notes suete of nyhtegales,
   Uch foul song singeth.

The threstelcoc him threteth oo,
Away is huere wynter wo,
   When woderove springeth;
The foules singeth ferly fele,
Ant wlyteth on huere wynter wele,
   That al the wode ryngeth.

The rose rayleth hire rode,
The leves on the lyhte wode,
   Waxen al with wille;
The mone mandeth hire bleo,
The lilie is lossom to seo,
   The fenyl ant the fille.

Wowes this wilde drakes,
Miles murgeth huere makes,
   Ase strem that striketh stille;
Mody meneth, so doh mo,
Ichot ycham on of tho,
   For love that likes ille.

The mone mandeth hire lyht,
So doth the semely sonne bryht,
   When briddes singeth breme;
Deawes donketh the dounes,
Deores with huere derne rounes,
   Domes forte deme.

Wormes woweth under cloude,
Wymmen waxeth wounder proude,
   So wel hit wol hem seme.
Yef me shal wonte wille of on,
This wunne weole y wole forgon,
   And wyht in wode be fleme.

In contrast with the *Spring-Song* quoted above, is the
so-called *Winter-Song*, beginning with the verse, "Wynter
wakeneth al my care". Here there is no description of the

wintry season, but the poet makes us feel that it is a time
of sadness and of mortality. A purely religious note dominates
the song, and the singer, mindful of the transitoriness of life,
looks to Christ as his only source of help.

Religious sentiment is again uppermost in the *Easter-
Song*[1]), beginning "Somer is com and winter gon", and the
reference to the changes in Nature is confined to the opening
stanza:

> Somer is comen and winter gon,
> Þis day biginniz to longe
> And þis foules everichon
> Joye him wit songe.

The *Song to the Virgin Mary*[2]) in the Sloane MS. 2593,
though it belongs to the fifteenth century, recalls the manner
of the earlier religious lyrics. The comparison of the coming
of Christ to the falling of dew is singularly gracious, and is
introduced by the poet in the manner of a refrain:

> I syng a of a mayden þat is makeles;
> Kyng of alle kynges to her sone che ches.
> He cam also stylle þer his moder was,
> As dew in Aprylle þat fallyt on þe gras;
> He cam also stylle to his moderes bowre,
> As dew in Aprylle þat fallyt on þe flour;
> He cam also stylle þer his moder lay,
> As dew in Aprille þat fallyt on þe spray.
> Moder and maydyn was never non but che,
> Wel may swych a lady godes moder be.

Somewhat similar to the place which external Nature
occupies in the religious lyrics is its place in the love-
lyrics of the same period. It forms here, in some cases, a
prelude to the love-sentiments which follow; in others, it
appears as a refrain preserved throughout. The latter is the
case with the love-song, *Blow, northerne wynd.*[3]) Here, at the
beginning of the song, and at the close of each stanza, are
found the following verses, which Ten Brink deemed to be
older than the song itself:

---

[1]) Wülcker, *Altenglisches Lesebuch,* Part II.
[2]) Wülcker, *Altenglisches Lesebuch,* Part II.
[3]) Wülcker, *Lesebuch,* Part I.

> Blow, norþerne wynd,
> Sent thou me my suetyng.
> Blow, northerne wynd, blow, blow, blow!

The old love-song, *Alysoun* [1]), opens with an idyllic picture of the springtide, which is regarded not only as the season of new life, but also of love; it reminds the singer of his love for his mistress Alison of the brown eyebrows, black eyes and slender waist:

> Bytuene Mershe ant Averil
>   when spray biginneth to springe,
> The lutel foul hath hire wyl
>   on hyre lud to synge;
> Ich libbe in love-longinge
> For semlokest of alle thynge,
> He may me blisse bringe,
>   icham in hire bandoun.
> An hendy hap ichabbe y-hent,
> Ichot from hevene it is me sent,
> From alle wymmen mi love is lent
>   ant lyht on Alysoun.

The opening verses of two other love-lyrics, both of them taken from Wright's *Specimens of Lyrical Poetry of the reign of Edward I,* may be quoted here, though the ideas introduced are almost identical with those found in other lyrics of the period, from which quotations have already been made. The one begins as follows:

> When the nyhtegale singes, the wodes waxen grene,
> Lef ant gras ant blosme springes in Averyl, y wene,
> Ant love is to myn herte gon with one spere so kene,
> Nyht and day my blod hit drynkes, myn herte deth me tene.

The other lyric also carries us away to the country-side, but here, instead of the nightingale's song, it is the play of the deer that is noticed: —

> In May hit murgeth when hit dawes,
> In dounes with this dueres plawes,
>   ant lef is lyht on lynde;
> Blosmes bredeth on the bowes,
> Al this wylde wyhtes wowes,
>   So wel ich under-fynde.

---

[1]) Wülcker, Part I.

Much more original, and in every way superior, is the lyric, entitled *The Contest of the Ivy and Holly* [1]), which is, however, of considerably later date. Ritson ascribed it to the reign of Henry VI. This is not exactly a *debate-poem*, for the trees themselves do not engage in the contest of words, yet it approaches the manner of this class of poems in respect of the general course of treatment. Incidentally, the poem reveals an appreciative study of Nature, though the poetically ubiquitous popinjay, as introduced among the other birds, weakens the fidelity of the painting:

> Nay, Ivy, nay,
>   Hyt shal not be, I wys;
> Let Holy hafe the maystry,
>   As the maner ys.
>
> Holy stond in the halle,
>   Fayre to behold;
> Ivy stond wythout the dore,
>   She ys ful sore a-cold.
>   Nay, Ivy, nay.
>
> Holy and hys mery men
>   They dawnsyn and they syng;
> Ivy and hur maydenys
>   They wepyn and they wryng.
>   Nay, Ivy, nay.
>
> Holy hath berys,
>   As rede as any rose;
> The foster and the hunter
>   Kepe hem fro the doos.
>   Nay, Ivy, nay.
>
> Ivy hath berys
>   As blake as any slo,
> Ther com the oule,
>   And ete hym as she goo.
>   Nay, Ivy, nay.
>
> Holy hath byrdys
>   A ful fayre flok;
> The nyghtyngale, the poppynguy,
>   The gayntyl lavyrok.
>   Nay, Ivy, nay.

---

[1]) Ritson, *Ancient Songs and Ballads,* Vol. II.

Gode Ivy,
　　What byrdys ast thu?
Non but the howlat,
　　That kreye, how! how!

Nay, Ivy, nay,
　　Hyt shal not be I wys,
Lef Holy hafe the maystry,
　　As the maner ys.

3. The English and Scottish Ballads.

The connection between the mediæval folk-song and the mediæval folk-ballad is very close, and pertains to the interpretation of Nature as well as to other things. Elaborate landscape painting was naturally as much out of place in the one as in the other; the aim of the ballad-writer was to tell his story as briefly and succinctly as possible, and the rapid movement of the ballad verse assisted materially in effecting this purpose. In the ballad, therefore, as in the popular song, the painting of landscape is kept within certain well-defined limits: in many cases it is introduced as a prelude to the story, and so enables the listener to realise the scenic background against which the story stands out. In other cases, there is found a running accompaniment of natural description mingling with the verses which develop the actual story. In the *Robin Hood Ballads* the painting of a landscape is confined to the introductory verses. Two of the oldest of these ballads — *Robin Hood and the Monk* and *Robin Hood and Guy of Gisborne* — set forth in the most telling manner the greenwood scene which is so closely associated with the adventures of the famous outlaw. In the former, these verses run as follows:

In somer, when the shawes be sheyne,
　　And leves be large and longe,
Hit is full mery in feyre foreste
　　To here the foulys song.

To se the dere draw to the dale,
　　And leve the hilles hee,
And shadow hem in the leves grene,
　　Undur the grene-wode tre.

> Hit befell at Whitsontide,
>   Erly in a may mornyng,
> The son up fayre can shyne,
>   And the briddis mery can syng [1]).

This is all quite simple, but the charm is as abiding as that of the opening passage of Chaucer's *Prologue to the Canterbury Tales*, of which Lowell said, "I repeat it to myself a thousand times, and still at the thousandth time a breath of uncontaminate springtide seems to lift the hair upon my forehead"[2]).

Similar, and not inferior, to these opening stanzas of *Robin Hood and the Monk*, are those of *Robin Hood and Guy of Gisborne*. Once again we are taken to the greenwood, and hear the song of the birds:

> When shaws beene sheene and shradds ful fayre,
>   And leaves both large and longe,
> Itt is merrye walkyng in the fayre forrest,
>   To heare the small birdes songe.
>
> The wood-weele sang, and wold not cease,
>   Sitting upon the spraye,
> So lowde, he wakened Robin Hood,
>   In the greenwood where he lay [3]).

The wood-weele is the green wood-pecker, whose laughing cry is in far closer association with the true life of the forest than are the notes of such birds as the thrush, robin or nightingale — the birds whose song is most frequently referred to in the poetry of the time. The later Robin Hood ballads, which were written in imitation of the original ones, frequently imitate also this prelude of natural description; but the true charm of the greenwood is not preserved in them, while at times it is replaced by something which is wholly sophisticated. The following stanza from *Robin Hood and the Ranger* illustrates the change:

---

[1]) Child: *English and Scottish Ballads*, Vol. III.
[2]) *My Study Windows.*
[3]) Child's Ballads, Vol. III.

> When Phoebus had melted the sickles of ice,
>   And likewise the mountains of snow,
> Bold Robin Hood he would ramble away,
>   To frolick abroad with his bow[1]).

Outside of the Robin Hood cycle, few English ballads can rival in excellence those composed on Scottish soil. Most of the latter introduce a love-story, and the reference to Nature takes the form of a running accompaniment to the main theme. In illustration of this, the following stanzas, taken from Scottish ballads edited by Professor Child in his monumental work, *English and Scottish Popular Ballads,* may by quoted:

> There was a lady of the North country
>   (Lay the bent to the bonny broom)
> And she had lovely daughters three,
>   Fa la la.

In like manner in the K version of the ballad entitled *The Elfin Knight:*[2])

> My father left me three acres of land,
>   Sing ivy, sing ivy;
> My father left me three acres of land,
>   Sing holly, go whistle, and ivy.

Or again in the B version of *Sir Lionel:*[3])

> A knicht had two sons o' sma' fame
>   Hey men nonny,
> Isaac-a-Bell and Hugh the Graeme,
>   And the norlan flowers spring bonny.

In the C version of *Gil Brenton*[4]), where the usual ballad-verse is replaced by the octosyllabic couplet, the reference to Nature is rather more elaborate, and some attempt is made to follow the course of the seasons:

> First blew the sweet, the simmer wind,
> Then autumn wi' her breath sae kind,
> Before that eer the guid knight came,
> The tokens of his love to claim

---

[1]) Child's Ballads, Vol. III.
[2]) Child, Vol. I.
[3]) Child, Vol. I.
[4]) Child, Vol. I.

> Then fell the brown an' yellow leaf
> Afore the knight o' love shawed prief.
> Three morns the winter's rime did fa,
> When loud at our yett my love did ca.

Many of the ballads show a simple yet heart-felt delight
in the blooming of the flowers. The flower to which most
frequent reference is made in these ballads is the broom,
but the primrose is also introduced, and in the following
stanzas from *Proud Lady Margaret* (A-Version) the reference
to this spring flower is full of charm:

> "Now what is the flower, the ae first flower,
>   Springs either on moor or dale?
> And what is the bird, the bonnie bonnie bird
>   Sings on the evening gale"?

> "The primrose is the ae first flower
>   Springs either on moor or dale,
> And the thristle-cock is the bonniest bird,
>   Sings on the evening gale".

The broom, besides being introduced incidentally into
many of the ballads, claims one — *The Broom of Cowden-
Knows* [1]) — as its own. The opening stanzas bring before us
a delightful picture of Scottish peasant life:

> The broom, the broom, and the bonny, bonny broom,
>   And the broom of the Cowden-knows!
> And aye sae sweet as the lassie sang,
>   I' the bought, milking the ewes.

> The hills were high on ilka side,
>   An the bought i' the lirk o' the hill,
> And aye as she sang, her voice it rang
>   Out-o'er the head o' yon hill.

G-Version.

In the romantic ballad, *Fair Margaret and Sweet William* [2]),
there occurs at the close a fancy which is more in keeping
with an Ovidian metamorphosis than with the sterner and
simpler character of the ballads. The lovers die, the one

---

[1]) Child, Vol. IV.
[2]) Child, Vol. II.

"for pure true love" and the other "for sorrow" and then
we are told, —

> Margaret was buried in the lower chancel,
> Sweet William in the higher:
> Out of her brest there sprang a rose,
> And out of his a brier.

> They grew as high as the church top,
> Till they could grow no higher:
> And then they grew in a true lover's knot,
> Which made all people admire.

Moreover, in the case of the English ballad entitled *The
Rose of England* [1]) a symbolic treatment of Nature is introduced. The reference in the following stanzas is to the red
rose of Lancaster, which is eventually rooted up by the boar,
Richard III.:

> Throughout a garden greene and gay,
> A seemlye sight itt was to see,
> How flowers did flourish fresh and gay,
> And birds doe sing melodiouslye.

> In the midst of a garden there sprange a tree,
> Which tree was of a mickle price,
> And there uppon sprang the rose soe redd,
> The goodlyest that ever sprang on rise.

In the magnificent Scottish ballad, *Sir Patrick Spens* [2]),
we pass from the associations of an inland landscape, such
as is usually met with in the ballads, to the storms of the
wild North Sea. There is no deliberate painting of sea-scenery
in this ballad, and yet the situation is brought before our
minds with weird force:

> "Yestreen I saw the new new moone,
> Wi' the auld moon in her arm;
> And if we gang to sea, master,
> I fear we'll come to harm."

> They hadna sail'd a league, a league,
> A league but barely three,
> When the lift grew dark, and the wind blew loud,
> And gurly grew the sea.

---

[1]) Child, Vol. III.
[2]) Child, Vol. II.

> The ankers brak, and the tap-masts lap,
>   It was sic a deidly storm:
> And the waves can owre the broken ship,
>   Till a' her sides were torn.

There is no wasting of words here: the narrative is throughout grimly curt, while an intensity of feeling, such as is found in some of the primitive epics of the Teutonic peoples, lends to the whole poem a strangely impressive dignity.

Chapter VII.

THE GAWAYNE-POET.

The history of Middle English literature before Chaucer presents nothing of greater interest to the modern reader than that revival of alliterative poetry which took place in the west-midland and northern counties about the middle of the fourteenth century. A study of the chief poems written between 1250 and 1350 produces the impression that the glorious heritage of Old English poetry has been almost entirely lost; the verse, the sentiments, the manners, and the interpretation of Nature, are all under the sway of French influences, and whatever is distinctively Saxon is excluded. But with the coalescence of the Norman and Saxon elements, which was almost fully accomplished by the middle of the fourteenth century, there came a mighty revival of Old English traditions, which was destined, not to overthrow the influence of French ideas, but to unite with this in the production of a literature at once original and of wide compass. At first, perhaps, it would seem that the renascence of Old English poetic traditions told against the foreign influence; if so, this was merely the natural reaction in favour of the earlier models, after they had been almost wholly neglected during the preceding hundred years.

William Langland calls for no comment in such a study as the present, and accordingly the foremost place in this alliterative revival must be assigned to the author of the romance, *Sir Gawayne and the Green Knight*[1]), which is beyond dispute the finest of all the Middle English metrical romances.

---

[1]) Edited by Dr. R. Morris (E. E. T. S., IV.).

Celtic in its theme, French in its chivalric sentiments, this poem is strictly Saxon in its verse, its diction, and its interpretation of Nature. In this work full amends are made for the general neglect of landscape-painting in Middle English romances. Here, as in pre-conquest poetry generally, Nature is studied and loved, not so much for the soft beauty and idyllic charm of a spring morning in garden or grove, as for the wild fury of winter storm. It is not Nature tamed by man and fashioned by art which is sought out, but Nature free and uncontrolled, Nature amid the ice-bound mountains and dense forests, Nature which is often at war with man, but which man loves, as a brave soldier loves the noble foe against whom he is pitted.

It would be out of place to give here an analysis of the plot of the romance. Such may be found in Dr. Morris's Introduction to his edition of the work for the Early English Text Society; or, more briefly, in the first volume of Ten Brink's *History of English Literature.* It is New Year's day when the poem opens, and at the beginning of the second 'fytte' the poet furnishes a highly appreciative description of the change of the seasons:

> Bot þenne þe weder of þe worlde wyth wynter hit þrepez.
> Colde clengez adoun, cloudez up-lyften,
> Schyre schedez þe rayn in schowrez ful warme,
> Fallez upon fayre flat, flowrez þere schewen,
> Bothe groundez and þe grevez grene ar her wedez,
> Bryddez busken to bylde, and bremlych syngen,
> For solace of þe softe somer þat sues þer-after,
>   bi bonk;
>   And blossumez bolne to blowe,
>   Bi rawez rych and ronk,
>   Þen notez noble in-noȝe,
>   Ar herde in wod so wlonk.

                                                       504—515.

Such is the poet's description of the coming of spring. The features introduced are extremely simple — the blossoming of flowers, the song of the birds — yet the picture is full of life, and we are made to feel the pleasure which not only man, but also the birds, experience at the departure of winter. A description of the other seasons follows immediately upon this:

After þe sesoun of somer wyth þe soft wyndez,
Quen zeferus syflez hym-self on sedez and erbez,
Wela-wynne is þe wort þat woxes þer-oute,
When þe donkande dewe dropez of þe levez,
To bide a blysful blusch of þe bryȝt sunne.
Bot þen hyȝes hervest and hardenes hym sone,
Warnez hym for þe wynter to wax ful rype;
He dryves wyth droȝt þe dust for to ryse,
Fro þe face of the folde to flyȝe ful hyȝe;
Wroþe wynde of þe welkyn wrastelez with þe sunne,
Þe levez lancen fro þe lynde and lyȝten on þe grounde,
And al grayez þe gres, þat grene watz ere;
Þenne al rypez and rotez þat ros upon fyrst,
And þus ȝirnez þe ȝere in ȝisterdayez mony,
And wynter wyndez aȝayn, as þe worlde askez
                No sage.

516—531.

Here the imagery is even more striking. The reference
to Zephyrus is suggestive of the conventions of courtly poetry,
but in other respects the description is quite unconventional.
The introduction of the wroth wind wrestling with the sun
is quite in the manner of the old Teutonic mythology, as is
also the implied personification of the seasons. English
descriptive poets have at all times been fond of describing
the fresh morning dew, but rarely has the exquisite delicacy
contained in the picture of the dank dew awaiting the blissful
blush of the sun been surpassed. In idea, if not in artistic
presentment, it is worthy of Shelley.

On All-Saint's day Gawayne sets out from Camelot on
his northward journey in search of the Green Knight. He
passes through North Wales as far as Holyhead; then,
turning eastwards, he reaches the "wilderness of Wirral" in
Cheshire, "where dwelt but few who loved with good heart
either God or man". Continuing his wanderings, he comes
to a rocky country beset with wolves, serpents and wild boars,
and with wild wood-men dwelling among the rocks. But
Gawayne finds that the hostility of the wintry season is
worse than the ravages of either man or beast:

For werre wrathed hym not so much, þat wynter was wors,
When þe colde cler water fro þe cloudez schadden,
And fres er hit falle myȝt to the fale erþe;

Ner slayn wyth þe slete he sleped in his yrnes,
Mo nyʒtez þen in-noghe in naked rokkez
Þer as claterande fro þe crest þe colde borne rennez,
And henged heʒe over his hede in hard isse-ikkles.

                                                    726—732.

From this point the action is laid entirely amid mountain
and forest scenery, the season being still that of winter. The
poet has not attempted to localise the scene, but it is not
difficult for us to estimate roughly Gawayne's situation. His
general direction has been a northward one, and he has left
behind him the mountains of North Wales, and the low-lying
tracts of Cheshire. Then, after long wanderings, he reaches in
mid-winter a land of mountains and forests. This must be
either the higher reaches of the Pennine Chain, or, as is more
likely, the mountain and forest land of the Lake District.
Remembering that the Gawayne-poet was in all probability
a Lancashire man, and remembering, too, his delight in the
wild scenes of Nature, it is permissible to think of him as
one who had penetrated as far as the mountain-fastnesses
which hem in that county to the north and north-east.
The intense realism of his descriptions betokens a close intimacy with mountain scenery; throughout his work we
feel that he was a poet nature-learned and not book-learned.
Thus while the Gawayne-poet reaches back with one hand
to the Old English poets, with the other he strains forward
to Wordsworth, in whose delight in the Lakeland mountains
he abundantly shares.

Christmas morning finds Gawayne still traversing this
land of hill and forest:

Bi a mounte on þe morne meryly he rydes,
Into a forest ful dep, þat ferly watz wylde,
Hiʒe hillez on uche a halve, and holt wodez under,
Of hore okez ful hoge a hundreth to-geder;
Þe hasel and þe haʒ-thorne were harled al samen,
With roʒe raged mosse rayled ay-where,
With mony bryddez unblyþe upon bare twyges,
Þat pitosly þer piped for pyne of þe colde.   740—747.

In the third 'fytte', after Gawayne's arrival at the castle,
there occurs a description, or rather three descriptions in

succession, of a hunting-scene. The first is a deer-hunt, the second a boar-hunt, and the third a fox-hunt. The manner of hunting is in each case different, and there is much diversity in the character of the scenery amid which each hunt takes place. The deer-hunt is now in the deep slades of the forest, and now on the heath; the boar-hunt takes place among the crags of the mountains, where the rocks echo the yelping clamour of the blood-hounds, till they come upon the boar,

> Bitwene a flosche in þat fryth, and a foo cragge;
> In a knot, bi a clyffe, at þe kerre syde,
> Þer as þe rogh rocher un-rydely watz fallen.
>
> 1430—32.

The fox-hunt is ushered in with a description of a winter sunrise:

> Ferly fayre watz þe folde, for þe forst clenged,
> In rede rudede upon rak rises þe sunne,
> And ful clere castez þe clowdes of þe welkyn.
>
> 1694—96.

The hunters soon catch sight of the fox, and pursue it in hot chase through the rough groves, spinneys, and rugged hillside tracks, till at last they run it to earth.

When the Christmas entertainments are over, New Year arrives, and is greeted by the poet with a vivid winter landscape :

> Now neȝez þe nwȝere, and þe nyȝt passez,
> Þe day dryvez to þe derk, as dryȝtyn biddez;
> Bot wylde wederez of þe worlde wakned þeroute,
> Clowdez kesten kenly þe colde to þe erþe,
> Wyth nyȝe in-noghe of þe norþe þe naked to tene;
> Þe snawe snitered ful snart, þat snayped þe wylde;
> Þe werbelande wynde wapped fro þe hyȝe,
> And drof uche dale ful of dryftes ful grete.
>
> 1998—2005.

Gawayne leaves the castle, accompanied by a guide who is to direct him to the chapel of the Green Knight. The journey of the two is described in the poet's most incisive manner, with the massing together of the boldest features which a rugged mountainous country can supply:

> Þay boʒen bi bonkkez þer boʒez ar bare,
> Þay clomben bi clyffez þer clengez þe colde;
> Þe heven watz up halt, bot ugly þer under,
> Mist muged on þe mor, malt on þe mountez,
> Uch hille hade a hatte, a myst-hakel huge;
> Brokez byled and breke, bi bonkkez aboute,
> Schyre schaterande on schorez þer þay doun schowved.
> Welawylle watz þe way, þer þay bi wod schulden,
> Til hit watʒ sone sesoun þat þe sunne rysez
> Þat tyde.   2077—2086.

Such verses as these, thanks to the rugged character of the alliteration and the boldness of the imagery, present a scene of wild sublimity in which the poet evidently takes a keen delight. Gawayne's guide leaves him, but he still continues his way through this land of wintry desolation, till at last he catches sight of —

> A balʒ berʒ, bi a bonke, þe brymme by-syde,
> Bi a forʒ of a flode þat ferked þare;
> Þe borne blubred þer-inne, as hit boyled hade.

*   *   *

> Þene herde he of þat hyʒe hil, in a harde roche,
> Bi-ʒonde þe broke, in a bonk, a wonder breme noyse,
> Quat! hit clatered in þe clyff, as hit cleve schulde,
> As one upon a gryndelston hade grounden a syþe;
> What! hit wharred and whette, as water at a mulne,
> What! hit rusched and ronge, rawþe to here.

2172—2204.

It is not necessary to follow the story any further, or to tell of Gawayne's encounter with the Green Knight, and its strangely impressive issue. It will be more to the point to try and form a summary view of the Gawayne-poet's attitude towards the manifestations of the natural world which he describes with such fidelity, and yet with such splendid imaginative power. With the exception of the passage in which the change of the seasons is described, his landscapes are all those of winter, — winter among the mountains. In concentrating his attention upon such scenery as this, he was opening up entirely new ground. The Old English poets, it is true, had loved to sing of winter, but they had confined themselves to the appearances of winter by sea and shore.

In his pictures of winter among the craggy ice-bound fells of the north of England, the Gawayne-poet is without rival. This originality stands out in yet bolder relief when his descriptions are compared with those of Middle English poets generally, whose feeling for Nature was so exclusively confined to the gentle influences of spring in garden and grove. In the landscapes of the Gawayne romance the beautiful gives place to the sublime. There is no placidity here: everything is in turbulent movement. The bitter wind is whistling among the crags, and driving the cruel snow-drifts along the dales. The streams descend in boiling torrents, the cloud-racks sweep along, and even the sunshine serves but to add a new element to the savagery of this landscape, by revealing the shadows of the jagged rocks. Our poet's colour-sense is not specially prominent, but he has a keen appreciation of natural form. He loves to describe the contours of the rocks, and of the oaks, hazels, and hawthorns, overgrown with rough moss; nor does he miss the grotesque shapes which the clouds and mists assume, nor the shadows thrown out by the rocks. Still more remarkable is his ready appreciation of the sounds of Nature: he notes, among other things, the torrent, which now whirrs like water in a mill-wheel, and now sounds shrilly as when one sharpens a scythe on a grindstone. He hears, too, the whistling of the wind, and the piteous piping of the birds frozen with the cold. All these features, so striking in themselves, and introduced for the most part in parallel clauses after the manner of the Old English poets, are made yet more impressive by the rugged grandeur of the alliterative verse, the alliterating syllables recurring sometimes with exaggerated frequency.

The question may possibly be asked, Did this poet really feel a sense of pleasure in such scenes of desolation as he describes? One can without hesitation reply that such was the case. Had it been otherwise, he would not have introduced these pictures with such frequency into the course of the romance, nor have brought into relief each single detail with such minute pencilling. Awesome as are these scenes, we feel that they appealed to his highly developed taste for natural

sublimity. He shared, indeed, in that same sense of exultation
in the presence of the majestic and devastating forces
of Nature which the Old English poets reveal in their descriptions of stormy sea and driving tempest. Moreover, he
was artist enough to see that a background of such landscapes as these was in keeping with the main action and
the human interest of his poem. The sudden appearance of
the Green Knight in the banqueting-hall of King Arthur,
his conduct there, and his reappearance at the close of the
poem, are all mysteriously impressive. To have set all this
against a background of May-day sunshine would have done
much to weaken the general effect of the poem. In this, as
in so much else, we trace the workmanship of a great,
though a somewhat untrained mind; the Gawayne-poet was
a man gifted with the sure touch of the true artist, a man
endowed with the power of revealing to men the poetry
which lies hidden in the mysterious and inevitable forces of
Nature.

In turning from *Sir Gawayne and the Green Knight* to the
Pearl, [1]) we pass from a romance to an elegy — an elegy robbed
of half its sadness by the vision of apocalyptic beauty which is
disclosed, and by the spirit of resignation which spreads
gradually over the poet's soul. This later work of the Gawayne-
poet, if indeed it is his, has become more familiar to readers
since Professor Gollancz's beautiful edition appeared, and little
need be said here with regard to the general course of the
story. As the poet stands sad at heart above the grave of
his lost Pearl, his gaze is directed first of all to the flowers
which spring from the ground:

> I entred in þat erber grene
> In auguste in a hyȝ seysoun,
> Quen corne is corven with crokez kene.
> On huyle þer perle hit trendeled doun,
> Schadowed þis wortez ful schyre and schene.
> Gilofre, gyngure and gromylyoun,
> And pyonys powdered ay betwene.   38—44.

As the father falls asleep by the grave of his vanished
daughter, he sees a heavenly vision. The mediæval mind,

---

[1]) *Early English Alliterative Poems,* ed. Morris (E. E. T. S., I.).

having its gaze averted from the things of earth and directed towards the world to come, found exquisite delight in the contemplation of paradise. Borrowing something from the classical imagery of the Elysian fields, the mediæval poets conceived of a heavenly landscape where all was sunshine and flowery mead, and it is into relationship with such descriptions of heaven that this vision of the Gawayne-poet must be brought. Yet our author was of too original a nature to rest satisfied with conventional outlines. Whereas heaven is usually described in mediæval poetry as a level plain, the Gawayne-poet, mindful of the mountain grandeur of his north-country home, conceives of it as a hilly land, where rocks and cliffs gleam in the eternal sunshine:

> Dubbed wern alle þo downez sydez
> With crystal klyffes so cler of kynde,
> Holte wodes bryӡt aboute hem bydez;
> Of bollez as blwe as ble of ynde,
> As bornyst sylver þe lef onslydez,
> Þat þike con trylle on uch a tynde,
> Quen glem of glodez aӡaynz hem glydez,
> Wyth schymeryng schene ful schrylle þay schynde.
> Þe gravayl þat on grounde con grynde
> Wern precious perlez of oryente;
> Þe sunne bemez bot blo and blynde,
> In respecte of þat adubbement.   73—84.

Here, too, are birds of every kind, and of every colour; these, as they beat their wings, sing so sweetly that neither zither string nor gittern can compare with them. The poet proceeds to describe the forest, the gardens, and then the river which flows between him and this blissful abode: —

> The dubbement of þo derworth depe
> Wern bonkez bene of beryl bryӡt;
> Swangeande swete þe water con swepe
> Wyth a rownande rourde raykande aryӡt;
> In the founce þer stonden stonez stepe,
> As glente þurӡ glas þat glowed and glyӡt,
> As stremande sternez quen stroþe men slepe,
> Staren in welkyn in wynter nyӡt;
> For uche a pobbel in pole þer pyӡt
> Watz Emerad, saffer oþer gemme gent,
> Þat alle þe loӡe lemed of lyӡt,
> So dere watz hit adubbement.   109—120.

When a poet attempts a description of heaven, he introduces into his picture those features which seem to him most beautiful: he furnishes us in fact with an ideal landscape. Looked at closely, the Gawayne-poet's description of heaven, at least as far as its general contour is concerned, bears a striking resemblance to that which he sets forth in *Sir Gawayne and the Green Knight.* Heaven is for him a land of hills with gleaming crags, and of deep forests, and these, as has already been noticed, are the chief features in the landscape of the romance. The difference is that whereas in the romance the scene is one of wintry desolation, in the elegy there reigns eternal sunshine, together with all the fairness of leaf and flower which the sunshine brings with it.

It was the Gawayne-poet's delight in purity of life which gave to his Arthurian romance so lofty a tone, and when in later years he turned from secular to sacred themes, his ideal of purity became yet more exalted, and suggested to him the composition of the poem, *Cleanness.* [1]) This poem is a homily in verse, wherein didactic lore is mixed with the exposition of Bible story. But the poet's powers of graphic description could not be repressed even in a theme which at first sight seems prosaic. In the course of the poem he relates the story of Noah, the destruction of Sodom and Gomorrah, and finishes with a review of the reigns of Nebuchadnezzar and Belshazzar. The story of Noah gives an opening for descriptions of ocean storm of which he avails himself to the full. The author of the Old English *Genesis* passes quickly over the actual scene of the flood, in order to dwell upon the flight of the raven and dove from the ark, while in the Middle English *Genesis* the story of the flood is treated in a somewhat cursory way, and with very little originality. The bolder imagination of the Gawayne-poet was quickened by the Bible story to a far higher degree than was the case with his predecessors, and he accordingly seizes upon the occasion to paint a picture of the raging waters which will bear comparison with the finest sea-pictures of Old English poetry:

---

[1]) *Early English Alliterative Poems,* ed. Morris (E. E. T. S., I.)

Þen bolne þe abyme and bonkez con ryse,
Waltes out uch walle-heved, in ful wode stremez,
Watz no brymme þat abod unbrosten bylyve,
Þe mukel lavande loghe to þe lyfte rered.
Mony clustered clowde clef alle in clowtez,
To-rent uch a rayn-ryfte and rusched to þe urþe;
Fon never in forty dayez and þen þe flod rysez,
Over-waltez uche a wod and þe wyde feldez;
For when þe water of þe welkyn with þe worlde mette,
Alle þat deth moʒt dryʒe drowned þerinne.

                                                    363—72.

The similarity of style between this passage and some
of the sea-pictures of Old English poetry, especially those of
the *Exodus,* is everywhere apparent, and is too close to be
merely accidental. The poet desires, moreover, not to omit
the human element from this scene of wild desolation. He
shows us the mother with her children fleeing to the hills, and
men and women casting themselves upon the mercy of
the waves to seek escape by swimming.

With equally realistic touch, the poet describes the
voyage of the ark through this troublous deep. It is heaved
up almost to the clouds by the hurtling billows, and then
fell winds bear it along, without mast, cable or anchor, till
at length the rain ceases, and the waters subside. Next
follows the story of the sending forth of the two birds: first
of all, "the bold raven that was ever a rebel":

He watz colored as þe cole, corbyal untrewe.
And he fongez to þe flyʒt and fannez on þe wyndez,
Hovez hyʒe upon hyʒt to herken tyþynges.
He croukez for comfort when carayne he fyndez;
Kest upon a clyffe þer costese lay drye,
He had þe smelle of þe smach and smoltes þeder sone,
Fallez on þe foule flesch and fyllez his wombe,
And sone ʒederly for-ʒete ʒisterday steven,
How þe chevetayn hym charged þat þe kyst ʒemed.

                                                    456—464.

The *naïveté* of this description recalls the manner of the
Old English riddles, and contrasts very effectively with the
subtle effects of such a highly finished poem as the *Pearl.*
Scarcely inferior to the description of the Deluge is that of

the destruction of Sodom and Gomorrah. Here again the
scale of the picture is of the widest, and the imagery almost
terrific in its sublimity. The poet tells how the winds from
all quarters wrestled together, how the clouds commingled,
and the thunderbolts pierced the rocks; rain, mixed with
fire and sulphurous smoke, rushed down, the great bars
that lock in the abyss were burst asunder, and the cliffs cleft to
fragments.

In the other verse-homily of the Gawayne-poet which
has been preserved, and which bears the title *Patience*[1]), there
is further illustration, if such were needed, of the poet's
rare descriptive powers. This poem deals with the story of
Jonah, and introduces, in this connection, a finely wrought
picture of the storm which precedes the expulsion of the
prophet from the ship:

> Anon out of þe norþ est þe noys bigynes,
> When boþe breþes con blowe upon blo watteres;
> Roӡ rakkes þer ros with rudnyng an-under,
> Þe see souӡed ful sore, gret selly to here;
> Þe wyndes on þe wonne water so wrastel togeder,
> Þat þe wawes ful wode waltered so hiӡe,
> And eft busched to þe abyme þat breed fysches.

> 137—143.

The language of the above passage is in its main features
similar to that of the description of the storm in *Cleanness*,
and the resemblance between the two passages becomes still
more marked in the further development of the picture.
Yet the poet's repetition, though reprehensible from the
artistic standpoint, is quite in keeping with the descriptions
of natural phenomena in Old English poetry, and thus serves
as a fresh link to connect the Gawayne-poet with those poetic
forbears of his, who lived at a time when the influence of
foreign schools of poetry was but slightly felt, and when
gleemen were free to follow the traditions which had come
down to them from the singers of the heroic age of the
Teutonic folk.

---

[1]) *Early English Alliterative Poems*, ed. Morris (E. E. T. S., I.).

Chapter VIII.

CHAUCER.

The well known cry of relief which escapes the lips of Boileau when, in the historical review of his *L'Art Poétique* he reaches at last the name of Malherbe, has, in spirit at least, been echoed by many a historian of English literature on arriving at Chaucer. *Enfin Chaucer vint*, and with him came regularity of structure, coherence, artistic finish and the true beginning of English poetry. Yet this cry of relief is almost as needless in the case of Chaucer as of Malherbe. It is true that with Chaucer modern English poetry begins, and it is also true that in him the continuous stream of English poetry finds its true source, but if this *enfin Chaucer vint* is meant to assert that before him everything was shadowy or chaotic, an arid waste of crude literary material valuable only to the philologist, then, indeed, it is a cry which is not only needless, but misleading as well.

Though a good deal of attention has been given to Chaucer's interpretation of Nature,[1] it must be confessed that his insight into the natural world is in many respects inferior to that of the Gawayne-poet. Chaucer was pre-eminently the student of humanity and of books, and Nature claimed only a third place in his esteem. His life of strenuous public service brought him into contact with men of every type, whose characters he deciphered with faultless accuracy. His leisure hours were devoted to literary study from which, as he tells us himself in the Prologue to his *Legend of Good Women*,[2] nothing could wean him, —

---

[1] See especially Ballerstedt, *Über ChaucersNaturschilderungen*, 1892.

[2] Chaucer's *Works*, ed. Pollard, 1898.

Save, certeynly, whan that the month of May
Is comen, and that I here the foules synge,
And that the floures gynnen for to sprynge, —
Farewel my boke, and my devocion!

B. Version, 36—39.

Chaucer's feeling for Nature underwent in the course
of his life a certain change. Seen in its true perspective,
his poetic career appears as a gradual passing from romanticism
to realism. This is a statement the full force of which
cannot be felt as long as we are uncertain of the exact
order in which the *Canterbury Tales* were written; but, if
we remove from that cycle those tales which are recognised
as belonging to an earlier period — such, for instance, as
The Second Nun's Tale and *The Knight's Tale* in its earliest
form — the realistic character of his later works, and the
romantic character of the early ones, appears in a clearer
light. This change is, moreover, in keeping with the changes
which took place in the poet's own life. The romantic and
idealistic outlook of the young man, spending his life in the
full splendour of courtly refinement or in foreign campaign,
passes into the more piercing yet less etherealised vision of
the full-grown man, engaged in shrewd diplomatic service,
or in the affairs of the mart, the inspection of the customs
and the scrutiny of men. An appreciation of Nature in its
beautiful or sublime manifestations is of the very essence
of romanticism, and it is therefore to the early works of
Chaucer that our attention must be chiefly directed in
order to discover what was his attitude towards Nature, and
what aspects of the natural world appealed to him most strongly.

With Chaucer we enter at once the courtly and conventional school of landscape poets, with which we have had
some contact while considering the descriptions found in the
later verse-romances, but from which we were very far
removed in the work of the Gawayne-poet. Based ultimately
upon the Greek poetry of the Hellenistic period, and more
immediately upon the Latin poetry of the Augustan and
post-Augustan ages, the landscape of the mediæval courtly
poets took its rise in France. It is common to the lyric

poetry of the Provençal Troubadours and the verse-romance of northern French poets, and through frequent repetition, both in France and other countries, it soon became stereotyped. In almost every case the landscape is that of a May morning in some garden, meadow, shady grove or rivulet-watered valley. The hour is usually that of the dawn, when it is neither too hot nor too cold, and when the sun has not yet dried up the dew from the leaves. The ground is thickly bestrewn with flowers of all kinds, the chief among them being the lily and the rose. Around, grow trees capable of giving ample shade from the midday sun, but not so thick or so tangled as to awaken a sense of desolation in the minds of those who wander among them. The hushed stillness of the forest aroused feelings of terror, and was rarely allowed to enter into this conventional May-morning landscape. From the trees there comes a chorus of birds of all sorts, the place of honour being, by universal agreement, given to the nightingale. Animals are less frequently introduced, though occasionally we hear of the squirrel playing among the branches of the trees. With the chorus of the birds is blended the murmur of the stream which glides softly through the valley, and the whisper of the wind in the trees. Such are the main features of this landscape of mediæval courtly poetry. Full of idyllic beauty as it is, and well-fitted to serve as background to romantic love-poetry, it soon wearies us by reason of the frequency of its recurrence. Fashioned in France, it soon passed into Germany, and stamped its impress upon the courtly romances of Gottfried von Strassburg, and the lyric poetry of the Minnesänger, with Walther von der Vogelweide as their coryphæus. In England there is a foretaste of this landscape in some of the descriptive passages of the *Phœnix*, but its real introduction took place at the time of the later verse-romances which were directly based on French models. With Chaucer, the courtly landscape comes into full vogue, and through him is handed down to his fifteenth century disciples, and to the Elizabethans.

Chaucer's delight in the spring season, so frankly expressed in the passage from the Prologue to the *Legend of*

Good Women already quoted, is attested by other of his poems. It is a May-morning landscape of which he dreams in *The Book of the Duchess*, and it is in April and May that the main action of *Troilus and Cressida* takes place; the Canterbury pilgrims start on their journey in mid-April, and several of the tales introduce the months of spring-tide. The only other season of which Chaucer takes cognisance is that of St. Valentine's day, which is introduced in the *Parliament of Fowls* and the *Complaint of Mars*, and which appealed to him because of its association with the life of birds.

In his pictures of the spring season, Chaucer rarely takes us very far away from the abodes of men. He loves before all else the garden rich in flowers, where Nature is brought under the restraining hand of art. It is in a garden that the birds meet in the *Parliament of Fowls* in order to choose their mates:

> A garden saw I, ful of blosmy bowes,
> Upon a river, in a grene mede,
> Ther as that swetnesse evermore y-now is,
> With floures white, blewe, yelwe and rede;
> And colde welle-stremes, no-thing dede,
> That swommen ful of smale fisches lighte,
> With finnes rede and scales silver-brighte.
>
> 183—189.

One must not, of course, attempt to identify such a garden as this with the walled enclosures of the present time. It is situated, as Chaucer himself tells us, in a meadow, and close to the woodland glades; there is no reference whatever to walls, and in the next stanza he relates how he sees the rabbits and squirrels playing, and farther off, "the dreadful roo, the buk, the hert and hynde".

There is another brief description of a garden in *Troilus and Cressida* (Book II, 820 et seq.), while it is in a garden "ful of braunches grene" that, in the *Knight's Tale,* Emily is first seen by the rival lovers. The plot of the *Merchant's Tale* is laid in a garden, and the delight which Chaucer experiences in describing such a spot is again seen in the *Franklin's Tale*:

> And this was on the sixte morwe of May,
> Which May hadde peynted with his softe shoures
> This gardyn, full of leves and of floures,
> And craft of mannes hand so curiously
> Arreyed hadde this gardyn, trewely,
> That never was ther gardyn of swich prys,
> But if it were the verray Paradys.
> The odour of floures and the fresshe sighte
> Woldë han maked any herte lighte
> That ever was born, but if to greet siknesse,
> Or to gret sorwe, helde it in distresse;
> So full it was of beautee with pleasaunce.
>
> 906—917.

Next to the garden in Chaucer's esteem would seem to come the meadow and the grove. In the *Book of the Duchess* there is an elaborate picture of such a grove of trees as the poet loved:

> Hit is no need eke for to axe
> Wher ther were many grene greves
> Or thikke of trees, so ful of leves;
> And every tree stood by him-selve,
> Fro other wel ten foot or twelve.
> So grete trees, so huge of strengthe,
> Of fourty, or fifty fadme lengthe,
> Clene, withoute bough or stikke,
> With croppes brode, and eek as thikke —
> They were nat an inche a-sonder —
> That hit was shadwe over-al under,
> And many a hert and many a hynde
> Was both before me and behynde.
> Of founes, soures, bukkes, does,
> Was ful the wode, and many roes,
> And many squirelles that sete
> Ful hye upon the trees and ete,
> And in her maner made festes.
>
> 416—433.

This description is in many ways interesting. Chaucer's delight in Nature, and especially in animal life, is apparent throughout, but no less apparent is the fact that his sympathies were not with the wild freedom of Nature, but with Nature curbed and formalised. The trees, here and elsewhere, are not allowed to grow naturally: they are planted at equal distances from each other, and are all of equal size,

as in the Dutch landscapes of the present time. This desire
to 'improve' Nature is not confined to Chaucer; he is, in
fact, only amplifying a descriptive passage of the *Roman de
la Rose* [1]), and bringing himself into line with the conventions
of landscape description. For the free forest-life, the charm
of which was so powerfully felt by many of the old ballad-
writers, Chaucer had little appreciation. The forest with its

> Knotty, knarry, bareyne trees olde
> Of stubbes sharpe, and hedouse to beholde,

in which dwelt neither man nor beast, is painted on the
walls of the temple of Mars in the *Knight's Tale,* and is
expressly calculated to excite the reader's sense of terror.
The well-known description of the trees in *The Parliament
of Fowls* (verses 176 et seq.), which Spenser had in mind when
he wrote the first canto of the *Faerie Queene,* is modelled
closely upon similar passages in classical poetry. There are
tree-lists corresponding to this in Ovid's *Metamorphoses* (X. 90),
Seneca's *Oedipus* (verses 352 et seq).; Statius' *Thebaid* (VI. 98)
and, amongst Italian and French works, in Boccaccio's *Teseide*
(XI. 22) and the *Roman de la Rose* (verses 1328 et seq.). Chaucer
is, indeed, if not the introducer, at any rate the populariser
of this literary convention in English poetry, whereby a
number of individual objects of the natural world are in-
discriminately massed together, instead of being introduced
amid their true surroundings. The practice, which became
only too popular in Elizabethan poetry, must be regarded as
unwholesome, leading as it did to strange incongruities, and
to the substitution of the dry catalogue for the living face
of Nature. Thus in the wood described in *The Parliament
of Fowls* there grow trees which have never existed side by
side in any known landscape. The palm and the olive grow
alongside of the oak and the fir, and trees of northern and
southern regions are massed together, contrary to all natural
grouping. Further, in this tree-list of Chaucer, the trees are
described not from an æsthetic, but from a utilitarian standpoint. He speaks of "the sayling firr" and "the sheter ew",

---

[1]) *Roman de la Rose,* verses 1373—1391.

while Milton's "branching elm star-proof" appears here as "the piler elm, the cofre unto careyne"!

Chaucer's interest in astronomy made him a keen observer of the heavens: he is extremely fond of following the sun through the zodiac, and in the *Complaint of Mars* he introduces somewhat intricate references to the astronomical systems of his time. Like all the courtly poets, he delights in the advent of dawn after the darkness of the night, and some of his most beautiful verses are those which describe a sunrise in spring. The following is from the *Knight's Tale:*

> The bisy larke, messager of day,
> Salueth in hir song the morwe gray,
> And firy Phebus riseth up so brighte
> That al the orient laugheth of the lighte,
> And with his stremes dryeth in the greves
> The silver dropes hangynge on the leves.
>
> > 1491—1496.

The exquisite thought introduced in the fifth verse is a translation of Dante's

> Faceva tutto rider l'oriente,
>
> > *Purgatorio,* 1. 20.

but enough remains to show Chaucer's own direct appreciation of such a scene.

In *Troilus and Cressida* he introduces an equally beautiful description of the twilight which precedes the dawn: —

> On hevene yit the sterres were y-sene,
> Although ful pale y-woxen was the mone,
> And whiten gan the orisonte shene
> Al estward, as it wont is for to done ;
> And Phebus with his rosy carte sone
> Gan after that to dresse him up to fare,
> Whan Troilus hath sent after Pandare.
>
> > V. 274—280.

The sun is referred to in quaint periphrases not unlike those of Old English poetry: it is "the dayes honour", "the hevenes ye" and "the nightes fo". Chaucer also found pleasure in the "shoures soote" of April, but his chief delight was in a cloudless sky, such as he describes in the ideal landscape of the *Book of the Duchess*, where there is no

cloud in the welkin, and the weather is neither hot nor cold.
Wind is repellent, except when it comes as a light breeze,
stirring a gentle murmur in the foliage:

> Therwith a wind, unnethe hit might be lesse,
> Made in the leves grene a noise softe,
> Acordant to the foules songe on-lofte.
>
> *Parl. of Fowls,* 201—203.

Chaucer expresses everywhere a sincere and naïve
delight in flowers; scarcely a single detailed landscape scene
can be found in his poems which does not introduce some
reference to them.   His favourite flower is, of course, the
daisy, which he describes in such affectionate terms in the
Prologue to the *Legend of Good Women:*

> This dayeseye, of alle floures flour,
> Fulfyld of vertu and of alle honour,
> And ever ilike fayr and frosh of hewe,
> As wel in wyntyr as in somyr newe,
> Fayn wolde I preysyn if I coude aright.
>
> First Version, 55—59.

Other flowers, however, are not referred to in detail.
The rose and the lily come in for their meed of praise, being
introduced chiefly by. way of comparison, while in the
Knight's Tale there is a reference to the woodbine; but with
these exceptions, Chaucer rarely attempts to discriminate
between the various kinds of flowers which deck his gardens
and meadows.   Nor does he follow the example of Dante
and give a symbolic interpretation to flowers. Symbolic
mysticism, even in its simplest forms, was foreign to his
mundane temperament even in his youth. Flowers are introduced because they add an element of cheerfulness to his
idyllic landscape, and because they appeal to his sense of
colour.

One of the most striking features in Chaucer's interpretation of Nature is his fine appreciation of colour-effects.
Discimination of colour, as has already been noticed, was in
a very undeveloped state in Old English poetry, even where
the delight experienced in the effects of light and shade was
so keen; and the same holds true in the case of most Middle
English poetry. But with Chaucer it is otherwise. In almost

all his pictures of landscape there is fine colouring, and if
he is writing of flowers, his aim is to describe their colours,
rather than to identify them. A good instance of this is
furnished by the description of the garden in the *Parliament
of Fowls* which has already been quoted. The flowers are
here spoken of as white, blue, and yellow, but are not
named; the fish in the streams have red fins and silver-
bright scales, but we are not told what fish they are. In the
House of Fame he notices the colour of the twigs of which
the labyrinthine house of Dædalus is built:

> And al this hous of whiche I rede
> Was made of twigges, falwe-rede
> And grene eek, and som weren whyte.
>
> III. 845—847.

But his keen colour-sense is, perhaps, most manifest in
the description of the cock, Chauntecleer, in the *Nun's
Priest's Tale:*

> His coomb was redder than the fyn coral,
> And batailled as it were a castle wal;
> His byle was blak, and as the jeet it shoon,
> Lyk asure were his legges and his toon,
> His nayles whiter than the lylye flour,
> And like the burned gold was his colour.   39—44.

This reference to the cock leads, in the next place, to
a consideration of Chaucer's pictures of bird and animal life.
The gay cheerfulness which is the prevailing feature of all
Chaucerian landscapes is due as much to the presence of
birds and animals as to the sunshine, the bright colours, and
the flowers. Like most of the Middle English poets, he was
fond of hunting scenes, and knew how to distinguish between
the different kinds of deer, and between deer of the same
kind at different ages. He found pleasure, too, in the merry
play of the squirrel in the trees, and of the rabbit on the
outskirts of the wood. But it is the birds which delight him
most of all. He never tires of the beautiful associations of
St. Valentine's day, when the birds choose their mates. The
idyllic *Parliament of Fowls* reads like a poem in honour of
the saint; the story of Mars and Venus in *The Complaint
of Mars* is told by a bird on the fourteenth of February,

while in the B. Version of the *Legend of Good Women* the
birds are introduced singing a song in honour of the gentle saint:

> And, for the newe blisful somers sake,
> Upon the braunches ful of blosmes softe,
> In hire delyt, they turned hem ful ofte,
> And songen, 'Blessed be Seynt Valentyne!
> For on this day I chees you to be myne,
> Withouten repentyng, myne herte swete!'
> And therewithal hire bekes gonnen meete,
> Yelding honour and humble obeysaunces
> To love, and diden hire othere observaunces
> That longeth onto love and to nature.

B. Version, 142—151.

In the *Parliament of Fowls*, and again in the *Nun's Priest's
Tale*, Chaucer comes under the influence of the mediæval
beast-fable. The latter poem is modelled partly upon Marie
de France's short fable, *Dou Coc et dou Werpil*, and partly
upon the more sustained *Roman de Renart*; but to Chaucer
belongs the poem's delicate humour, and the homely charm
of the situation. His story of Chauntecleer and Dame Pertelote
breathes the air of an English farm-yard, and the consternation
which spreads over the peacefulness of farm-life when the
fox carries off his prize is depicted with a sureness of touch
and a vividness of which Chaucer had a perfect mastery:

> Ran Colle, our dogge, and Talbot, and Gerland,
> And Malkyn, with a dystaf in hir hand;
> Ran cow and calf, and eek the verray hogges,
> So were they fered for berkynge of the dogges,
> And shoutyng of the men and wommen eek;
> They ronne so, hem thoughte hir herte breek.
> They yolleden as feendes doon in helle;
> The dokes cryden as men wolde hem quelle;
> The gees, for feere, flowen over the trees;
> Out of the hyve cam the swarm of bees;
> So hydous was the noys, *a benedicitee!*

563—573.

The extremely sympathetic interpretation of bird-life
given in the *Parliament of Fowls* owes its inspiration to
the *De Planctu Naturæ,* a twelfth century work of the French
poet Alein Delille. Many of the forcible epithets applied to
the birds in Chaucer's poem are taken from Delille, but in

the work of the French poet the birds are merely figured on the vesture of the goddess Nature, whereas in Chaucer they are real living birds which flock around "the vicaire of thalmyghty lorde", and do her homage. To Chaucer, and not to Delille, belongs, too, the exquisite gracefulness with which the story of the wooing of 'the formel egle' by the three rivals is set forth. Chaucer's unique gift of humour, which, at the time when this poem was written, had but rarely cast its genial radiance upon the characters of men, is here allowed to play upon the manners of the birds. The comments of the goose, cuckoo, sparrow-hawk and merlin, which are dramatically introduced in order to relieve the somewhat formal speeches of the three rivals, are brimful of the daintiest and merriest humour, while the charm of the poem, which deepens as the story progresses, is exquisitely rounded off by the closing song of the birds in honour of Queen Nature:

> Now welcom somer, with thy sonne softe,
> That hast this wintres weders over-shake,
> And driven awey the longe nightes blake!
> Seynt Valentyn, that art ful hy on-lofte; —
> Thus singen smale foules for thy sake —
> Wel han they cause for to gladen ofte,
> Sith ech of hem recovered hath his make:
> Ful blisful may they singen whan thay wake.
>
> 680 *et seq.*

In Chaucer's other poems references to bird-life, though brief, are yet eloquent in attesting his delight in the feathered world. In the *Book of the Duchess* he relates how he is wakened by the birds singing in harmony "the most solempne servyse", and again, in the opening verses of the Prologue to the *Canterbury Tales*, he notices the melodious song of the small birds,

> That slepen al the nyght with open ye.

References to the nightingale, the poet's bird *par excellence*, are, of course, frequent, but of greater insight into bird-life are those which tell of the swallow. This bird is described as singing mournfully in *Troilus and Cressida* (II. 64.) and is introduced in simile in the *Miller's Tale:*

> But of hir song, it was as loud and yerne,
> As any swalwe chitteryng on a berne.
>
> 71—72.

  All that has been said, and all that has been quoted,
will serve to show to how great a degree the prevailing
mood of all Chaucer's landscapes is one of cheerfulness and
pleasant animation. Sunshine, the song of birds, the bright
colours of flowers — these are the materials with which he
constructs his landscapes. He was no lover of solitude or
silence. His pictures, too, are all foreground; very rarely
do they give us any sense of distance or wide range. For
the sublimity of Nature he had absolutely no appreciation.
The mountains with their jagged crags, which appealed so
forcibly to the Gawayne-poet, aroused in Chaucer only a
feeling of discomfort and terror. The words which he places
on the lips of Dorigen in *The Franklin's Tale*, and which
give such clear utterance to this sense of repugnance for
mountainous scenery, express Chaucer's own feelings:

> Eterne God, that thurgh thy purveiaunce,
> Ledest the world by certein governaunce,
> In ydel, as men seyn, ye nothyng make;
> But, Lord, thise grisly, feendly, rokkes blake,
> That semen rather a foul confusioun
> Of werk than any fair creacioun
> Of swich a parfit wys God, and a stable, —
> Why han ye wroght this werk unresonable?
> For by this werk, south, north, ne west, ne est,
> Ther nys y-fostred man, ne bryd, ne beste;
> It dooth no good, to my wit, but anoyeth.
>
> 139—150.

  Nor did Chaucer find pleasure in the ever-changing
appearances of the sea, in spite of the fact that his journeys
to foreign lands must have made him in some measure
acquainted with it. In *The Former Age* he refers to the
"wawes grene and blewe", and again in *The Knight's Tale*,
he speaks of "wawes grene and brighte as any glas", but
these references serve chiefly to illustrate his keen delight
in colour. In the *Man of Law's Tale* the sea plays an important part in the story, but nowhere in that poem is any

attempt made to describe the appearances of the sea, either in calm or storm.

Chaucer's interpretation of Nature is, further, objective and naïve. Nature in his poems stands apart from man, delighting man by reason of its idyllic repose or bright colours, but never responding to his sentiments or yearnings. He was essentially a narrative poet, with strongly marked dramatic tendencies; for lyrical poetry in the highest sense he had no gift. That lyric intensity which finds in the forms of the natural world a certain sympathy even with a poet's deepest feelings, such as is found in the Old English *Seafarer* and *Wanderer*, is quite foreign to his temperament.

In all this Chaucer takes his stand as the foremost English representative of the mediæval school of courtly poets. The reaction in favour of Old English traditions of landscape painting, which began in the west-midland district about the middle of the fourteenth century, and to which the Gawayne poet owed allegiance, encountered in the poetry of Chaucer a counter-action. Sublimity once more yields place to idyllic beauty, the grandiose to the picturesque, just as the rugged alliterative verse is replaced by the shapely rhymed decasyllabics of one who would not "geeste rum ram ruf by lettre".

Chapter IX.

THE
ENGLISH POETS OF THE FIFTEENTH CENTURY.

The disciples and imitators of Chaucer, great as was their admiration for their master, failed to recognise the full extent of his greatness. The realism and fine character-isation of Chaucer's later works were scarcely appreciated by them; the Chaucer whom they knew and reverenced was the Chaucer of the early works, in which the prevailing note is one of courtly romanticism fraught with allegory and symbolism, and in which the conventional setting is that of a May-day dream. Of the poems ascribed to Chaucer, either falsely, or on insufficient evidence, *The Flower and the Leaf*, *The Cuckoo and the Nightingale*, *The Court of Love* and *Chaucer's Dream* demand a passing notice [1]. In each of these poems the landscape is that of a spring morning at sunrise, the chief features introduced belonging in each case to the regular *répertoire* of the courtly fourteenth and fifteenth century poets. There is the pleasant grove where the oaks grow straight as a line;

> and an eight foot or nyne
> Every tree wel fro his felawe grew,
> With braunchis brode, laden with leves new,
> That sprongen out ayein the sonne shene;
> Som very rede, and som a glad light grene.
> *The Flower and the Leaf*, 31—35.

Among the trees is the sun-proof arbour where the knights und ladies rest, listen to the song of the birds, and discourse on love, life and immortality. In *The Flower and*

---

[1] These poems have all been edited by Prof. Skeat in the seventh volume of the *Complete Works of Chaucer*.

the Leaf the birds are the goldfinch — a bird beloved of Scottish poets at all times, but not introduced into Chaucer's *Parliament of Fowls* — and the nightingale. Here the disputants are human, but in *The Cuckoo and the Nightingale*, which Professor Skeat has shown to be the work of Sir Thomas Clanvowe, it is the birds themselves which engage in the debate. This poem, which by its title recalls *The Owl and the Nightingale,* is inferior to that work in fine insight into Nature as also in humour; but the May landscape which serves as a scenic background to the debate merits quotation, if only by reason of its Chaucerian reminiscences:

> And than, anon as I the day espyde,
> No lenger wolde I in my bedde abyde,
> But unto a wode, that was faste by,
> I wente forth alone, boldely,
> And held my way doun by a broke-syde;

> Til I com to a launde of whyte and grene;
> So fair oon had I never inne been;
> The ground was grene, y-poudred with daisye,
> The floures and the gras y-lyke hye,
> Al grene and whyte; was nothing elles sene.

> Ther sat I doun among the faire floures,
> And saw the briddes trippe out of her boures
> Ther-as they had hem rested al the night.
> They were so joyful of the dayes light
> That they begonne of May to don hir houres.

56—70.

The debate which follows, instead of turning upon the mediæval theme of asceticism, is all of love and love's service. The character of the disputants is not brought out with that dramatic mastery shown by the author of *The Owl and the Nightingale,* but Professor Skeat[1]) has drawn attention to the interesting fact that Milton had before him this pseudo-Chaucerian poem when writing his *Sonnet to the Nightingale.*

The *Court of Love* is also rich in bird-song, May-day flowers and Chaucerian memories. The close of the poem gives an account of the orisons which the birds render to the Lord of Love. The paramount literary influence is that of

---

[1]) Chaucer's Works, vol. VII. p. LXI.

The Parliament of Fowls, and the songs and speeches show
something of that dramatic correspondence with the traditional
characters of the different birds which is the source of so
much delight in Chaucer's romantic poem:

> The second lesson robin redebrest sang,
> "Hail to the god and goddess of our lay"!
> And to the lectorn amorously, he sprang: —
> "Hail", quod he eke, "O fresh seson of May,
> Our moneth glad that singen on the spray!
> Hail to the floures rede, and white, and blewe.
> Whiche by ther vertue make our lustes newe!"

> The third lesson the turtill-dove took up,
> And thereat lough the mavis as in scorn:
> He said, "O god! as mot I dyne or sup,
> This folissh dove will give us al an horn!
> There been right here a thousand better born.
> To rede this lesson, which, as wel as he,
> And eke as hot, can love in all degree."

> The turtill-dove said, "Welcom, welcom, May,
> Gladsom and light to loveres that ben trewe!
> I thank thee, Lord of Love, that doth purvey
> For me to rede this lesson al of dewe;
> For in gode sooth of corage I pursue
> To serve my make till deth us must depart:
> And than *"Tu autem"* sang he al apart.

1380—1400.

John Gower, the author of the *Confessio Amantis,* though
senior to Chaucer by about ten years, may in some respects
be regarded as his disciple. Without Chaucer's brilliant
example before him, it is scarcely likely that he would have
written English verse at all, while in the actual composition
of his long cyclical romance there is frequent trace of
Chaucerian imitation both in respect of subject and style.
The curious medley of prurient love-story and sententious
moral which the *Confessio Amantis* [1]) presents has somewhat
puzzled readers, and perhaps Gower is himself the best critic
of his poem when he describes it as one "which stant betwene

---

[1]) Ed. Pauli, 1857.

ernest and game". Gower is neither a profound, nor a far-
reaching, student of external Nature. For the most part, he
is too absorbed in his love-story and his often ill-fitting moral
to have any eye for landscape. He opens his poem with a
reference to the conventional May-morning, and in the first
Book, whilst describing the adventures of Acteon, he turns
aside for a moment to paint a woodland landscape:

> So him befelle upon a tide,
> On his hunting as he cam ride,
> In a foreste alone he was,
> He sigh upon the grene gras
> The faire fresshe floures springe;
> He herd among the leves singe
> The throstel with the nightingale.
> Thus, er he wist, into a dale
> He came, wher was a litel pleine,
> All rounde aboute wel beseine
> Wit busshes grene and cedres high,
> And there within he caste his eye.
>
> Vol. I, p. 53.

Every feature in this landscape is painfully trite, and
nowhere is there any trace of actual study of Nature. Of
a similar character is the following passage from the story
of Rosiphele in Book IV.

> Whan come was the month of may,
> She wolde walke upon a day,
> And that was er the sonne arist.
> Of women but a fewe it wist.
> And forth she wente prively
> Unto the park was faste by.
> All softe walkend on the gras,
> Til she came there the launde was,
> Through which ther ran a great rivere.
>
>   * * *
>
> She sigh the swote floures springe,
> She herde gladde foules singe,
> She sigh the bestes in her kinde,
> The buck, the doo, the harte, the hinde,
> The male go with the femele.
>
> Vol. II. p. 44.

The picture of the cave of Morpheus in the same Book
is evidently based on Ovid and Chaucer, but the description

of a storm in Book VIII., slight as it is, seems more original,
and certainly marks a departure from the conventional : —

> Within a time, as it betid,
> Whan they were in the see amid,
> Out of the north they sigh a cloude,
> The storme aros, the windes loude
> They blewen many a dredeful blast ;
> The welken was all overcast.
> The derke night the sonne hath under ;
> There was a gret tempest of thunder.
> The mone and eke the sterres bothe
> In blacke cloudes they hem clothe,
> Whereof her brighte loke they hide.

Vol. III. p. 310.

The most faithful of Chaucer's long line of disciples in
the poetic craft was Thomas Occleve. In his *Governail of
Princes* he tells us something of the affectionate esteem and
reverence which he bore towards his master, while the
general conduct of his poems tells us a good deal more.
Amongst other things, Occleve reproduces some of the striking
features in the Chaucerian landscape — the delight in the
freshness of a May morning, and in the song of birds. But
in some of his minor poems he introduces into his descriptions
of Nature a certain personal feeling and an inwardness of
manner, which are rarely to be met with in the purely objective landscape painting of Chaucer. Occleve is prone to
melancholy. He seems, indeed, to have been dominated by
that sense of the transitoriness of the things of this world
which is so frequently met with among the Old English
poets. In *Occleve's Dialogue* he tells us, —

> Welthe of the world and longe and faire dayes
> Passen as dooth the shadwe of a tree ;

and this idea recurs very frequently in other poems. One
feels that it is quite in place in a picture of an Autumn
landscape such as he gives us very briefly in his *Complaint*,
for Autumn is pre-eminently the season of decay ; but the
same idea is found even in his description of a May-morning,
where one would expect to meet with feelings of gladness
and hope :

As that I walkid in the monthe of May
Besyde a grove, in a hevy musynge,
Floures dyverse I sy, right fressh and gay,
And briddes herde I eek lustyly synge,
That to myn herte yaf a confortynge.
But evere o thought me stang unto the herte,
That dye I sholde, and hadde no knowynge
Whanne, ne whidir, I sholde hennes sterte.

Ballad to the Virgin and Child.[1]

In spite of the gladness of the May season, rich in song and floral colour, the poet's thoughts turn to death, and give to an otherwise cheerful picture a tinge of melancholy.

The generally accepted idea that the poems of John Lydgate, the Benedictine monk of Bury St. Edmund's, are as dull as they are voluminous stands in need of some correction. Their volume is scarcely greater than their versatility of manner, and their dulness is again and again relieved by picturesque description, wealth of colour, and landscape scenes of great charm.   Lydgate, in donning the cowl, refused to forswear his appreciation for the beauty of Nature, and his poems are accordingly fraught with passages of natural description which are evidently based on actual observation. In his interpretation of Nature, as in everything else, he owes much to Chaucer. Thus he imitates Chaucer's pictures of a spring morning:

First Zephirus with his blastys soote,
Erspireth Ver with newe buddys greene,
The bawme ascendith out of every roote,
Causyng with flourys ageyn the sonne sheene
May among moneths sitte lyk a queene,
Hir sustir April wattryng hir gardynes,
With holsom shoures shad in the tendyr vynes.

Lydgate's Testament.

But, as the passage shows, he was much more than an imitator.   In fact Chaucer was for Lydgate rather an inspiration than a model, as far as his descriptions of Nature are concerned. Thus it is Chaucer who awakens his admiration for the daisy, but his reference to that flower is different from that of the poet of the *Legend of Good Women:*

[1] Hoccleve's Minor Poems vol. I. ed. Furnivall (E. E. T. S. Extra Series LXI.).

Now mercy, Fortune, and have pyte
On myn gret adversyte,
And on my woful maladye;
And graunte that the dayesye,
The whiche is callyd margaret,
So fayr, so goodly and so meke
Of flour, of stalk, of crop and rote,
So frosch, so benygne and so sote,
Whos croune is bothe whit and red,
The stalke evere grene and nevere ded.
In medewe, valeyis, hillys and clyf,
The whiche flour pleynly ʒif
I myghte at leyser onys se,
And abyde at lyberte,
When as it doth so faire sprede
Ageyn the sunne in every mede,
On bankys hy among the bromys
Wher as these lytelle herdegromys
Floutyn al the longe day,
Both in aprylle and in may,
In here smale recorderys,
In floutys and in rede sperys
Aboute this flour, til it be nyght;
It makyth hem so glade and lyght,
The grete beute to beholde
Of this flour.

Lydgate's Complaint.

The whole of this description of the daisy has been given, became of the graceful fancies which the poet gathers round the flower. His independence of manner is apparent throughout, while in his introduction of the shepherd-boys playing all day upon their flutes and recorders, he breaks entirely away from Chaucer, and anticipates the pastoralists of the Elizabethan era.

In the same way Lydgate looks to Chaucer for inspiration in his delineation of bird-life, yet follows the bent of his own genius in matters of detail. In his short poem, *The Devotions of the Fowls,* suggested, no doubt, by Chaucer's *Parliament of Fowls,* the poet tells us how on a Easter morning he goes forth into the fields and listens to the "voyce celestial" of the birds, praising God "with a hevenly ympne and a holsum", and breaking out into songs of joy because of the risen Christ.

Lydgate's fine appreciation of natural scenery is again illustrated by his poem on *The Mutability of Human Affairs*[1]) and by *The Complaint of the Black Knight*[2]). In the former poem he gives us another May picture all atune with the song of nightingales, cuckoos, woodpeckers and other birds, and then, by way of contrast, introduces a winter scene:

Constreynt of colde makith flouris dare
With winter frostes, that thei dar not appere:
All clad in russet, the soil of grene is bare:
Tellus and Ymo be dullid of their chere.
By revolucion and turnyng of the yere,
A gery march his stondis doth disclose;
Now reyne, now storme, now Phebus bright and clere.
All stant in chaunge like a mydsomer rose.

Lydgate's most elaborate landscape painting is found in his *Complaint of the Black Knight,* and it is in this poem too that he reminds us most of Chaucer. The Proem to the *Complaint* introduces the usual May morning scene in a beautiful park "walled with grene stoon", but though conventional in its general outlines, the landscape which the poet reveals is instinct with a genuine appreciation of country life. Amongst other things he notices the dew —

lyk silver in shyning
Upon the leves, as any baume swete;

and listens to the birds which sang so loudly —

that al the wode rong,
Lyke as it shulde shiver in peces smale.

He tells us what trees grow in the park — the cedar, filbert, ash, fir, oak and hawthorn, the last-named being finely characterised, and attesting Lydgate's first-hand study of Nature:

Ther saw I eek the fresshe hawethorn
In whyte motle, that so swote doth smelle.

But what is most noticeable in this landscape is Lydgate's fine sense of colour, in which he rivals, if indeed he does

---

[1]) Lydgate's *Minor Poems* ed. Halliwell (Percy Society Publications) p. 24.

[2]) Skeat's *Supplement to Chaucer's Works.*

not surpass, Chaucer himself. His references to the hawthorn,
the silver dew, the golden gravel, the soil "clad in grene, rede
and whyte", and the green stones of the park wall — all serve
to bring this fine perception of colour into prominence, while
the passage from *The Mutability of Human Affairs* given
above shows that the russet hues of winter had also been
observed by this great colourist. However much of the
sublimity of Old English landscape painting had been lost
in Middle English times, the works of Chaucer and Lydgate
show that in the appreciation of colour-effects there had been
a very marked advance.

Stephen Hawes, the chief poet who graced the court of
Henry VII, brings down some of the Chaucerian traditions
of poetry into the sixteenth century, while his chief work,
The Pastime of Pleasure, has been described as "the link
between *The Canterbury Tales* and *The Faerie Queene*". Its
connection with the former work must be acknowledged to
be very slight, and if Hawes himself is to be believed, it
was Lydgate rather than Chaucer whom he regarded as "the
chefe orygynal of my lernyng". The meagre references to
external Nature which occur in his allegoric *Pastime of
Pleasure* [1]) are conceived in faint imitation of the Chaucerian
style. In the first Canto he brings his hero, Graunde Amour,
into a meadow — the meadow of youth according to the
allegory — which he describes in the jejune and conventional
manner of the mediæval courtly poets:

> When that Aurora did well appeare
> In the depured ayre and cruddy firmament,
> Forth then I walked without impediment
>
> Into a medowe both gaye and glorious,
> Whiche Flora depainted with many a colour,
> Lyke a place of pleasure moste solacious,
> Encensyng out the aromatike odoure
> Of Zepherus breath, whiche that every floure
> Through his fume doth alwaye engender.

No less conventional is the garden where the poet's
heroine, La Bell Pucell, takes the air "among the floures

---

[1]) Percy Society Publications, vol. XVIII.

of aromatyke fume". Like all other gardens of mediæval poetry, that of Hawes contains its arbour, —

> Set all about with flours fragraunt,
> And in the myddle there was resplendyshaunte
> A dulcet spring and marvaylous fountaine
> Of golde and azure made all certaine.

Canto XVIII.

The inability of the courtly poets of the Middle Age to speak of dawn, sunrise or sunset, without dragging in the threadbare myths of classical poetry, finds only too ample illustration in the pages of Hawes's allegory. In the thirty-third canto of his *Pastime of Pleasure* he describes a sunrise scene in which this mannerism is especially prominent:

> Ryght in the morowe, when Aurora clere
> Her radiaunt beames began for to spreade,
> And splendent Phebus, in his golden spere,
> The cristalle ayr did make fayre and redde,
> Dark Dyane declining pale as any ledde,
> When the lytle byrdes swetely dyd syng
> Laudes to their maker early in the mornyng.

Alexander Barclay (1475? — 1552?) the first of a long line of English eclogue-writers is now chiefly remembered as a fore-runner of Spenser. Yet Barclay's *Eclogues*[1]) have an intrinsic and self-dependent interest as well. His pictures of country life have a certain warm colouring and sincerity of manner which are only too often wanting in the works of later eclogue-writers. Barclay is usually free from pastoral conventions and arcadianism, and his "uplondyshman" is as faithful in his picture of rural England as is his "Cytezen" in that of London. His insistence on the rivalry of town and country, and on the respective merits and demerits of each, introduces a new note into English poetry, and one which was to claim the attention of Spenser, Shakespeare, and of many another Elizabethan. In this, as in much else, Barclay shows himself to be an apt disciple of Mantuan and Æneas Sylvius, as they in their turn were of Virgil and Theocritus. The actual appearance of the country-side appealed far less strongly to Barclay than the life of the peasantry, so that descriptions

---

[1]) Ed. Fairholt (Percy Society Publications) 1847.

of Nature are rare in the course of his five eclogues. It is, in fact, curious that in the first three, in which the prominent features in the life of a courtier and a peasant are placed in antagonism, the chief landscape scene is one which is introduced into the picture of court life. This is found in the second eclogue, where Cornix describes the courts of the Middle Age, and among the things in which courtiers find pleasure mentions the following:

> Gardeyns and medowes or place delicious,
> Forestes and parkes well furnished with dere,
> Colde pleasaunt streames, or welles fayre and clere,
> Curious cundites or shadowie mountaynes,
> Swete pleasaunt valleys, laundes or playnes,
> Houndes, and suche other thinges manyfolde
> Some men take pleasour and solace to beholde.

It is difficult to reconcile the shadowy mountains or even the pleasant streams with the every-day life of the Tudor courtier, and of this Barclay himself seems to be aware; for he adds, —

> But all these pleasoures be much more jocounde
> To private persons, which not to court be bounde,
> Then to suche other whiche of necessitie
> Are bounde to the court as in captivitie.

In the fifth and last eclogue more attempt is made to introduce country scenery. But such is Barclay's dogged honesty that he will not paint it on its most attractive side. Though a fierce satirist of court and town, he will not shut his eyes upon the hardships of the peasant. He gives us no alluring picture of May mornings, rich in verdure and song, but seems to find a grim pleasure in recalling the bitterness of the winter season:

> In colde January whan fyre is comfortable,
> And that the feldes be nere intollerable,
> Whan shepe and pastoures leveth felde and folde,
> And draw to cotes for to eschewe the colde,
> What tyme the verdure of grounde, and every tre,
> By frost and stormes is pryvate of beaute,
> And every small byrde thynketh the wynter longe,
> Which well apereth by ceasynge of theyr songe; —

At this same season two herdes fresshe of age,
At tyme apoynted met both in one cotage.

Prologue to *Eclogue V.*

This wintry landscape is further developed in the eclogue itself, when Amyntas, introducing the debate, describes in faithful and homely detail the "uplandishman's" winter both without and within doors:

The wynter snowes, all covered is the grounde,
The northe wynde blowys all with fereful sounde,
The longe yse sycles at the howsys honge,
The streames frosen, the nyght is colde and longe:
Where botes rowed now cartes have passage,
From yoke the oxen be lowsed and bondage;
The ploweman resteth avoyde of all busynesse,
Save whan he tendeth his harnes for to dresse:
Mably his wyfe sytteth byfore the fyre,
All blacke and smoke, clothed in rude atyre;
Sethynge some grewell, and sterynge the pulment
Of peese or frument, a noble meete for lent.

In sheer fidelity of description, and in keen insight into the life of an English peasant, Barclay claims kinship with Crabbe. The one is the founder of the English eclogue, the other the poet who, by his unswerving truth-telling, aimed a death-blow at the stilted affectation of a later and feebler generation of eclogue-writers.

We are prone to think of John Skelton [1]) (1460? —1529?) vicar of Diss, either as a writer of morality plays and satires, or as the master of that racy doggerel verse which historians of literature have named after him. Yet there is another side to Skelton's genius. He was the author of poems which bear the impress of Chaucerian discipleship as clearly as anything of Lydgate or Occleve; these are written in Chaucer's rhyme-royal, and borrow both motives and brocade from the fourteenth century master. Such, for instance, is his *Garland of Laurel*, in which he follows Chaucer's lead, not only in the general plan and choice of verse, but also in the occasional descriptions of Nature which adorn the work. The Chaucerian accent is unmistakable in the following stanza:

---

[1]) *Poetical Works*, ed. Dyce, 1843.

> Lyke as the larke, upon the somers day,
> Whan Titan radiant burnisshith his bemis bryght,
> Mountith on hy with her melodious lay,
> Of the soneshyne engladid with the lyght,
> So am I supprysyd with pleasure and delyght
> To se this howre now, that I may say,
> How ar ye welcome to this court of aray.
>
> 533—539.

Equally so in this: —

> The clowdis gan to clere, the mist was rarifiid:
> In an herber I saw, brought where I was,
> There birdis on the brere sange on every syde;
> With alys ensandid about in compas,
> The bankis enturfid with singular solas,
> Enrailid with rosers, and vinis engrapid;
> It was a new comfort of sorowis escapid.
>
> 651—657.

Of Skelton's lyrics, notice may be taken of his *Philip Sparrow*, reminiscent in its general idea of the famous dirge of Catullus, but developed with far greater detail. Skelton calls upon all the birds in turn to lament the death of his favourite bird. He falls at once into the catalogue-description, which, though pleasing for a time, soon becomes monotonous:

> The goldfynche, the wagtayle,
> The janglynge jay to rayle,
> The flecked pye to chatter
> Of this dolorous mater;
> And robyn redbrest,
> He shall be preest,
> The requiem masse to synge,
> Softly warbelynge,
> With helpe of the red sparow,
> And the chattrynge swallow,
> This herse for to halow.

Philip Sparrow has a certain affinity to the poem entitled *The Harmony of Birds*[1]), which was once attributed to Skelton, but which has since been shown to be by another hand, and of a somewhat later date. This fanciful study of bird-life has rapidity of movement and a pleasing quaintness

---

[1]) Percy Society Publications, Vol. VII.

of fancy, but the fidelity with which the different birds are
portrayed is somewhat marred by the inclusion of such
"wildfowl" as the popinjay, phœnix and pelican. The opening
stanzas express the poet's delight in the dawn of a spring
morning:

> Whan Dame Flora
> In die Aurora
> > Had coverd the meadow with flowers,
> And all the fylde
> Was over distylde
> > With lusty Aprell showers :

> For my disporte,
> Me to conforte,
> > Whan the day began to spring.
> Foorth I went,
> With a good intent
> > To here the byrdes syng.

The birds then appear, and each in turn breaks out
into singing, the theme of their song being the praise of
Him who, —

> > for mannes love
> Was borne of mayden milde.

Among the more truly English birds introduced are the
thrush, the lark, the nightingale, the partridge, the magpie,
the cock, the eagle and the swallow. The lark sings as follows: —

> Than sayd the larke,
> Bycause my parte
> > Is upward to ascend,
> And downe to rebound
> Toward the ground,
> > Singyng to discend.

> Than after my wunt,
> "Pleni sunt
> > Celi et terra", quod she,
> Shall be my song,
> On briefe and long,
> > "Majestatis glorie tue".

In due course comes the song of the swallows:

> The swalowes syng swete,
> To man we be mete,
> > For with him we do buylde;

Lyke as from above,
God, for mannes love,
    Was borne of mayden milde.

The Harmony of Birds, written at a time when mediævalism was slowly giving place to the ideals of the Renascence,
owes its inspiration to *The Parliament of Fowls:* but the keen
interest in bird-life which the poem displays was in existence
in England long before Chaucer, and by virtue of that interest, the poem comes into line with the thirteenth century
Owl and the Nightingale, and even with those Old English
riddles which dwelt so fondly on the forms and movements
of birds.

Chapter X.

THE SCOTTISH POETS OF THE FIFTEENTH AND SIXTEENTH CENTURIES.

After the death of Chaucer and Gower the centre of gravity of British poetry passed from England to Scotland and remained there throughout the fifteenth century, and indeed until the great Elizabethan age began. Remembering this, it is at the same time necessary to bear in mind how largely Scottish poetry was influenced during this period by the earlier English models. Two streams of influence may be traced flowing through the poetry of King James I., Dunbar and Douglas; the one is Chaucerian, the other Virgilian, and it is difficult to say which of the two was the stronger. The influence of Chaucer is most marked in the case of King James I. of Scotland (1394—1437). Thanks to his long enforced sojourn in England, he came into closest touch with the works of the English poet, and on every page of *The King's Quair* [1]) we see signs of this Chaucerian influence.

Nowhere is this influence more marked than in the delineation of landscape. King James, like Chaucer, preferred the scenery of the garden, where Nature is brought under the sway of art, to the wild freedom of the mountains and woods. His description of the birds in the garden, and of their song in honour of the return of spring, is evidently suggested by Chaucer's *Parliament of Fowls*, though the Scottish King is no mere imitator. While the general design of his landscape is Chaucerian, the details and the filling in of the picture are original, and display a gracefulness of

[1]) Edited by Professor Skeat (Publications of the Scottish Text Society).

touch which is entirely his own. King James is not free
from a certain conventionality in his pictures, any more
than Chaucer and Gower, his "maisteris dere". There is the
trite reference to classical Nature-myths, and to the course
of the sun through the zodiac, but with the conventional
and artificial there is mingled a fine sense of the life which
is in Nature, and of the joy which even the flowers feel
at the return of spring. Thus in stanza XXI. he describes
how the sun had —

> Passyt mydday bot foure greis evin,
> Off length and brede his angel wingis bryght
> He spred upon the ground doun fro the hevin,
> That, for gladnesse and comfort of the sight,
> And with the tiklyng of his hete and light,
> The tendir flouris opnyt thame and sprad,
> And, in thaire nature, thankit him for glad.

The royal bard then brings his readers to a beautiful
garden, in the midst of which is an arbour:

> So thik the bewes and the leves grene
> Beschadit al the aleyes that there were,
> And myddis every herbere myght be sene
> The scharpe, grene, suete Ienepere,
> Growing so faire with braunchis here and there,
> That, as it semyt to a lyf without,
> The bewis spred the herbere all aboute.
>
> Stanza XXXII.

Then comes a description of the birds which haunt the
garden, and of the spring-song which they sing in chorus:

> Worschippe, ye that loveris bene, this May,
> For of your blisse the Kalendis are begonne,
> And sing with us, away, winter, away!
> Cum, somer, cum, the suete sesoun and sonne!
> Awake, for schame! that have your hevynnis wonne,
> And amorously lift up your hedis all;
> Thank Lufe that list you to his merci call.
>
> Stanza XXXIV.

This follows, of course, the model of the birds' roundel
to Queen Nature in Chaucer's poem, but King James enters
into the spirit of the song with fresh vigour, and infuses
into a new grace.

While King James's interpretation of Nature is, for the most part, as naïve as that of Chaucer, he at times has an inkling of that sympathetic affinity between Nature and humanity, which finds its fullest development in modern lyric poetry. An instance of this occurs in stanza CXVIII.: —

> And eke, in takin of this pitouse tale,
> Quhen so my teris dropen on the ground,
> In thaire nature the lytill birdis smale
> Styntith thaire song, and murnyth for that sound,
> And all the lightis in the hevin round
> Of my grevance have suich compacience,
> That from the ground they hiden thaire presence.

This picture of the stars hiding their presence in sympathy with the poet's grief opens up a new vista in English literature: its spirit is Petrarchian, not Chaucerian.

In stanza CLII. King James takes his readers beyond the garden, and out into the meadow by the side of a river, —

> Quhare, throu the gravel, bryght as ony gold,
> The cristall water ran so clere and cold,
> That in myn ere maid contynualy
> A maner soun, mellit with armony.

The cheerful animation and gay colour of Chaucer's landscapes are rivalled by this river scene of the Scottish poet. In the succeeding stanza he paints the fish which swim in the water:

> That full of lytill fischis by the brym,
> Now here, now there, with bakkis blewe as lede,
> Lap and playit, and in a rout can swym
> So prattily, and dressit thame to sprede
> Thaire curall fynnis, as the ruby rede,
> That in the sonne on thaire scalis bryght
> As gesserant, ay glitterit in my sight.

The description of the river which begins so felicitously in the above stanzas is, however, spoiled by the reference to the animals found by its banks. The desire to bring together a number of animals in what is little better than a long catalogue, like the tree-catalogue of Chaucer's *Parliament of Fowls*, leads King James into gross unnaturalness. Almost every animal of which he had any knowledge

at all is dragged into the list — the lion, the panther, "the
lytill squerelle ful of besynesse", the porcupine, the lynx,
the unicorn, the tiger, "the wyly fox, the wedewis inemye",
and a host of other beasts far too numerous to mention.
The epithets applied to some of the animals are often strikingly
faithful, but the impression which the whole passage makes
is a discordant one.

Robert Henryson[1]) whose poetic career probably extended over the greater portion of the latter half of the
fifteenth century, is one of the most original and certainly
one of the most attractive of our line of poets. Though
we think of him chiefly as a fabulist, he was also the
author of courtly romances, while, by virtue of his *Robin
and Makyne,* he may be fitly regarded as the first of
our pastoral poets. As an interpreter of Nature Henryson
also holds a post of distinction. In this, as in much else, he
is the true disciple of Chaucer, but, like the other Scottish
poets of the fifteenth and sixteenth centuries, his allegiance
to the English master is always tempered with distinct originality, and with the resolve to rely wherever possible upon
actual observation. The accent of locality is unmistakable
in Henryson, and his landscape painting is never so fine
as when it unfolds the scenery of his own northern home.

Most of the *Fables,* though they reveal a very shrewd
insight into animal life, together with the capacity of looking
upon that life on its most attractive and most humorous
side, lie somewhat apart from the present field of study.
The several fables which introduce the fox — "Sir Chante-
cleer and the Fox", "The Fox, the Wolf and the Moon's
Shadow", "The Fox, the Wolf and the Cadger" — claim
comparison with the famous Low German beast-epic, and
Henryson can scarcely be said to suffer by the comparison.
The first-named fable also recalls Chaucer's *Nun's Priest's
Tale,* just as another of the fables — "The Parliament of
Beasts" — is directly reminiscent of his *Parliament of Fowls.*
But it is the fable entitled *The Preaching of the Swallow*
which chiefly calls for notice in this place. In this poem

---

[1]) *Works,* ed. Laing 1865.

Henryson anticipates Gawin Douglas in giving to his readers a graphic picture of the different seasons of the year. As we have already seen, Henry the Minstrel does the same thing in his *Wallace*, but there is no evidence to show which of the two poets was the first to write.

Henryson starts his poem with a picture of summer arrayed "in jolye mantill of grene", and in the next stanza passes on to autumn. But it is in depicting winter and spring that he puts forth his chief strength. Nothing is more noticeable in the interpretation of Nature by Scottish poets than the intense realism and zest introduced into descriptions of a wintry landscape. It may easily be argued that these winter scenes are inspired rather by shrinking dread than by appreciation, yet it can scarcely be questioned that the realism of these pictures implies a certain interest and even delight in what is at first sight only repellent. Such at least is the impression which Henryson gives us in his winter landscape: —

> Syne Wynter wan, quhen austern Eolus,
> God of the wynd, with blastes boreall,
> The grene garment of somer glorious
> Hes all to rent and revin in pecis small;
> Than flouris fair, faidit with frost, mon fall,
> And birdis blyith changit thair noitis sweit
> In still murning, neir slane with snaw and sleit.
>
> Thir dailis deip with dubbis drownit is,
> Baith hill and holt heillit with frostis hair;
> And bewis bene are laiffit bair of bliss
> By wickit windis of the Wynter wair.
> All wyld beistis than from the bentis bair
> Drawis for dreid unto their dennis deip,
> Coucheand for cauld in coiffis thame to keip.

Henryson's language is a little quaint — though less so than that of the later poet Douglas — but no quaintness of language can hide the force of the picture. As winter passes into spring, the last of the four landscapes appears, and the poet breaks out into gladness when he sees once more the blossoming of the flowers, and hears the newly awakened voices of the birds:

Syne cummis Ver, quhen Winter is away,
The secretar of Somer, with his seeill,
Quhen columbine up keikis throw the clay,
Quhilk fleit wes befoir with frostis feeill.
The maveis and the merle beginnis to mell;
The lark on loft, with uther birdis small,
Then drawis furth fra derne, over doun and dail.

In his courtly poem, *The Testament of Cressid*, Henryson follows the excellent custom of prefixing to the story an Introduction setting forth the occasion on which the poem was written, and bringing in, incidentally, a good deal of landscape painting. What is most pleasing in this Introduction is the recognition on the poet's part that the tragic theme of his story requires a sombre winter landscape to correspond to it. As he himself expresses it, —

Ane dooly sesoun to ane cairfull dyte
Suld correspond, and be equivalent;

and he forthwith proceeds to tell of "shouris of haill", frosts, and bitter blasts that "fra pole Artyk come quhisling loud and shill". This association of a "dooly sesoun" with a "cairful dyte" is not quite such a simple matter as may at first sight appear. It implies, in fact, the recognition of certain moods in Nature, if not also of a certain sense of sympathy between Nature and man.

In the *Prologue* to the *Fables* there is no demand for a sombre wintry landscape, and Henryson accordingly gives us one of the most brilliant of his colour-passages, fitly called forth by a description of flaming June:

Sweit was the smell of flouris quhite and reid,
The noyis of birdis richt delitious,
The bewis braid bloomit abone my heid,
The ground growand with gersis gratious:
Of all plesance that place wes plenteous,
With sweit odouris and birdis harmonie,
The morning myld, my mirth was maire forthy.

The roisis reid, arrayit on rone and ryce,
The prymerois and the purpour viola;
To heir it wes ane poynt of Paradice,
Sic mirth the mavis and the merle couth ma.
The blossumis blyith brak up on bank and bra,

> The smell of herbis and of foullis cry,
> Contending quha suld haif the victorie.

This is a joyous picture, and the feelings which the June season calls forth from the Scottish poet are wholly spontaneous. There is no suspicion of book-learning in the above description: the birds and the flowers are those of a Scottish woodland, and no false note brings discord into this well-ordered landscape.

Although *Robin and Makyne* is the best known of Henryson's poems, it does not call for special attention here. As a faithful and yet romantic picture of shepherd life its charm is perennial; for the scene which it presents is no make-believe, like so many of the pastoral poems of a later and more sophisticated age, but bears throughout the stamp of truth. At the same time, little attempt is made in the course of the pastoral to introduce landscape, even in the form of a scenic background, such as is found in the Robin Hood Ballads, and in many Middle English lyrics. The dialogue form of the poem no doubt accounts for this, for on other occasions, as has already been seen, Henryson paints a landscape with considerable fulness. Yet in reading the poem, we feel that there is everywhere an open-air freshness, and that we are carried away to the greenwood just as surely as in the ballad-poems which open with natural description. It is worthy of notice, too, that in the only stanza in which there occurs anything approaching landscape painting it is the greenwood to which reference is made:

> Makyne, the nicht is soft and dry,
> The wether warm and fair;
> And the grene wod richt neir hard by,
> To walk attowre all where.

Contemporary with Robert Henryson is the somewhat unfamiliar figure of Sir Richard Holland the author of the *Book of the Howlat,* [1]) written about 1453. This study of bird-life falls into the large class of poems which, directly or indirectly, are fashioned after the model of Chaucer's *Parliament of Fowls.* The poem opens with the picture of a

---

[1]) Edited by Laing (Publications of the Bannatyne Club) 1823.

morning "in the middis of May", and relates how the poet goes forth into a meadow where flowers and herbs of all kinds are in bloom. The landscape is a pleasing one, but the elements which go to the making of it are somewhat commonplace, and there is an absence of that finer individualisation which is not content with generalities, but seeks to introduce distinctive and specialised features. Holland does not distinguish between the different flowers in the meadow, nor, when he proceeds to describe the river which flows through it, does he attempt to identify the birds which are singing on the overhanging trees: —

> I walkit till a riveir,
> That ryallye rered.
> The ryver ran down, but resting or rove,
> Throu a forest on fauld, that ferlye was fair;
> All the brayis of that buyrne buir brenchis above,
> And birds blithest of ble on blossomes bair.
> The birth that the ground bure was broudyn in bredis.
> With gerss gay as the gold, and granis of grace,
> Mendis and medicine for all menis neidis;
> Help till hert, and till hurt, helefull it was.

The most interesting figure in British poetry between Chaucer and the Elizabethans is William Dunbar,[1] "the Rhymer of Scotland" (1465?—1530?). Inferior to Chaucer in the greatest things, he surpasses him in versatility. Whether he essays lyric poetry, allegoric romance, or satire, he shows himself a perfect master of his art. Like almost all the Scottish poets of the fifteenth and sixteenth centuries, he is very much under Chaucer's influence, especially in his allegoric romances. Descriptions of landscape occupy an important place in his poems, though the field from which these descriptions are drawn is somewhat limited. For the sublime effects of Nature, and indeed for most things which are not to be found in a spring landscape of quiet beauty, he has scarcely any appreciation. In spite of the fact that he spent much of his time on the threshold of the Scottish Highlands, he shows no interest in mountain or loch. His landscapes, indeed, have little in them

---

[1] *Works,* ed. Laing, 1834.

which is characteristically Scottish, and in this respect differ considerably from those of his contemporary, Gawin Douglas.

The romantic allegory entitled *The Golden Targe* is full of sensuous delight in the beauty of a May morning, which the poet paints with extraordinary richness of colour:

> For mirth of May, wyth skippis and wyth hoppis,
> The birdis sang upon the tender croppis,
> With curiouse notis, as Venus chapell clerkis:
> The rosis yong, new spreding of thair knoppis,
> War powderit brycht with hevinly beriall droppis.
> Throu bemes rede, birnyng as ruby sparkis;
> The skyis rang for schoutyng of the larkis,
> The purpur hevyn, our-scalit in silvir sloppis.
> Ourgilt the treis, branchis, leivis and barkis.
>
> Doun throu the ryce a ryvir ran with stremys.
> So lustily agayn thai lykand lemys,
> That all the lake as lamp did leme of lycht,
> Quhilk schadowit all about wyth twynkling glemis :
> That bewis bathit war in fecund bemys,
> Throu the reflex of Phebus visage brycht :
> On every syde the hegeis raise on hycht,
> The bank was grene, the bruke was full of bremys.
> The stanneris clere as sternis in frosty nycht.

There is, perhaps, little in this well-filled landscape which has not been met with before. The May season, the birds, the flowers, and the river with its fish, are all constituent parts of the landscapes of Chaucer and King James. But in richness of colour and in luminosity Dunbar here surpasses both of his predecessors. The picture is ablaze with sunshine — a sunshine which illumines the sky, the branches, leaves and bark of the trees, as well as the river with the shingle lying in its cool, clear depths. Dunbar also strives to outdo Chaucer, but this time with less success, in his appreciation of bird-life. Yet the line quoted above, —

> The skyis rang for schouting of the larkis —

is magnificent.

His famous allegoric poem, *The Thistle and the Rose,* celebrating the marriage of James IV. and Margaret Tudor, is in many ways reminiscent of Chaucer's *Parliament of Fowls.* There is in both the same personification of Dame Nature, though

Dunbar extends his personification to the dawn (Aurora), and to May, both of whom are represented as coming to the poet's bedside to rouse him from sleep. As with Chaucer, too, the landscape does not extend beyond the garden:

> I went
> In to this garth most dulce and redolent
> Off herb and flour, and tendir plantis sueit,
> And grene levis doing of dew doun fleit.

But most of the landscape-painting in this poem is of the conventional, courtly school, showing little of that direct contact with Nature which his shorter and more independent poems reveal.

In his sacred lyric, *Rorate cœli desuper*, Dunbar passes from the purely objective treatment of Nature to something deeper. This is a song in celebration of Christ's nativity, which is not unworthy of being placed side by side with the *Nativity Ode* of Milton. Dunbar, like Milton, assimilates the spirit of the Hebrew psalmists, and calls upon Nature to rejoice in the wondrous birth of the Christ-child:

> Celestiall fowlis in the air,
> Sing with your nottis upoun hicht;
> In firthis and in forrestis fair,
> Be myrthfull now, at all your mycht:
> For passit is your dully nycht,
> Aurora hes the cluddis perst,
> The sone is rissin with glaidsum lycht,
> Et nobis Puer natus est.

Then, turning from the birds to the flowers, he calls also upon them, and invites them to come into bloom, —

> In honour of the blissit frute
> That raiss up fro the rose Mary.

Dunbar's love for birds, and for all forms of animal life, leads him into the well-trodden paths of the Fable. In *The Tod and the Lamb* the fable forms but a very thin disguise for a spirited account of one of King James IV.'s amours. Of greater interest in this place is *The Merle and the Nightingale*, in which there is a debate similar to that of *The Owl and the Nightingale.* Here the theme under discussion is love for woman as opposed to love for God, but whereas in *The Owl and the Nightingale* the latter bird was represented as having set its affections on the things of earth, here all its longings are heavenwards, and opposed to the earthly desires of the merle or blackbird. The poem opens with the dawn of a bright May morning: a merle, seated upon "a blisful brenche of lawryr grene", is descanting of love in merry notes:

> This wes hir sentens sueit and delectable:
> "A lusty lyfe in luvis service bene".

Hard by is a nightingale, whose thoughts on this bright May morning are otherwise directed:

> Under this brench ran doun a revir bricht,
> Of balmy liquour, cristallyne of hew,
> Agane the hevinly aisur skyis licht,
> Quhair did, upon the tothair syd, persew
> A nychtingall, with suggarit notis new,
> Quhois angell fedderis as the pacock schone:
> This wes hir song, and of a sentens trew:
> "All luve is lost bot upone God allone".

The comparison of the sombre plumage of the nightingale to the gorgeous hues of the peacock is the one element of discord in an otherwise charming picture, and calls to mind the fact that, in Scotland at any rate, the nightingale is a bird more often read about than seen. The irrepressible joyance of the merle makes itself felt in the following stanza:

> With notis glaid and glorious armony,
> This joyfull merle so saluit scho the day,
> Quhill rong the woddis of hir melody,
> Saying, "Awalk, ye luvaris, of this May.
> Lo! fresche Flora has flurest every spray,
> As natur hes hir taucht, the noble quene,
> The feild bene clothit in a new array;
> A lusty lyfe in luvis service bene".

The debate between the two birds now grows warm: arguments of all kinds are introduced, till at last a definite understanding is reached. The nightingale brings the merle round to his opinion that there is something far better than "a lusty lyfe in luvis service bene", inasmuch as "all luve is lost bot upone God allone".

A curious feature in Dunbar's descriptions of landscape is that they are not confined to his serious and courtly poems, but find also an occasional place in his comic and satirical verse. In his alliterative poem, *Two Married Women and the Widow,* he introduces a highly realistic picture of bourgeois life, set forth with much merriment and satire. But the opening and close of this poem are formed by two beautiful and idealised landscape scenes, rarely surpassed by Dunbar in his most exalted moments. He describes how after midnight he wanders forth alone, —

> Besyde ane gudlie grene garth, full of gay flouris,
> Hegeit, of ane huge hicht, with hawthorne treis ;
> Quhairon ane bird, on ane bransche, so birst out hir notis,
> That never ane blythfullar bird was on the beuche harde.

Under cover of a ditch the poet listens to the unrestrained chatter of the two married women and the widow, and when they have gone he still lingers there, watching for the dawn, and closes his poem with another exquisite landscape : —

> Thus draif thai our that deir nicht with danceis full noble,
> Quhill that the day did up daw, and dew donkit the flouris ;
> The morow mild wes and meik, the mavis did sing,
> And all remuffit the myst, that the meid smellit;
> Silver schouris doun schuke, as the schene cristall,
> And berdis schoutit in shaw, with thair schill notis:
> The goldin gliterand gleme so gladdit thair hertis,
> Thai maid a glorious gle amang the grene bewis.
> The soft souch of the swyr, and soune of the stremys,
> The sweit savour of the sward, and singing of foulis,
> Myght confort ony creatur of the kin of Adam,
> And kindill agane his curage, thocht it were cald sloknyt.

The alliterative rhythm and the archaic and dialectical diction must not obscure for us the rare beauty of this dawn-landscape. The poet, it is true, attempts to bring too much on to his canvas, but his insight into Nature and his sense of the power of natural beauty to quicken the spirit of man are wonderfully keen. Dunbar's perception of the beauty in Nature was, within its limits, singularly intense. We have already illustrated his delight in colour and in effects of light and shade. In his references, in the above passage, to the soughing of the wind in the col (*'swyr'*) of the hill, and to the sweet savour of the greensward, he shows that not only his eye, but also his other senses were singularly acute to appreciate whatever in Nature was sensuously beautiful. In this respect he is the nearest to Keats of all the pre-Spenserian poets.

Though he does not approach Dunbar in originality or in versatility of poetic power, Gawin Douglas[1] (1474?—1522?) is by no means his inferior as an interpreter of Nature. His range of vision is wider, and he has the faculty of detecting beauty in many humble and minute forms of the natural world which escaped the notice of Dunbar. Douglas's most elaborate descriptions of scenery are to be found in the Prologues to his translation of Vergil's *Æneid*. The fashion of introducing pictures of the seasons and months into a poem has already been referred to more than once. The May landscapes which prelude some new departure in the narrative of the verse-romances had passed into the more elaborate pictures of April, June and September found in the *Wallace* of Henry the Minstrel, or the descriptions of the four seasons of the year which find a place in Henryson's *Preaching of the Swallow*. The practice had thus become peculiarly Scottish in the course of the fifteenth century, and as such made a special appeal to a poet like Gawin Douglas, whose poetry, alike in its sentiment and its diction, is strikingly, almost perversely, national. Douglas contributes a Prologue to each of the books of the *Æneid*, and in the case of the seventh, twelfth and thirteenth books, this Prologue is wholly occupied with landscape painting of the most detailed character. The introduction of landscape is much less noticeable in his allegorical romance, *King Hart,* but in his early work, *The Palace of Honour*, it comes again into prominence.

Douglas, like so many of his English and Scottish predecessors, is fond of the serenely beautiful moods and aspects of Nature; he finds delight in the splendour of a May morning or a June evening, of which he never seems to tire. At the same time he is a very keen observer of winter scenery. He finds in it, it is true, little that is really beautiful, and much that awakens a sense of dread. Yet he loves to paint such scenery, and to mass together a wealth of details which

---

[1] *Works,* ed. Small. 1874.

quicken the reader's imagination. Professor Veitch,[1]) writing
of Douglas's famous winter landscape in the Prologue to the
seventh Book of the *Æneid,* defines the poet's feeling
for winter as one of "shivering repugnance". It may, however,
be doubted whether this is really true. The description in
question extends over one hundred verses, every verse bearing
witness to the poet's close intimacy with all the aspects
of a winter landscape. Such intimacy the poet could have
acquired only by dint of careful observation. Were his mental
attitude really one of "shivering repugnance", he would
scarcely have elaborated his picture to such an extent, for
repugnance would be much more likely to lead him to turn
away from such a scene than to describe it with an almost
exhaustless wealth of detail. To the modern reader, indeed,
his winter landscape, by virtue of its striking originality,
is more interesting than the more conventional descriptions
of spring and summer. He sings of "the raging storm our-
walterand wally seis", of rivers in spate, and of mountain
peaks covered with snow; of the landslip, "rumland rudely with
sic beir", of ragged whinstone rocks, and of cold, stony cleughs,
shining with frozen faces. Over the fields sweep "sour bitter
blasts", while "drumlie" shadows darken the heavens: —

> Dym skyis oft furth warpit feirfull levyne,
> Flaggis of fyir, and mony felloun flawe,
> Scharp soppis of sleit, and of the snypand snawe.
> The dowy dichis war all donk and wait,
> The law vaille flodderit all wyth spait,
> The plane stretis and every hie way
> Full of fluschis, doubbis, myre and clay.
> Laggerit leys wallowit farnys schewe,
> Broune muris kithit thair wysnit mossy hewe,
> Bank, bra, and boddoum blanschit wolx and bair;
> For gurll weddir growyt bestis haire.
> The wynd made wayfe the reid weyd on the dyk,
> Bedovin in donkis deyp was every syk.
> Our craggis and the front of rochis seyre
> Hang gret isch schoklis lang as ony spere.
> The grund stude barrand, widderit, dosk and gray,
> Herbis, flouris, and gersis wallowit away;
> Woddis, forestis, with nakit bewis blout,
> Stud strypyt of thair weyd in every hout.

---

[1]) *The Feeling for Nature in Scottish Poetry,* Vol. I, p. 274.

In all this there is undeniable power, together with a keen insight into Nature in her wildest moods. Nor does the above passage exhaust Douglas's store of observation. He next describes the birds chirming and cheeping as they fly in search of some hiding-place, the rush of the linns, and the whistling of the wind. Then the scene changes to night, and the poet, now within the house, listens to the hooting of the owl, and the sound of the flying geese:

> Hornit Hewbade, quhilk clepe we the nycht owle,
> Within hir caverne hard I schowt and yowle;
> Laithlie of forme, wyth crukit camschow beik,
> Ugsum to heir was hir wyld elriche screik.
> The wyld geis claking eik by nychtis tyde
> Attoure the citie fleand hard I glyde.

When dawn comes, the owl and the geese give place to other birds — the cock, "Phebus crowned byrd", the jackdaw cackling on the roof above, the cranes, "the birds of Palamede" and the kite uttering its plaintive cry — until at last the long description is brought to a close. Douglas's landscape poetry, and this picture of winter more especially, has been subjected to a fierce attack by James Russell Lowell, who, like Taine, saw little that was valuable in English poetry between Chaucer and Spenser. This winter landscape, writes Lowell in his essay on Spenser[1] "is a mere bill of parcels, a *post-mortem* inventory of nature, where imagination is not merely not called for, but would be out of place. Why, a recipe in the cookery-book is as much like a good dinner as this kind of stuff is like good word-painting. The poet with a real eye in his head does not give us everything, but only the *best* of everything. He selects, he combines, or else gives what is characteristic only; while the false style of which I have been speaking seems to be as glad to get a pack of impertinences on its shoulders as Christian in the *Pilgrim's Progress* was to be rid of his". This criticism is correct in as far as it points out the lack of unity and of perspective in Douglas's landscape, nor is the censure passed upon its inventory character unmerited. But in refusing

---

[1] *Essays on the English Poets.*

to recognise the poetic value of such a passage, Lowell himself loses that sense of perspective — historic perspective
in this instance — the absence of which he deplores in
Douglas. The merit of this winter-landscape lies mainly in
the fact that its author, tired of the conventional landscape-
painting of the courtly poets, tired of May-morning scenes
in some curiously disposed garden, turns to the open country
and to scenes of a wholly different character. He escapes
from the conventional to the real, and paints, instead of some
garden of Provence, the wind-swept hills and dales of Scotland; while instead of declaring that all the poetry of Nature is
summed up in the serene beauty of a May morning, he proceeds
to reveal, if not beauty then grandeur and sublimity, in a
Scottish winter. In thus extending the horizon of poetry,
Douglas plays the part of an intrepid adventurer. It is true
that the Gawayne-poet had moved in the same direction, but
his example had not been followed. Scottish poets before
Douglas occasionally go outside of the season of May, and
Henryson, as we have seen, gives us a short winterlands-
cape in *The Preaching of the Swallow;* but most of the
landscapes of the fifteenth century Scottish poets are confined
to the month of May. Dunbar in his *Meditation in Winter*
reflects indeed the general feeling of the time for winter
scenery. Winter is the time of "dirk and drublie dayis", when
the poet's spirits are saddened, and his heart lost in languor
"for laik of symmer with his flouris". Scottish poetry soon
after Douglas's death fell into a state of decay, but with its
revival in the eighteenth century, his appreciation of winter
scenery became a potent source of inspiration. Thomson began
his *Seasons* with *Winter*, while in the lyric poetry of the
century this feeling for winter deepens until it culminates in
the memorable verses of Burns :

> The sweeping blast, the sky o'ercast,
> The joyless winter day,
> Let others fear, to me more dear
> Than all the pride of May.

The weakness of Douglas's landscapes, both in his Prologues to the *Æneid* and in the *Palace of Honour,* lies in

the fact that his artistic sense lags far behind his power to recognise the beautiful or the grandiose in Nature. The inventory landscape, against which even so great an artist as Chaucer was not altogether proof, is developed to an inordinate degree by Douglas. Yet his dryest catalogues have the rare merit of fidelity to the scenes which lay immediately before him in his Scottish home, and bear further witness to his powers of observation. Thus in his description of the flowers of May in the Prologue to the twelfth book of the *Æneid* he is not content to enumerate only the conventional flowers — the rose, lily and daisy — but includes in his list the wild banewort, clover, trefoil and camomile, "the columby blank and blew", and the ivy, whose rank leaves overspread the castle tower: —

> Seyr downis smaill on dent de lion sprang,
> The ying grene blomyt straberry levis amang;
> Gymp gerraflouris thar royn levys unschet,
> Fresch primros and the purpour violet.

There is a delightful homeliness in the association of such flowers as these, and the same is true of the bird-list which follows. With the exception of the poetically ubiquitous nightingale, the birds are all true to a Scottish spring. Among them are the lark, "loud releschand in the skyis", the merle or blackbird, and the mavis or thrush. Then with singular truth to Nature he adds:

> The cowschet crowdis, and pirkis on the rys,
> The sterlyng changis divers stevynnys nys,
> The sparrow chyrmis in the wallis clift,
> Goldspynk and lyntquhyte fordynnand the lift.
> The gukgo galis, and so quyteris the quaill,
> Quhill ryveris rerdyt, schawis and every vaill,
> And tender twystis trymlyt on the treis,
> For byrdis sang, and bemyng of the beis.

Within his self-appointed limits, Douglas overlooks nothing of interest or beauty. In reading his descriptive passages, we are reminded of a man who, though deeply read, had not allowed book-lore to dim his powers of vision into the world of Nature as it lay around him. The sky with its planets and fixed stars, the earth with its woods and beryl streams,

its birds, its insect-life and floral beauty, were all familiar
to him. Though he tells us very little of the sea, or of mountain scenery, he does not ignore them altogether. His
landscapes, however, are chiefly those of the Scottish Lowlands, in painting which he combines extraordinary wealth
of detail with the closest fidelity. Had his artistic touch and
power of co-ordination been equal to these, he would rank
among the greatest poets who have sought to portray the
face of Nature. As it is, his place is an exalted one.

Of the great Scottish poets of the fifteenth and sixteenth
centuries, whose works claim all the more attention because
of the comparative dearth of high poetry in England during
the same period, the last is Sir David Lyndsay [1]) (1490—1555).
Living as he did at a time of great religious controversy, his poems
bear a close relation to the various phases of religious feeling
of that time, and many of them are accordingly poems "with a
purpose". This means, of course, a partial exclusion of that
romantic element which prevails in *The King's Quair* and
The Golden Targe; for Lyndsay, even when he introduces
into his poetry the romantic framework of his age, is primarily
a moralist and a satirist. Yet so strong, even in the middle
of the sixteenth century, was the Chaucerian tradition as to
the course which a poem should follow, that Lyndsay found
himself bound to abide by it in many points, and to this we
owe those passages of natural description, conceived wholly
in the Chaucerian manner, which occur in many of his works.
Such description, it is true, is absent from his chief work,
A Satire on the Three Estates, but that poem is simply a
morality play "writ large". In A *Dialogue betwixt Experience
and a Courtier,* on the other hand, there occurs a Prologue
introducing a May morning scene, in which the poet is
represented as leaving his bed at dawn and wandering forth
into a park where he can hear the birds sing and smell "the
aromatik odouris" of the flowers. All this is modelled upon
Chaucer, as is also the introduction of the astronomical lore
current at the time. The sun is "Phebus, that king etheriall",

---

[1]) *Works,* ed. Laing 1879.

whose rising, "in habyte gaye and glorious", means that Cynthea, "the hornit nychtis quene", together with the stars and planets, must speedily grow pale. Next he describes how at sunrise the birds break out into song and greet Nature with their glad melody. The picture is a beautiful one, though scarcely original, and Lyndsay mars to some extent the truthfulness of his description by falling into the error of some of his Scottish predecessors, and introducing the peacock side by side with such native birds as the lark, goldfinch and blackbird :

> All warldlie cure anone did fro me wend,
> Quhen fresche Flora spred furth hir tapestrie,
> Wrocht be dame Nature, quent and curiouslie
>
> Depaynt with mony hundreth hevinlie hewis ;
> Glaid of the rysing of thare royall Roye,
> With blomes breckand on the tender bewis.
> Quhilk did provoke myne hart tyl natural joye.
> Neptune, that day, and and Eoll held thame coye,
> That men on far mycht heir the birdis sounde,
> Quhose noyis did to the sterrye hevin redounde.
>
> The plesande powne prunyeand his feddrem fair ;
> The myrthfull maves maid gret melodie ;
> The lustye lark ascending in the air,
> Numerand hir naturall notis craftelye :
> The gay goldspink, the merle rycht myrralye :
> The noyis of the nobyll nychtingalis
> Redundit throuch the montans, meids and valis.
>
> Prologue, *vv.* 178—194.

Thus much of natural description is introduced in deference to Chaucer and the courtly poets generally : but Lyndsay's heart is not in all this, and growing impatient, he turns from such description to the main purpose of the poem :

> I lose my tyme, allace ! for to rehers
> Sic unfruitful and vaine discriptioun,
> Or wrytt in to my raggit rurall vers
> Mater without edificatioun ;
> Consydering quhow that myne intentioun
> Bene tyll deplore the mortall misereis,
> With continuall cairfull calamiteis,
>
> Consisting in this wracheit vaill of sorrow.
>
> Prologue, *vv.* 202—209.

He then enters upon his main theme, which consists of
a conversation, extending over four Books, between an aged
man called Experience and himself as Courtier. When the
conversation is at length over, Lyndsay reverts once again
to natural description, and in the closing section of the work,
which may be regarded as an Epilogue, he paints a sunset
picture in terms which correspond exactly to those of the
description of sunrise with which he introduced his main
theme. The day has been given up to conversation, and now
"Dame Synthea" rises "with vissage paill" in the eastern sky,
announcing the approach of night. As in the picture of
sunrise Lyndsay introduces the song of the morning birds
and the opening of the flowers, so here he describes the
birds of evening and the closing up of the flower-petals:

> The dew now dounkis the rosis redolent:
> The mareguildis, that all day were rejosit
> Of Phebus heit, now craftelly ar closit.

> The blysfull byrdis bownis to the treis,
> And ceissis of thare hevinlye armoneis:
> The cornecraik in the croft, I heir hir cry,
> The bak, the howlat, febyll of thare eis,
> For thare pastyme, now in the evenyng fleis:
> The nychtyngaill, with myrthfull melody,
> Hir naturall notis persith throw the sky,
> Tyll Synthea, makand hir observance,
> Quhilk on the nycht dois tak hir dalyance.
>
> *A Dialogue,* Book IV., *vv.* 6309—6320.

The minor Scottish poets contemporary with, or subsequent
to, Sir David Lyndsay, who carried forward the poetic traditions of Henryson, Dunbar and Douglas, and helped to
defer that period of atrophy which fell upon Scottish poetry
at the close of the sixteenth century, have received full and
appreciative treatment at the hands of the late Professor
Veitch in the first volume of his work, *The Feeling for
Nature in Scottish Poetry*. The ample quotations from their
poems, illustrating their interpretation of Nature, which Professor Veitch gives, justify a more cursory treatment of them
in this place. Montgomerie, Scott and Hume were all true
lovers of a Scottish landscape, which they painted with

considerable feeling. Alexander Montgomerie[1] (1556? — 1610?)
in the opening stanzas of his debate-poem, *The Cherry and the
Sloe,* furnishes an extremely spirited picture of that landscape
as it appears in the month of May. It is true that in this description the poet cannot forget his classical scholarship, and sacrifices simplicity through his desire to introduce the classic
fables of Progne, Tereus, Narcissus, Amphion and Apollo; but
he has at his command a good deal besides book-learning, and
certainly shows a true appreciation of the actual sights and
sounds of Nature. He devotes one stanza to the song of the
birds, another to the forms and movements of the beasts,
and then proceeds to range through the whole field of vision
which the landscape presents. In this he takes us beyond the
idyllic associations of the garden, park and meadow, and
describes with considerable power the mountain-stream descen-
ding in cascades along its rocky bed:

> But as I mused, mine alone,
>   I saw ane river rin
> Out oure ane craggy rock of stane,
>   Syne lighted in ane lin;
> With tumbling and rumbling
>   Among the rockis round,
> Dewalling and falling
>   Into that pit profound.
>
> To hear thae startling streamis clear,
> Methought it music to the ear,
>   Where discant did abound.
> With treble sweet and tenor just,
> And aye the echo repercust
>   Her diapason sound.

The gaiety of spirit which characterises these opening
stanzas of *The Cherry and the Sloe,* is again found in his
song "Hey, now the day dawis". Here, too, all is movement
and life, for birds and beasts vie with each other in the
attempt to lend animation to the landscape:

> Hey, now the day dawis,
> The jolie cock crawis,
> Now shrouds the shawis
>   Throu Nature anone.

---

[1] *Works* ed. Cranstoun (Scottish Text Society) 1886.

> The thristell-cock cryis
> On lovers wha lyis,
> Now skaillis the skyis;
> The night is neir gone.

Alexander Scott, in his purely descriptive poem, *O Lustie May,* is much less original. He is content to follow the traditions of the mediæval courtly poets, and confines himself entirely to generalities. This is not the case with Hume, the author of another descriptive poem, *The Day Estivall,* written in stanzas of four verses, towards the close of the sixteenth century. In extent of range Hume is superior to Montgomerie, and is scarcely his inferior in respect of animation. His poem, like Milton's *L'Allegro* and *Il Penseroso,* is panoramic in character; the poet, starting with daybreak, follows the whole course of the summer day. The dawn-song of the birds — the lark, lapwing and snipe — is succeeded by a picture of the husbandman and shepherd going forth to the fields, and then the poet glances over the landscape, and notes each feature in it: —

> The misty reek, the clouds of rain,
>   From tops of mountains skaills;
> Clear are the highest hills and plain,
>   The vapours takes the vales.
>
> Calm is the deep and purpour sea,
>   Yea, smoother than the sand;
> The wallis that weltering wont to be,
>   Are stable like the land.
>
> The rivers fresh, the caller streams
>   Oure rocks can softly rin;
> The water clear like crystal seems,
>   And makes a pleasant din.
>
> The clogged, busy humming-bees,
>   That never thinks to drown,
> On flowers and flourishes of trees
>   Collects their liquor brown.

Noontide comes, and man and beast seek shelter from the heat; but in the afternoon their labours are renewed, till at length, —

> The gloaming comes, the day is spent,
>   The sun goes out of sight,
> And painted is the occident
>   With purpour sanguine bright.

With a description of the home-coming of the cattle and the labourers the poem draws to a close :

> All labourers draws hame at even,
>   And can till other say,
> Thanks to the gracious God of Heaven,
>   Whilk sent this summer day.

From the stanzas which have been quoted, some idea may be gained of the simple dignity and beauty of this poem. No false note, no pedantic turn, mars its homely charm, while for extent of range, genuine appreciation of the country, and richness of colouring, it will rank with the finest descriptive poems in our literature. In reading it, it is difficult not to believe that it belongs to the great romantic revival of the latter half of the eighteenth century. Yet this poem, like those of Montgomerie, follows the lines laid down by the earlier Scottish poets of the fifteenth century. No attempt is made to describe Nature except in a purely objective manner; the lyric feeling of the Renascence, bringing with it a sympathetic interpretation of Nature is wholly absent. The poet feels pleasure in contemplating the beauty of the summer day, but he does not attempt to bring the landscape into association with his own personal feelings. Nowhere is there any recognition on his part of a mystic bond of sympathy between Nature and man. The Scottish poets of the fifteenth and sixteenth centuries come under the influence of the Revival of Learning, but the full spirit of the Renascence, which is as much Italian as classical in its origin, and which called forth the profuse strains of the Elizabethan poets reached Scotland and Scottish poetry only with Drummond of Hawthornden.

Chapter XI.

THE EARLY ELIZABETHANS.

The publication of Tottel's *Miscellany* in the year 1557 is so prominent a landmark in English literary history and in the poetic interpretation of Nature, that it may prove of service to review very briefly the steps which have been taken in the foregoing chapters. Old English poetry reveals an interpretation of Nature which, in its sharp contrast to the mediæval interpretation which first became general after the Norman Conquest, may, without unduly straining the import of the word, be called heroic. The descriptions of Nature in *Beowulf,* in the *Riddles,* and in most of the other pre-conquest poems, is the direct heritage of the old Teutonic world, in which Latin ideas and Latin predilections had as yet scarcely made themselves felt. What the Old English poets felt for Nature was not love but awe — an awe which evoked wonder and admiration, and which had in it no element of benumbing fear. The peculiar fascination exercised on the minds of Old English poets by the contemplation of the stupendous forces of Nature is revealed in all their works, and the landscapes which they paint with surest hand are those of winter storm at sea or by some wind-swept coast. For the most part, their painting is objective, but not infrequently we catch glimpses of that vanishing mythopœic conception of Nature which saw in the hurricane or in the lashing of the waves the play of superhuman personal agents at war with man. After the Conquest all this was changed. The inrush of foreign ideas, and the domination exercised upon English poetry by the works of the French *trouvères,* caused the Old English interpretation of Nature to be superseded by something entirely different. Instead of demanding as scenic background for their tales of human prowess a landscape which is wintry, maritime and northern, English poets now have neither eye nor ear for anything in Nature which lies outside of garden or park. The sublime yields place to the idyllic, the north is conquered by the south. A reaction to all this takes place with the revival of alliterative verse in the middle of the fourteenth century, and in the works of the Gawayne-poet, in the *Troy-Book*, and to a less extent in the *Morte Arthur*, much of the Old English delight in the sublimer aspects of Nature is re-captured. The influence of Chaucer was exerted wholly on the side of the foreign interpretation of Nature, and this influence makes itself felt on all the English poets of the fifteenth century; but in the works of some of the Scottish poets the native tradition endures side by side with the foreign. If in the Prologue to the Twelfth Book of the Æneid Gawin Douglas gives us a picture of a May morning which would have satisfied the most exacting Chaucerian, his winter landscape prefixed to the Seventh Book would have evoked applause had it been recited by some primitive Teutonic *scop* in the mead-hall of Hrothgar.

But the mediæval interpretation of Nature, whether it follows native or foreign traditions, or assimilates both, remains objective. Even in the lyric poetry, the sentimental regard for Nature, which is so prevalent in Renascence poetry, is rarely found. The only escape in Middle English poetry from the objective description of a landscape was in the direction of allegory and symbolism. The allegoric interpretation of Nature, practised first of all in the interests of religion by the authors of bestiaries and works of a similar nature, became in course of time the possession of secular and chivalrous poets whose prowess was claimed for the high ritual of the Courts of Love. In Chaucer's *Prologue to the Legend of Good Women*, in the *Pearl*, and in Dunbar's *Thistle and Rose* the symbolic interpretation of Nature is paramount. Akin to, and often blending with, this symbolism of Nature in the service of chivalrous allegory and love, was its application for the purpose of the beast-epic and fable. In France that purpose was mainly satiric, but in England, while much of the playful humour of satire is preserved, the fable often becomes, as is the case with Henryson and others, an instrument in the hands of the moralist.

The English Renascence, of which Tottel's *Miscellany* was the unmistakable herald, can scarcely be said, as far as its interpretation of Nature is concerned, to have broken with the past. The mediæval delight in a May morning in garden or grove, and the application of external Nature for the purpose of fable and allegory, are almost as common to Elizabethan poetry as to that of the fourteenth or fifteenth centuries; while there is, indeed, a continuity between Chaucer and Spenser, and even between Chaucer and Shakespeare, which has not yet been fully grasped. Acknowledging this, it is at the same time necessary to recognise the fresh departures made by the Elizabethan poets in regard to Nature. A new influence, that of Petrarch and the Petrarchian school of poetry, makes itself felt. Poetry now becomes steeped in lyricism, the direct aim of which is self-revelation. From being impersonal and naïve, poetry now becomes subjective and intense. The causes which determined this change have often been made the theme of literary criticism and need not be directly referred to here. It is enough for our purposes to ascertain in what ways, and how far, the new forces which were at work in poetry coloured the interpretation of Nature.

With the growth of lyricism in poetry, Nature is no longer regarded as forming simply a background to the play of human forces, as was the case in the mediæval romance, but is drawn into close relationship with humanity. Poets now project their own personal feelings into Nature, and discover there, sometimes a sympathetic response to their own emotions, at other times a harsh repulse. When they are glad and prosper in their love, they find that the contemplation of Nature's beauty increases their gladness, while at other times the beauty of a spring morning brings only cruel mockery to the rejected lover. Or again, they go to Nature to discover there something which in its beauty and winsomeness can be compared with the beauty and winsomeness of their Stella, their Delia, or their Phyllis. The simile, which is infrequent in Middle English poetry, now becomes extremely common, and all Nature is ransacked by courtly Euphuists bent on discovering in it analogies to something human and personal. The following song by "Shepherd Tony" (? Anthony Munday), which finds a place in that matchless anthology, *England's Helicon,*[1]) may serve to illustrate this attitude of Elizabethan poets towards the natural world:

> I serve Aminta, whiter than the snow,
> Straighter than cedar, brighter than the glass;
> More fine in trip than foot of running roe,
> More pleasant than the field of flow'ring grass;
> > More gladsome to my withering joys that fade
> > Than Winter's sun or Summer's cooling shade.
>
> Sweeter than swelling grape of ripest wine,
> Softer than feathers of the fairest swan;
> Smoother than jet, more stately than the pine,
> Fresher than poplar, smaller than my span;
> > Clearer than Phœbus' fiery-pointed beam,
> > Or icy crust of crystal's frozen stream.
>
> Yet is she curster than the bear by kind,
> And harder hearted than the aged oak;
> More glib than oil, more fickle than the wind,
> More stiff than steel, no sooner bent but broke:
> > Lo! thus my service is a lasting sore,
> > Yet will I serve, although I die therefor.

The simple charm of these allusions to Nature will probably be felt by every reader, but only too often in Elizabethan poetry this quest after Nature-similes betrays the exercise of a laboured ingenuity which muffles poetic feeling. In its fondness for simile, its sentimental attitude towards Nature, and its indulgence in "the pathetic fallacy", Elizabethan poetry owns allegiance to Italian and French models, all of which derive ultimately from Petrarch. From Italy, too, came the pastoral sentiment which impelled men, in fiction if not in fact, to eschew courts and cities, and

---

[1]) Ed. Bullen, p. 135.

11

recapture the golden age in the society of shepherds and
shepherdesses. Here again affectation is rife, but the pastoral
fiction, in that it brings country life into prominence, is a
potent instrument in widening the horizon of Nature-poetry,
while in plays such as *As You Like It*, or poems like
Drayton's *Muses' Elysium*, the fresh breath of the English
greenwood purges the pastoral atmosphere of its Arcadian
vapours and gives to the poetry refreshment and tone.

But non-literary as well as literary influences go to the
making of Elizabethan poetry, and make their presence felt
in the poetic interpretration of Nature. The Elizabethan age
was an age of maritime discovery, and the strange tales which
mariners brought back of wonderful lands across the seas,
and which have been preserved for us in the pages of
Hakluyt, must be taken into account in our present study.
The direct bearing of maritime discovery upon the interpretation of Nature by Elizabethan poets is slight, and the
new world which had swum into their ken is an unconsidered
trifle in comparison with the riches brought from Italy and
Greece. Elizabethan England possesses no Camoens, and even
for such slight poetic descriptions of American scenery as
those found in Waller's *Battle of the Summer Islands* or
Marvell's *Bermudas* we have to wait until the middle of the
seventeenth century. But in the pages of Spenser's *Faerie
Queene*, and more clearly in some of the plays of Shakespeare,
we see in poetry a reflection of that wonder-land which the
enterprise of Spanish, Portuguese and English sailors had
revealed. Una's wanderings among the "salvage nation" that
strew the ground with branches before her, and

> "worship her as Queene with olive girlond cround",

are something more than a transference to English soil of the
Roman Satyr fable, while for Shakespeare, whose mind was
as a sensitised film to all impressions from without, the
western continent was full of the elements of wonder and
mystery. The stories of

> "the Cannibals that each other eat,
> The Antropophagi, and men whose heads
> Do grow beneath their shoulders —"

are the love-charms with which Othello steals away the heart
of Desdemona, and these tales, as Dr. Anders has recently
pointed out,[1]) are probably based on Shakespeare's reading of
Raleigh's *Discovery of Guiana*. *The Tempest*, again, is conceived in that spirit of wonder which the discovery of a new
world bred, and the romantic potentiality of which Shakespeare
keenly felt.

Of greater importance than the discovery of America as
a determining factor in the growth of interest in Nature was
the awakening of that national consciousness which followed
so swiftly upon the defeat of the Spanish Armada. The
historical play and the historical poem are the first-fruits of
this new sense of national consciousness, but the same spirit
which impelled English poets to emblazon in patriotic verse
the past history of their country led them also to study its
natural features and to rejoice in the beauty and grandeur
of its scenery. It is the fashion with many critics to speak
of Drayton's *Polyolbion* as a fatuous emprise — a creation
of the gazetteer rather than the poet — but in Drayton's
stupendous untertaking we see the work of a man deeply
imbued with patriotic feeling, and whose object was to pay
a poet's homage to his fatherland.

These then are some of the new influences at work upon
the interpretation of Nature in English poetry. As stated before, they do not replace the old influences of mediæval poetry,
but, wherever possible, blend with them. Nowhere is there
reaction, but everywhere advance.

Sir Thomas Wyatt (1503?—1542), who, with Lord Surrey,
was the chief contributor to Tottel's *Miscellany*, assimilated
with remarkable ease the half-sentimental and half-sympathetic
interpretation of Nature which he found in Petrarch and in
Petrarch's Italian and French imitators. In his sonnets and
other lyrics Nature is not described for its own sake, nor
symbolised after the manner of the courtly and didactic
allegorists of mediæval times; Wyatt's aim throughout is to
bring the external world into direct relationship with his own

---

[1]) *Shakespeare's Books*, p. 229.

individual feelings, and to discover in Nature points of analogy with his own spiritual life. Many of Wyatt's sonnets are written in direct imitation of those of Petrarch or of the French sonneteer, Melin de St Gelais; but even where imitation goes as far as actual translation from the original, it is not difficult for the reader to recognise and appreciate Wyatt's forceful individuality. The delight in the Nature-simile, which we have already indicated as one of the striking features of Renascence poetry, is frequently met with in Wyatt. Thus in the following lyric he compares love to a stream falling from the Alps:

> From these hie hilles as when a spring doth fall,
> It trilleth downe with still and suttle course;
> Of this and that, it gathers aye and shall,
> Till it have just down flowed to streame and force:
> Then at the fote it rageth over all.
> So fareth love, when he hath tane a course.
> Rage is his raine, resistance vayleth none,
> The first eschue is remedy alone.
>
> *Tottel's Miscellany*, ed. Arber, p. 46.

The mountain torrent, which had kindled the imagination of the Gawayne-poet, was entirely ignored by Chaucer and the courtly school of poets. Its re-introduction here is interesting as marking the widening of the poetic horizon as well as the new manner of regarding Nature. In the following sonnet, translated from Melin de St Gelais, Wyatt again brings before his readers the aspects of mountainous country, and finds there an analogy to his own love:

> Lyke unto these unmesurable mountaines,
> So is my painefull life, the burden of yre.
> For hye be they, and hye is my desire;
> And I of teares, and they be full of fountaines.
> Under craggy rockes they have barren plaines;
> Hard thoughtes in me my wofull minde doth tyre;
> Small frute and many leaves their toppes do attire,
> With small effect great trust in me remaines.
> The boystrous windes oft their hye boughes do blast,
> Hote sighes in me continually be shed.
> Wilde beastes in them, fierce love in me is fed,
> Unmoveable am I, and they stedfast.
> Of singing birdes they have the time and note,
> And I alwaies plaintes passing through my throte.
>
> *Ibid.* p. 70.

In this sonnet the search for objects in Nature which shall offer comparisons with human life interests the reader by reason of its novelty: in the course of a few decades it was to develop into the over-subtlety and mannerism of fantastic Euphuism. On another occasion Wyatt, imitating both Petrarch and St Gelais, compares the lover's state to that of a galley, "charged with forgetfulness", which cleaves its way through storm-tossed, rocky seas; or again to a willow "which stoopeth with the wind", and afterwards regains its erect position. Nor is Wyatt content with the mere search for comparisons. In one of his poems he calls upon Nature to listen to his griefs and to echo his love-plaint: —

Resownde my voyce ye woodes that heare me plaine:
Both hilles and vales causyng reflexion,
And rivers eke, record ye of my paine,
Which have oft forced ye by compassion,
As judges, lo, to heare my exclamacion;
Amonge whom ruth (I finde) yet doth remaine.
Where I it seke, alas, there is disdaine.
Oft ye rivers, to hear my wofull sounde,
Have stopt your cours, and plainely to expresse,
Many a teare by moisture of the grounde
The earth hath wept to hear my heavinesse,
Which causelesse I endure without redresse.
The hugy okes have rored in the winde,
Ech thing me thought complayning in their kinde.

Ibid. p. 43.

Here again Wyatt strikes a new note in English poetry. Nature is addressed as a conscious being, and is called upon to sympathise with the poet's sorrows. There are poems both in Old and Middle English poetry which, drawing their inspiration from the Hebrew psalmists, conceive of Nature as a conscious being paying homage to the Creator, but this second step whereby Nature is invited to show sympathy with humanity is the immediate outcome of the Renascence; it entered English poetry with Wyatt, and found its loftiest utterance in the refrain of Spenser's *Epithalamion*:

So I unto my selfe alone will sing;
The woods shall to me answer, and my Eccho ring.

Lord Surrey (1517?—1547), like Sir Thomas Wyatt, is
prompted to commune with and interpret Nature by the
impulse of an unrequited love-passion. Yet while it is only
in his love-poems that he refers to the natural world, he is
far less anxious than Wyatt to bring natural objects into
connection with his own love-sentiments, or to grasp the hidden
sympathies which subsist between Nature and the life of
man. Lyric poet as he is, his treatment of Nature is often
objective, or if he brings it into comparison or contrast with
his own subjective feelings, he does this very lightly. The
fact is, as Ten Brink has pointed out,[1] that Surrey is quite
as much under the influence of the descriptive and objective
Chaucer, as under that of the lyric and subjective Petrarch.
Whereas Wyatt is purely Petrarchian, Surrey grafts the exotic
growth upon the native Chaucerian stock. Thus in the fine
sonnet on early summer, the pure description of Nature holds
the first place, and the personal feelings are reserved for the
final clause:

> The soote season that bud and blome furth bringes.
> With grene hath clad the hill, and eke the vale:
> The nightingale with fethers new she singes;
> The turtle to her mate hath tolde her tale.
> Somer is come, for every spray nowe springes:
> The hart hath hung hys olde hed on the pale:
> The buck in brake his winter cote he flinges:
> The fishes flote with newe repaired scale:
> The adder all her sloughe awaye she flinges;
> The swift swalow pursueth the flyes smale,
> The busy bee her honye now she minges;
> Winter is worne, that was the flowers' bale:
> And thus I see among these pleasant thynges
> Eche care decayes, and yet my sorow sprynges.

> *Tottel's Miscellany,* p. 4.

Surrey is so far a descriptive poet as to localise his
pictures of landscape: the scenery which he loves most of
all being that of the Windsor district. At Windsor some of
the happiest years of his boyhood and youth had been spent
in the company of the Duke of Richmond, and when in later
years he found himself a prisoner in Windsor Castle, his mind
reverted to the scenes of his youth. He remembers, —

---

[1] *History of English Literature,* Vol. III, p. 242.

The pleasant spot revested green with warme,
The blossomd bowes with lusty Ver yspred:
The flowred meades, the wedded birdes, so late
Mine eyes discover.

Tottel's Miscellany, p. 11.

He remembers, too, the wide vales where the night was often spent, and the secret groves which resounded with his love-plaints. In the two poems which tell of the Windsor scenery there is description, but description tinged with elegiac sentiment. In his poem, "The Complaint of a Lover that defied Love", the influence of Chaucer makes itself strongly felt. It begins with a description of the overthrow of winter by summer. Summer has

clothed fayre the earthe about wythe grene,
And every tree new garmented, that pleasure was to sene.

The poet is then impelled by the genial sunshine to walk abroad, and listen to the song of the birds :

So on a morow furth, unwist of any wight,
I went to prove how well it would my heavy burden light:
And when I felt the aire, so pleasant round about,
Lorde, to my self how glad I was that I had gotten out.
There myght I se how Ver had every blossom hent,
And eke the new betrothed birdes ycoupled how they went:
And in their songes, me thought, they thanked nature much,
That by her lycence all that yere to love their happe was such,
Right as they could devise to chose them feres throughout:
Wyth much rejoysing to their Lord, thus flew they all about.

Ibid. p. 7.

Then his thought turns inwards, and he contrasts his own love-weariness with the joys of the birds.

Thomas Sackville[1]) (1536—1608), the author of *The Induction to The Mirror of Magistrates* and of *The Complaint of Henry, Duke of Buckingham*, was endowed with a powerful imagination and great originality of thought. His imaginative power is seen in the creation of those luridly impressive allegoric forms which, in *The Induction*, the poet encounters in his journey through Hell, and also in the landscape painting introduced at the commencement of this poem. His landscape is

---

[1]) *The Works of Thomas Sackville*, edited by Lord Delawarr, 1859.

in this place a wintry one, which is elaborated with singular fidelity, and is in strictest congruity with the central theme. A winter background, Sackville felt, was alone fitted for the stage on which figures so gruesome and tragic as Misery, Revenge, War and Sorrow were to pass. His picture of winter is to a large extent taken up with the appearance of the sky : there is some parade of astronomy and classical mythology in his descriptions, but in many of the stanzas the delineation is simple and direct: —

> The wrathful winter proaching on apace,
> With blustering blasts had all ybar'd the treen,
> And olde *Saturnus*, with his frosty face,
> With chilling cold had pierc'd the tender green:
> The mantels rent, wherein enwrapped been
> The gladsome groves that now lay overthrown,
> The tapets torne, and every bloom **down** blown.
>
> Hawthorn had lost his motley livery,
> The naked twigs were shivering all for cold,
> And dropping down the tears abundantly;
> Each thing, methought, with weeping eye me told
> The cruel season, bidding me withhold
> Myself within, for I was gotten out
> Into the fields, whereas I walk'd about.
>
> And sorrowing I to see the summer flowers,
> The lively green, the lusty leas forlorn,
> The sturdy trees so shatter'd with the showers,
> The fields so fade that flourish'd so beforn;
> It taught me well, all earthly things be born
> To die the death, for nought long time may last;
> The summer's beauty yields to winter's blast.
>
> *Induction*, 1 *et seq.*

The poet, it is clear, finds little in winter which is not repulsive. He has far less appreciation for the season than Douglas, yet he paints it with considerable detail, because it is in keeping with what follows. Superior to his picture of winter, is that of midnight introduced in *The Complaint of Henry, Duke of Buckingham.*

> Midnight was come, and every vital thing
> With sweet sound sleep their weary limbs did rest;

The beasts were still, the little birds that sing,
Now sweetly slept beside their mother's breast;
The old and all well shrowded in their nest
The waters calm, the cruel seas did cease,
The woods, the fields, and all things, held their peace.
The golden stars were whirl'd amid their race,
And on the earth did laugh with twinkling light,
When each thing nestled in his resting place,
Forgat day's pain with pleasure of the night:
The hare had not the greedy hounds in sight,
The fearful deer of death stood not in doubt,
The partridge dream'd not of the falcon's foot.

vv. 547—560.

In every line of this picture it is easy to trace the poet's keen appreciation of the scene which he portrays. Each feature in the landscape bears the stamp of truth. The horizon which the poet brings before us is a wide one; sky, sea and earth are all included in the picture, each detail of which brings with it a sense of restfulness, giving to the whole landscape a prevailing mood of idyllic calm.

George Gascoigne[1]) (1525? — 1577), in describing himself on one occasion as "Chaucer's boy and Petrarch's journeyman", quaintly indicates that blending of native with foreign influences which distinguishes most of the early Elizabethan poetry. His *Steel Glass* does not concern us here, but the volume of poems which he published in 1575 with the title of *Posies* contains amongst its "Flowers", "Herbs" and "Weeds" some felicitious description of Nature. Thus in the poem *Philomene* the poet gives us a pleasant picture of an evening in April:

In sweet April, the messenger to May,
When hoonie drops do melt in golden showres,
When every byrde records his lovers lay,
And westerne windes do foster forth our floures,
Late in an even I walked out alone,
To heare the descant of the nightingale;
And as I stood I heard hir make great moane,
Waymenting much, and thus she tolde hir tale.

These verses make it clear that Gascoigne had some excuse for calling himself Chaucer's boy, while the complaint

---

[1]) *Poems,* ed. W. C. Hazlitt, 1869.

of the nightingale which follows is endued with a poetic
fancifulness which comes at times within reasonable distance
of the parliamenting of Chaucer's birds. The nightingale
compares her lot with that of other birds — the thrush,
finch, lark, linnet, etc. — and derives small comfort from the
comparison: —

> The Finche, which singeth never a note but 'peepe',
> Is fedde aswel, nay better farre than I.

While all the other birds live a life of gladness, it is
the melancholy duty of the nightingale to "forpine" herself, —

> that lovers might delight
> To heare the notes that breake out of my breste.

In the poem, *The Praise of Philip Sparrow,* — one of
the "weeds to be avoided" — Gascoigne associates himself
with both Skelton and Sidney in singing the praises of
Lesbia's bird. The sprightliness of the poem may be gauged
by its first stanza:

> Of all the byrdes that I doe know,
> Phillip my sparrow hath no peare:
> For sit she high or lye she lowe,
> Be she farre off or be she neare,
> There is no byrde so faire, so fine,
> Nor yet so freshe, as this of myne.

Several pieces of landscape painting in the *Arcadia* show
that Sir Philip Sidney (1544—1586) was a ready observer
of natural beauty, and looked upon Nature with the eyes of
a poet[1]; but when he exchanged prose diction for that of
verse, there comes over much of his poetry of Nature that
hardness and artificiality from which the Elizabethan sonneteer,
unless he be a Shakespeare, so rarely escapes. The "pathetic
fallacy", to which the surcharged sentiment of the art-lyric
too often leads, is common enough with Sidney. It finds the
frankest expression in the following sonnet:

> In wonted walks since wonted fancies change,
> Some cause there is which of strange cause doth rise,

---

[1] What, for instance, can be more poetic than the following:
"Her breath is more sweet than a gentle south-west wind, which
comes over flowery fields and shadowed waters in the extreme heat
of summer"? (*Arcadia,* Book I.)

> For in each thing whereto my mind doth range,
> Part of my pain, meseems, engraved lies.
> The rocks, which were of constant mind the mark,
> In climbing steep, now hard refusal show;
> The shading woods seem now my sun to dark,
> And stately hills disdain to look so low.
> The restful caves now restless visions give;
> In dales I see each way a hard ascent;
> Like late-mown meads, late cut from joy I live;
> Alas, sweet brooks do in my tears augment.
> Rocks, woods, hills, caves, dales, meads, brooks answer me:
> Infected minds infect each thing they see. [1]

The last line shows that Sidney introduced the pathetic fallacy into his poetry with open eyes. He makes no pretence that Nature does in reality vary with the mood of the poet, but acknowledges that all this is illusion — the infection of infected minds. The picture of early morn in the ninety-first *Astrophel and Stella* sonnet is full of beauty, though in the fourth verse Sidney falls into the trap of the sonneteer and sacrifices beauty to tasteless ingenuity:

> But when birds charm, and that sweet air which is
> Morn's messenger, with rose-enamelled skies,
> Calls each night to salute the flower of bliss,
> In tomb of lids then buried are mine eyes,
> Forced by their lord, who is ashamed to find
> Such light in sense, with such a darkened mind.

Still steeper is the descent to rococo prettiness in his sonnet to the moon. It opens with two verses of undeniable grandeur and resonance, which stand on an altogether different level from those which come after:

> With how sad steps, O Moon, thou climb'st the skies!
> How silently, and with how wan a face!
> What, may it be that even in heavenly place
> That busy archer his sharp arrow tries!
>
> *Astrophel and Stella*, Sonnet XXXI.

The sonneteers who follow in the wake of Sidney present, with the exception of Shakespeare, whose sonnets are considered in another place, very little that is of importance for our present study. The industry with which they prosecute their search through the natural world for analogies with

---

[1] *The Complete Poems of Sir Philip Sidney*, ed. Grosart, Vol. I, p. 177.

their own emotions is, for the most part, as misplaced as it
is undeniable, while the sentimental attitude towards Nature
which they usually assume leads them into all forms of
affectation. The following verses from the ninth of Constable's
Diana sonnets is fairly typical of the sonneteer's manner.

> My lady's presence makes the roses red,
> Because to see her lips they blush for shame:
> The lily's leaves, for envy, pale became,
> And her white hands in them this envy bred.
> The marigold the leaves abroad doth spread,
> Because the sun's and her power is the samé.
> The violet of purple colour came,
> Dyed in the blood she made my heart to shed.
> In brief: all flowers from her their virtue take [1]).

Yet even in the sonnet the simple delight in a spring
landscape makes itself felt at times, and occasionally the
sonneteer, breaking away from the trammels of laboured ingenuity, yields himself up to this pleasure and speaks from
the heart instead of from the head. The following sonnet
from Richard Carleton's *Madrigals,* 1601, may serve to illustrate
this direct contact with the world of reality :

> When Flora fair the pleasant tidings bringeth
> Of summer sweet with herbs and flowers adorned,
> The nightingale upon the hawthorn singeth,
> And Boreas' blasts the birds and beasts have scorned ;
> When fresh Aurora with her colours painted,
> Mingled with spears of gold, the sun appearing,
> Delights the hearts that are with love acquainted,
> And maying maids have then their time of cheering;
> All creatures then with summer are delighted,
> The beasts, the birds, the fish with scale of silver;
> Then stately dames by lovers are invited
> To walk in meads or row upon the river.
> I all alone am from these joys exiled,
> No summer grows where love yet never smiled! [2])

In regard to the interpretation of Nature, the songs and
lyrics which appeared in the various song-books at a time
when England was a nest of singing-birds are of greater
importance than the more formal sonnets. Even where these

---

[1]) Elizabethan Sonnets, ed. Sidney Lee, Vol. II, p. 83.
[2]) Bullen: *Lyrics from Elizabethan Song-Books.* p. 109.

songs approach closest to foreign models, they are imbued with spontaneity and freshness. The themes of these songs are always simple: most of them tell of love, and love demands a background of spring sunshine in valley or wood. The pastoral sentiment is infused into many of them and brings with it, at this early period in its history, an idyllic mirage. The features of the natural world which had most attraction for the Elizabethan lyrist are all contained in Marlowe's famous song, *The Passionate Shepherd to his Love*, and are presented there in their most attractive form:

> Come live with me and be my love,
> And we will all the pleasures prove,
> That valleys, groves, hills and fields
> Woods or steepy mountains yields.

> And we will sit upon the rocks,
> Seeing the shepherds feed their flocks,
> By shallow rivers, to whose falls
> Melodious birds sing madrigals.

> And I will make thee beds of roses,
> And a thousand fragrant posies,
> A cap of flowers and a kirtle,
> Embroider'd all with leaves of myrtle.

These verses show clearly enough that the poet's world of natural beauty has extended its frontiers since the coming of the Renascence. It is no longer bounded by the enclosure of a garden, or by the stream which waters the flowery meadow. The poet's eye now ranges freely over woods, mountains and rocky hills, and sees beauty in these no less than in meadow or shady grove. But the season of Nature's beauty is still pre-eminently that of spring. In the following lyric, from Thomas Campion's *Two Books of Airs*[1]) (circ. 1613), the joy which the poet feels in the return of spring is the same as that of the mediæval lyrists or romance-writers:

> The peaceful western wind
> The winter storms hath tamed,
> And Nature in each kind
> The kind heat hath inflamed:
> The forward birds so sweetly breathe
> Out of their earthly bowers,

---

[1]) Bullen, *Lyrics from Elizabethan Song Books*, p. 113.

That heaven, which views their pomp beneath,
　Would fain be decked with flowers.
See how the morning smiles
　　On her bright eastern hill,
　And with soft steps beguiles
　　Them that lie slumbering still!
The music-loving birds are come
　　From cliffs and rocks unknown,
To see the trees and briars bloom
　　That late were overblown.

In the following, taken from Dowland's *Second Book of Airs*,[1]) 1600, the beauty of Nature is blended with love-sentiments with a graciousness of fancy that defies analysis:

Clear or cloudy, sweet as April show'ring,
　Smooth or frowning, so is her face to me.
Pleased or smiling, like mild May all flow'ring,
　When skies blue silk, and meadows carpets be:
Her speeches, note of that night-bird that singeth,
Who, though all sweet, yet jarring notes outringeth.
Her grace, like June, when earth and trees be trimmed
　In best attire, of complete beauty's height:
Her love again, like Summer's days be dimmed
　With little clouds of doubtful constant faith;[2])
Her trust, her doubt, like rain and heat in skies,
Gently thundering, she light'ning to mine eyes.
Sweet Summer, Spring, that breatheth life and growing,
　In weeds, as into herbs and flowers,
And seeds of service, divers sorts in sowing,
　Some haply seeming, and some being yours:
Rain on your herbs and flowers that truly seem,
And let your woods lack dew, and duly starve.[3])

Akin to this is the following song from Morley's *Madrigals*, 1600:

Now is the gentle season, freshly flowering,
　To sing, and play, and dance, while May endureth,
　And woo, and wed too, that sweet delight procureth.
The fields abroad with spangled flowers are gilded,
　The meads are mantled, and closes[4]);
　In May each bush arrayed, and sweet wild roses.

---

[1]) ed. Bullen, *Shorter Elizabethan Poems*, 1903.
[2]) The editor reads 'faith', but the rhyme seems to require 'light'.
[3]) The rhyme here shows the reading to be false.
[4]) A defective verse.

The nightingale her bower hath gaily builded,
And full of kindly lust and loves inspiring,
I love, I love, she sings, hark, her mate desiring. [1]

In other songs and lyrics this unquestioning delight in the beauty of Nature is replaced by something deeper and more metaphysical. Thus in the following *Palinode* of Edmund Bolton (1575? — 1633?) we see- how the poet, instead of abandoning himself whole-heartedly to Nature, goes to her to find support for his own brooding thoughts:

As withereth the primrose by the river,
As fadeth summer's sun from gliding fountains,
As vanisheth the light-blown bubble ever,
As melteth snow upon the mossy mountains;
So melts, so vanisheth, so fades, so withers,
The rose, the shine, the bubble and the snow,
Of praise, pomp, glory, joy (which short life gathers),
Fair praise, vain pomp, sweet glory, brittle joy.
The withered primrose by the mourning river,
The faded summer's sun from weeping fountains,
The light-blown bubble vanished for ever,
The molten snow upon the naked mountains,
    Are emblems that the treasures we uplay,
    Soon wither, vanish, fade and melt away.

For as the snow, whose lawn did over-spread
Th'ambitious hills, which giant-like did threat
To pierce the heaven with their aspiring head.
Naked and bare doth leave their craggy seat;
Whenas the bubble, which did empty fly
The dalliance of the undiscerned wind,
On whose calm rolling waves it did rely,
Hath shipwreck made, where it did dalliance find;
And when the sunshine which dissolved the snow,
Coloured the bubble with a pleasant vary,
And made the rathe and timely primrose grow,
Swarth clouds withdrawn (which longer time do tarry) —
    Oh what is praise, pomp, glory, joy, but so
    As shine by fountains, bubbles, flowers or snow? [2]

Or again, we see Elizabethan poets turning to Nature in order to find there solitude and freedom from care after the distractions of a life of activity. This is the prevailing

---

[1] From Carpenter's *English Lyric Poetry* (Warwick Library) p. 77.
[2] Bullen: *England's Helicon*, p. 25.

mood of the pastoralist, and as such is weighed in the balance
of Shakespeare's *As You Like It;* but whereas in pastoral
poetry this desire to escape from the life of courts and cities
often fails to carry conviction with it, it is, we feel assured,
wholly sincere when it escapes the lips of that ill-starred
courtier, Elizabeth's Earl of Essex:

> Happy were he could finish forth his fate
>   In some unhaunted desert most obscure
> From all societies, from love and hate
>   Of worldly folk; there might he sleep secure,
> Then wake again, and ever give God praise,
>   Content with hips and haws and bramble-berry;
> In contemplation spending all his days,
>   And change of holy thoughts to make him merry:
> Where, when he dies, his tomb may be a bush,
> Where harmless robin dwells with gentle thrush [1]).

---

[1]) Hannah: *Poems of Sir Walter Raleigh and other Courtly Poets.*

Chapter XII.

SPENSER.

In Edmund Spenser we reach a poet who not only had
an appreciation for whatever was beautiful in life and in
the world around him, but who also sought to analyse beauty,
and to refer all beautiful things to an original archetype. This
was an altogether new departure in English poetry; the
earlier poets had been content to recognise the beautiful
and the sublime in Nature, and to give poetic expression to
what they saw, or fain would see, of the world's loveliness
of form, colour, or grouping. In Spenser's abstract reasoning
as to the origin of man's æsthetic feelings he is unmistakably
influenced by Greek philosophy. His master is Plato, whose
doctrine of the perfect *idea* of the beautiful was assimilated
by him, and forms the basis of his *Hymn in Honour of
Beauty*. In this exquisite poem the teaching of Plato's
Symposium is faithfully reproduced :

> What time this worlds great Workmaister did cast
> To make al things such as we now behold,
> It seemes that he before his eyes had plast
> A goodly Paterne, to whose perfect mould
> He fashioned them as comely as he could,
> That now so faire and seemely they appeare,
> As nought may be amended any wheare.
>
> That wondrous Paterne, wheresoere it bee,
> Whether in earth layd up in secret store,
> Or else in heaven, that no man may it see
> With sinfull eyes, for feare it to deflore,
> Is perfect Beautie, which all men adore ;
> Whose face and feature doth so much excell
> All mortall sence that none the same may tell.

> Thereof as every earthly thing partakes
> Or more or lesse, by influence divine,
> So it more faire accordingly it makes,
> And the grosse matter of this earthly myne
> Which clotheth it thereafter doth refyne,
> Doing away the drosse which dims the light
> Of that faire beame which therein is empight. [1]

Yet another famous Platonic idea finds utterance in the same Hymn. Beauty is made identical with goodness:

> For all that faire is, is by nature good.

The working of this thought may be traced in every page of Spenser's poetry. Beauty, physical and spiritual, is Spenser's life-long quest. In his characters ugliness and moral obliquity become synonymous: beauty and virtue are made one. The æsthetic emotions acquire a moral and spiritual significance, and whatever is beautiful in life or in external Nature is sought after and loved, not for its own sake only, but because of its bearing upon the sphere of morality as well.

In his delineation of the natural world Spenser is under the sway of both native and foreign influences. In the first place, he is the lineal descendant of Chaucer and the mediæval school of English poetry. The breach which is sometimes thought to yawn between mediævalism and the Renascence is less wide than it appears. It is bridged over by Spenser and other Elizabethan poets who, while absorbing the new influences which came to them from abroad, yet clung tenaciously to what was best in mediæval thought and art. In the second place, Spenser is a disciple of the Renascence: he came profoundly under the influence of Ariosto and of other Italians, and through them under that of the Greek poets. In his interpretation of Nature it is sometimes difficult to distinguish between these two influences, which, it must be remembered, are not always directly opposed to each other.

From Chaucer and the mediæval poets he learnt the use of the nature-fable. In his earlier poems fables are somewhat frequently introduced, being employed, as in mediæval times, for the presentation of moral truths, social satire, or general reflection on life. Thus in *The Shepherd's Calendar*

---

[1] *Spenser's Works* ed. Morris (Globe Edition).

there is the fable of the Oak and the Brier, in which the
opposition of youth and age — a theme so popular with the
writers of the older *debates* — is sympathetically treated.
In his delineation of the oak Spenser is more graphic than
is his wont:

> There grewe an aged Tree on the greene,
> A goodly Oake sometime had it bene,
> With armes full strong and largely displayd,
> But of their leaves they were disarayde:
> The bodie bigge, and mightely pight,
> Throughly rooted, and of wonderous hight;
> Whilome had bene the King of the field,
> And mochell mast to the husband did yielde,
> And with his nuts larded many swine:
> But now the gray mosse marred his rine;
> His bared boughes were beaten with stormes,
> His toppe was bald, and wasted with wormes,
> His honor decayed, his braunches sere.
>> *The Shepherd's Calendar: February.*

To *The Shepherd's Calendar* belongs also the fable of
the Fox and the Kid, an early study of the beast-fable which
Spenser afterwards developed with such masterly power in
Mother Hubberd's Tale. In this work, as in the prototype of
the mediæval fable, *Reynard the Fox,* the main purpose is
a satirical one, and as far as the interpretation of Nature
and of animal life is concerned, *Mother Hubberd's Tale* is
inferior to such a poem as *The Owl and the Nightingale.*
The interest of Spenser's work is social and human; the fox,
ape and lion are at bottom simply human beings under an
animal disguise. In Spenser's maturer work, when he came
more under the influence of the Renascence and of Italian
models, the Fable was abandoned.

Spenser follows Chaucer again in his tendency to introduce natural objects, such as trees, flowers, or animals, in
a mass, without much idea of perspective, or even of naturalness;
in other words, he falls into the habit of substituting a cut
and dried inventory of natural objects for a well-ordered and
harmonious landscape. He repeats the tree-list of Chaucer's
Parliament of Fowls in the opening canto of the *Faerie
Queene,* and elsewhere long lists of birds, animals, or flowers

appear, drawn up in the same tasteless manner. Further, there is occasionally in Spenser a trace of that fondness for stiff and formal regularity in the outline of a landscape which is so noticeable in Chaucer: in his description of the garden of Venus he tells us:

> And all without were walkes and alleyes dight
> With divers trees enrang'd in even rankes;
> *Faerie Queene,* IV. 10. 25.

a passage reminiscent of the wood described in Chaucer's *Book of the Duchess.*

Spenser shares, too, Chaucer's delight in the season of spring, and his horror of winter. He makes a certain advance upon Chaucer's naïve delight in a May morning, beautiful with flower and song, yet the landscape which he paints with surest hand is one which is closely associated with the springtime. Winter is for him a season of dreariness; he speaks of 'winter's wastful spight', and with his characteristic fondness for the personification of nature-forces, he depicts the arrival of the wintry season in the following manner:

> But eft, when ye count you freed from feare,
> Comes the breme Winter with chamfred browes,
> Full of wrinckles and frostie furrowes,
> Drerily shooting his stormy darte,
> Which cruddles the blood, and pricks the harte.
> *Shepherd's Calendar : February.*

Increased experience did not change Spenser's attitude towards this season of the year: the picture of winter in the procession of the seasons, introduced into the fragmentary seventh Book of the *Faerie Queene*, has much in common with that of his first poem.

In most respects, however, Spenser's advance upon Chaucer is considerable. The latter, as has been already pointed out, rarely takes his readers beyond the garden, or, at farthest, the flower-bestrewn meadow which skirts it. Spenser, while retaining Chaucer's love for the garden and its flowers, finds his favourite landscape in some well-watered and well-wooded valley among the hills. Such a spot is described in detail in the third Book of the *Faerie Queene:*

> Into that forest farre they thence him led,
> Where was their dwelling, in a pleasant glade,

With mountaines rownd about environed,
And mightie woodes which did the valley 'shade,
And like a stately Theatre it made,
Spreading it selfe into a spatious plaine :
And in the midst a little river plaide
Emongst the pumy stones, which seemd to plaine
With gentle murmure that his cours they did restraine.

Beside the same a dainty place there lay,
Planted with mirtle trees and laurells greene,
In which the birds song many a lovely lay
Of Gods high praise, and of their loves sweet teene,
As it an earthly Paradize had beene.   III. 5. 39—40.

The landscape which is here described differs in many
respects from that of Chaucer. It is much more extensive,
and includes, in addition to the foreground of valley, stream
and myrtle grove, a background of forest and mountain. In
his earlier works Spenser seems to share Chaucer's dread of
the forest, and speaks on more than one occasion of "wast-
full woods"; but at the time when he was engaged upon the
Faerie Queene, his taste had widened, and he represents most
of the adventures of his great romance as taking place
either in, or in the immediate neighbourhood of, some forest.
Again, in the noble refrain to the *Epithalamion* —

The woods shall to me answer and my Eccho ring —

we see how his appreciation of woodland scenery included
the recognition of a bond of sympathy between it and himself.

This change may have been due in part to the influence
of the new school of pastoral poetry. The pastoral poetry of
the Renascence begins with Petrarch, whose Latin Eclogues
were written between 1346 and 1356.[1]) Proceeding from
Italy, pastoralism soon came into vogue throughout western
Europe and exercised a certain influence upon the attitude
of poets towards external Nature. Spenser is steeped in
pastoralism; he began his career as a pastoral poet with *The
Shepherd's Calendar;* adopted the pastoral convention in both
Colin Clout's Come Home Again and *Daphnaïda,* and towards
the close of his life, wrote those surpassingly beautiful pastoral

---

[1]) It is worthy of note that Boccaccio's pastoral romance, *Ameto,*
is even earlier than these Eclogues of Petrarch; its date is 1342.

scenes of the sixth Book of the *Faerie Queene* which describe the life of Pastorella among the shepherds. Pastoral poetry, in its true form, owes its vogue almost entirely to the desire which filled men's hearts at the time of the Renascence to escape from the storm and stress of city life, and to seek seclusion in the country. In almost every case the desire was an idle one, as far as its practical fulfilment was concerned, but it called into being the pastoral fiction, the magic spell of which was felt not only by the romantic dreamer Spenser, but to some extent even by Shakespeare, whose grasp of the realities of life was so sure.

In removing the centre of interest from the city to the country, the Pastoral brought the painting of landscape into greater prominence. The trim and formal town garden of the earlier courtly poetry was exchanged for the freedom of the woodland, or the well-watered plain. More than this, it helped to change the naïve and objective interpretation of Nature into a sentimental one, for the sentimental interpretation of Nature is almost as strong in the pastoralists as in the lyrists. But while in one sense the advance made by pastoral poetry was so great, in another there was rather retrogression than progress. Renascence pastoralism was at best a pleasing fiction, having very little hold on the realities of life. Only half sincere at the outset, the pastoral ideal soon became an artificial convention, which, in its interpretation of Nature, substituted certain formal, stereotyped ideas for actual communion with the external world. Its defiance of truth is seen in its choice of a locality wherein the pastoral ideal could be most satisfactorily realised. The Arcadia of the Peloponnesus is a mountainous, and, for the most part, barren region, but in the works of the pastoralists it assumes the form of a paradisaic land of gently flowing streams and loveliest verdure, the inhabitants of which live a life of refined simplicity, unaffected by the strife of the outer world. Stamped even at its birth by the impress of unnaturalness, the pastoral grew more and more artificial the farther it passed from its Italian home. In Sannazaro's *Arcadia* and Tasso's pastoral play, *Aminta,* the scenery is fairly true to an Italian sky, but in English pastorals the element of artificiality becomes more distinctly felt. Thus when Spenser describes groves of myrtle trees under which his heroes and heroines seek protection from the raging heat of "Phebus fiery carre", or rivers which murmur sweetly "over pumy [pumice] stones", the reader is convinced that the description is book-learned, and not based on actual observation.

But Spenser's horizon is at the same time far wider than that of the conventional pastoralists. Whether mindful or not of the traditions of Old English poetry, he delights in painting the sea. His attitude towards the sea is not quite the same as that of the pre-conquest poets; he paints the sea in the hour of storm, and is conscious of the sublimity of such a scene, but the prevailing feeling which an ocean tempest awakens within him is one of shrinking terror. He fails to share in that delight in sea-voyaging which was experienced by the Elizabethan sea-dogs, the lineal descendants of the early Vikings. His attitude towards the sea is, perhaps, best expressed in a familiar passage of *Colin Clout's Come Home Again:*

> 'So to the sea we came; the sea, that is
> A world of waters heaped up on hie,
> Rolling like mountaines in wide wildernesse,
> Horrible, hideous, roaring with hoarse crie'.
> 'And is the sea (quoth Coridon) so fearfull?'
> 'Fearful much more (quoth he) then hart can fear;
> Thousand wyld beasts with deep mouthes gaping direfull
> Therin stil wait poore passengers to teare.
> Who life doth loath, and longs death to behold,
> Before he die, alreadie dead with feare,
> And yet would live with heart halfe stonie cold,
> Let him to sea, and he shall see it there'.

In the account of the voyage of Guyon and the Palmer to the island where dwells the siren Acrasia (*Faerie Queene* II. 12.), there is detailed painting of the sea both in calm and in storm. In his description of the "griesly Wasserman", the horrible Sea-satyre" and the "monsters thousand-fold" of the deep, he clings tenaciously to the superstitions which were in vogue in Old English times, when poets told of the nickors and other beasts of rapine which were thought to inhabit the depths of the ocean. In his account of this voyage Spenser brings out with much artistic mastery the contrast between the sea in calm and the sea in storm. At first all is quiet:

> . . . the hoare waters from his frigot ran,
> And the light bubles daunced all along,
> Whiles the salt brine out of the billowes sprong.
>
> II. 12. 10.

Storm follows, and the change is described with bold imagery and a fine appreciation of colour:

> Ye might have seene the frothy billows fry,
> Under the ship as thorough them she went,
> That seemd the waves were into yvory,
> Or yvory into the waves were sent;
> And otherwhere the snowy substaunce sprent
> With vermell, like the boyes blood therein shed,
> A piteous spectacle did represent;
> And otherwhiles, with gold besprinkeled,
> It seemd thenchaunted flame which did Crëusa wed.
>
> II. 12. 45.

Elsewhere, and especially in *The Faerie Queene*, the sea is frequently introduced in simile. Usually it is the sea in storm, the sea battling with the rocks, or trying to engulf the ship which sails across it, which is described; but on one occasion it is the sea in calm, when

> the sunny beams do glaunce and glide
> Upon the trembling wave.

Compared with earlier English poets, Spenser makes a significant advance both in the frequency of his similes, and in the range of objects from which they are drawn. They are for the most part taken from natural phenomena or animal life, and are often apt and forcible. In his employment of simile he is largely under the influence of Ariosto; many of his similes, indeed, are either borrowed from foreign models, or are drawn from his imagination instead of from actual observation. Thus the similes of conflicts between lions and tigers, or lions and wolves, or again that of wolves breaking into the fold, such as appears in *The Faerie Queene*

(IV. 4. 35), are manifestly not the outcome of personal knowledge. Others, however, — and these are always the most interesting — are appropriate to English life, and come within the range of the poet's own experience. Among the homeliest of these is that of the gnats attacking a shepherd, described in the opening canto of *The Faerie Queene*:

> As gentle shepheard in sweete eventide,
> When ruddy Phebus gins to welke in west,
> Hygh on a hill, his flocke to vewen wide,
> Markes which doe byte their hasty supper best;
> A cloud of cumbrous gnattes doe him molest,
> All striving to infixe their feeble stinges,
> That from their noyance he no where can rest;
> But with his clownish hands their tender wings
> He brusheth oft, and oft doth mar their murmurings.
>
> I. 1. 23.

Several similes, scattered throughout *The Faerie Queene*, bear witness to Spenser's keen observation of the phenomena of the sky, and the beauty of cloud forms. This is how he describes the clouds driven by the wind:

> As when a windy tempest bloweth hye,
> That nothing may withstand his stormy stowre,
> The clowdes, as things affrayd, before him flye;
> But all so soone as his outrageous powre
> Is layd, they fiercely then begin to showre;
> And, as in scorne of his spent stormy spight,
> Now all attonce their malice forth do poure:
> So did Prince Arthur beare himselfe in fight,
> And suffred rash Pyrochles waste his ydle might.
>
> II. 8. 48.

Not unlike this is the simile which introduces the mist:

> As, when a foggy mist hath overcast
> The face of heven, and the cleare ayre engroste,
> The world in darkenes dwels; till that at last
> The watry Southwinde, from the seabord coste
> Upblowing, doth disperse the vapour lo'ste,
> And poures it selfe forth in a stormy showre;
> So the fayre Britomart, having disclo'ste
> Her clowdy care into a wrathfull stowre,
> The mist of griefe dissolv'd did into vengeance powre.
>
> III. 4. 13.

The great bulk of the similes of *The Faerie Queene,*
however, as is only natural in a work mainly concerned with
martial adventure, paint the conflicts between various kinds
of beasts and birds, or birds in pursuit of their prey. As an
instance of the latter class the simile which introduces the
falcon may be given; here the description is evidently based
on actual observation:

> As when a Faulcon hath with nimble flight
> Flowne at a flush of Ducks foreby the brooke,
> The trembling foule dismayd with dreadfull sight
> Of death, the which them almost overtooke,
> Doe hide themselves from her astonying looke
> Amongst the flags and covert round about.
>
> V. 2. 54.

Perhaps the most interesting of Spenser's similes are
those in which the accent of locality is heard, and the poet
introduces some pleasing sketch of his Irish life and Irish
home. The action of *The Faerie Queene* is so undefined, so
untrammelled by the fetters of space and time, that such
local references as occur have a special interest. Amongst
these is the simile in which the tide of battle is compared
with the tide in the river Shannon:

> Like as the tide, that comes fro th'Ocean mayne,
> Flowes up the Shenan with contrarie forse,
> And over-ruling him in his owne rayne,
> Drives backe the current of his kindly course,
> And makes it seeme to have some other sourse;
> But when the floud is spent, then backe againe,
> His borrowed waters forst to redisbourse,
> He sends the sea his owne with double gaine,
> And tribute eke withall, as to his Soveraine.
>
> IV. 3. 27.

There are also occasional references to "father Mole,
that mountaine hore", which, like "the shiny Mulla", bordered
on the poet's home at Kilcolman. These references to Irish
scenery, taken in connection with the affectionate manner
in which he speaks of his Irish life in *Colin Clout's Come
Home Again,* serve to modify the view suggested by other
passages in his works, that his Irish life was for him nothing
more than a period of dreary exile. His occasional crossing

of the Irish sea gave rise to one of the most vigorous of
his sea-similes, in which he paints the hurtling together of
two opposing billows:

> As when two billowes in the Irish sowndes,
> Forcibly driven with contrarie tydes,
> Do meete together, each abacke rebowndes
> With roaring rage ; and dashing on all sides,
> That filleth all the sea with fome, divydes
> The doubtfull current into divers wayes.
> So fell those two in spight of both their prydes.

IV. 1. 42.

Spenser rarely ventures on elaborate description of an
objective character, except where he has a literary model
before him. *The Faerie Queene* opens with the figure of the
Red Cross Knight "pricking on the plaine", but no attempt
is made to describe this plain or the country through which
the hero passes in his wanderings. This absence of localisation
and particularisation gives to the whole work an element of
vagueness which contrasts in a very marked way with the
clearly outlined and carefully surveyed regions through which
Dante leads his readers in the *Commedia*. The Spenserian
student is left with an ill-defined impression that the adventures of *The Faerie Queene* are somehow or other bound
up with forest-life, and occasionally with the sea-shore ; but
for the rest, he is wandering through the land of *Weiss-
nichtwo,* a land in which Spenser is loftily regardless of
topography. But where there were classical or Italian models
to direct him, as in the description of the Garden of Adonis,
or the yet more famous Bower of Acrasia, he displays considerable power in outlining his landscape, and in grouping
together a number of sensuously beautiful details into a well-
ordered picture. In his description of the Bower of Acrasia,
visited and despoiled by Guyon in the second Book of *The
Faerie Queene*, he drew upon all possible sources for his
material and his colours. All that classic poets had sung of
the Elysian fields, or modern romanticists had fabled of an
earthly bower of bliss, is pressed into the picture. The model
which was chiefly before his eye when he painted this picture
was Tasso's *Gerusalemme Liberata,* in the fifteenth and six-

teenth books of which is described, in colours scarcely less
gorgeous than those of the English poet, the bower of the
siren Armida. Spenser is, however, no slavish imitator; he
shows his originality at the outset by bringing into contrast the
utter loveliness of the siren's bower and the wild fury of
the sea which rings it round. Guyon and the Palmer steer
their way across a sea made perilous by rocks, quicksands,
whirlpools and monsters of the deep. Escaping from these,
they at last arrive at port:

> And now they nigh approched to the sted
> Whereas those Mermayds dwelt: it was a still
> And calmy bay, on th' one side sheltered
> With the brode shadow of an hoarie hill;
> On th' other side an high rocke toured still,
> That twixt them both a pleasaunt port they made,
> And did like an halfe Theatre fulfill:
> There those five sisters had continuall trade,
> And usd to bath themselves in that deceiptfull shade.
>
> II. 12. 30.

It is most probable that when Spenser wrote this he had
in mind the haven in the Fortunate Islands which Tasso's
knights reach in their search for Rinaldo:

> A secret place they found in one of those,
> Where the cleft shore sea in his bosom takes,
> And 'twixt his stretched arms doth fold and close
> An ample bay; a rock the haven makes,
> Which to the main doth his broad back oppose,
> Whereon the roaring billow cleaves and breaks,
>   And here and there two crags, like turrets high,
>   Point forth a port to all that sail thereby.
> *Gerusalemme Liberata,* Fairfax's Translation, *XV. 42.*

There follows next the description of the bower of Acrasia,

> A place pickt out by choyce of best alyve,
> That natures worke by art can imitate.

In describing this bower, Spenser brings together all the
sensuous delights that imagination, tricked out with classic
inventions, could devise. The profusion of sweetnesses is
cloying, and before the end is reached, the reader longs for
the healthy breath of an east wind which shall purify the
scent-laden air, and bring with it tone and energy. There

is very little in the picture which can be regarded as the outcome of the poet's own insight into Nature. Here, as in the somewhat similar Garden of Adonis (III. 6.) or the Garden of Venus (IV. 10.) we look in vain for that touch of the realist which reveals itself in the simpler and more beautiful garden-scene of *Muiopotmos*. The poet brings his readers to a dream-world of sensuous delight, and holds them, as it were, in a web of voluptuous beauty which at first enchants, but soon only satiates. This is, perhaps, no more than Spenser's clear intention in his description of Acrasia's Bower of Bliss. He doubtless finds no small pleasure in setting forth the sensuously beautiful, but he never lets us forget that his sympathies are with the knight of temperance. The whole conduct of the second Book clearly points to this. Hedonism is painted gorgeously but frankly, and the bower of sensual pleasure is on all sides beset with the "Rocke of Vile Reproch", "the Whirlpool of decay", and "the quicksand of Unthriftyhed".

The prevailing characteristic of Spenser's more elaborate landscapes is romantic fancifulness, shot with classic imagery, as opposed to naturalness and literalism. The same applies also to his pictures of sunrise and sunset, and to many other of his representations of natural phenomena. In these he adopts the fiction of classical mythology and delights in personification. The dawn is "fayre Aurora", rising from "the deawy bed of aged Tithone"; sunset, the laving of Phœbus' steeds beneath the waves; night is ever attired in sable mantle; the north wind is "fell Boreas", and the sea, "Tethys bosom faire". This tendency to personify nature-forces is, of course, in no sense confined to Spenser. Instances of it occur in Chaucer, and more frequently in Gawin Douglas, while the poetry of the Renascence is saturated with similar and equally trite imagery. No poet delighted in such things more than Tasso, whereas Ariosto preferred to paint what he actually saw, and generally refused to adopt a classical convention which centuries of use had worn threadbare.

Whatever his shortcomings or excesses may be, Spenser stands pre-eminent among his own generation of poets as a

word-painter of some of the most opulent scenery which eye
has seen or the imagination conceived. His connection with
Chaucer as an interpreter of Nature has been already shown,
and it must also be borne in mind that he himself established
a new poetic tradition, and won for himself a band of disciples through whom his influence was handed down to Milton.
The melody of the Spenserian stanza and the gorgeousness
of the Spenserian landscape aroused little enthusiasm among
the poets of the Augustan school, but when the beginnings
of modern romanticism appeared in the poems of James
Thomson, it was from the pages of *The Faerie Queene*, no less
than from those of *L'Allegro* and *Il Penseroso* that the Scottish
poet drew his inspiration.

Chapter XIII.

THE MINOR ELIZABETHANS.

Contemporaneous with Shakespeare and Spenser, there existed a galaxy of English poets, whose radiance, though dimmed by the presence of those greater luminaries, shines not ineffectually when they are withdrawn. Of these minor Elizabethans — many of them minor only in a strictly relative sense — some follow the Spenserian tradition of the poetic art, others pursue an independent course, while one, Donne, may be regarded as a sturdy opponent of the Spenserian richness and fluidity of style, and as the establisher of a more rugged form of poetry. Almost all forms of poetry were essayed by these contemporaries of Spenser and Shakespeare. The art-lyric and the song-lyric, the historical poem, the metaphysical poem, the descriptive poem and the satire are all well represented, while perhaps the best evidence of the deeply poetic spirit of the age is to be found in the choice of apparently unpromising themes for poetic treatment.

Most of these poets had an eye for the beauty of Nature, and though generally content with a superficial observation of the natural world, recognised the poetic value of descriptions of country life and scenery; while one of them — Michael Drayton[1]) (1563—1631) — blending his appreciation of English scenery with his patriotism, produced a work, the *Polyolbion,* which, in spite of its unpromising theme and its excessive length, must be regarded as one of the most remarkable poems of a remarkable age. Drayton, like Shakespeare, was a Warwickshire man, and like Shakespeare, too,

---

[1]) Anderson's *British Poets,* Vol. III.

he had a true appreciation for the scenery of the English midlands. In one of his *Idea* sonnets he celebrates the Warwickshire river Ankor, —

> Clear Ankor, on whose silver-sanded shore
> My soul-shrined saint, my fair Idea lies; —

and calls the Forest of Arden his Tempe. In his youth he came under the sway of the pastoral convention, and wrote eclogues after the manner of Spenser; then, after the completion of historical poems, dramas, and the topographical *Polyolbion*, the Arcadian fantasy once more moved him to poetry, and in his *Muses' Elysium* (1630) he gave to his countrymen some of the most graceful pastoral dialogues of the time. Here he avoids all allusion to religious or political affairs, and reverting to the purer style of Theocritus, makes his Doron and Dorilus, Cloris and Mertilla — Greek in name, but English in everything else — engage in song-contests. Introduced into these pastoral dialogues, or "nymphals" are some charming pictures of country scenery. Listen, for instance, to Doron and Dorilus in the third nymphal:

Doron. The sun out of the east doth peep,
And now the day begins to creep
    Upon the world at leisure.

Dorilus. The air enamour'd with the greaves,
The west wind strokes the   gentle leaves,
    And kisses them at pleasure.

Doron. The spinners' webs, twixt spray and spray,
The top of every bush make gay,
    By filmy cords there dangling.

Dorilus. For now the last day's evening dew
Even to the full itself doth shew,
    Each bough with pearl bespangling.

When the shepherds are breathless, the shepherdesses, Naiis and Cloe, take their place, and discover new fancies in the fair scene before their eyes:

Naiis.   Behold the rosy dawn
        Rises in tinsell'd lawn,
        And smiling seems to fawn
        Upon the mountains.

Cloe. Awaked from her dreams,
Shooting forth golden beams,
Dancing upon the streams,
Courting the fountains.

Naiis. The gentle winds sally
Upon every vally,
And many times dally
And wantonly sport;

Cloe. About the fields tracing
Each other in chasing,
And often embracing
In amorous sort.

There is a grace and delicacy in verses such as these which reveals a side of Drayton's nature undreamed of by the reader of the *Polyolbion.* And the nymphals are full of such things, with the rich perfume and abiding charm of the country-side ever about them. In the sixth nymphal he brings together a woodman, fisherman and shepherd — Silvius, Halcius, Melanthus — and makes each of them extol his own peculiar craft. The idea, it should be noticed, is that which Isaak Walton subsequently developed in prose diction in the conversations of Piscator, Auceps and Venator in *The Compleat Angler.* The poem shows an exact knowledge of each of the three crafts, but our attention here must be confined to the landscape scene with which the poem begins:

Clear had the day been from the dawn,
All chequer'd was the sky,
Thin clouds, like scarfs of cobweb lawn,
Veil'd heaven's most glorious eye.
The wind had no more strength than this,
That leisurely it blew,
To make one leaf the next to kiss,
That closely by it grew.
The rills that on the pebbles play'd
Might now be heard at will;
This world they only music made,
Else every thing was still.

Drayton is content in these nymphals to sing of simple things in simple fashion; but there is a charm in his colours and an opalescent purity in his atmosphere which recall the Sicilian idylls of Theocritus.

The better-known *Nymphidia*, a mock-epic of fairy-lore, is as graceful as it is whimsical, while *The Quest of Cynthia*, and some of Drayton's other shorter poems, display the same delicate painting of English scenery which we have noticed in the *Muses' Elysium*.

The *Polyolbion* is of a different character. Here the short lilting verse of the lyric poems is exchanged for the heavy-footed Alexandrine, and Drayton, instead of allowing himself to dally with fairy-lore or the song-contests of imaginary shepherds, has a serious duty to perform. A chorographical description in verse must be given of each of the counties of England. To raise so prosaic a theme to a poetic level, Drayton has recourse to various devices; to atone for the lack of human interest, he personifies the streams and mountains, introduces as much of the pastoral element as is possible, and furnishes Christian England with a complete equipment of nymphs, dryads and hamadryads. We are not called upon to criticise the poem as a whole, but only to consider its landscape art. The range of this is necessarily wide. The poet who traverses each of the English counties has to go outside of the palings with which the land of Arcady is closely fenced: not only grove and stream call for notice, but mountain and sea as well. But in extending his horizon, Drayton shows that he possesses a healthy taste. In Song II., while speaking of the Hampshire coast, he describes with considerable power the shoreward rush of the waves in time of storm:

> Some coming from the east, some from the setting sun,
> The liquid mountains still together mainly run;
> Wave woundeth wave again; and billow, billow gores,
> And topsy-turvy so fly trembling to the shores.

In the next Song he bestows high praise upon the "smooth-brow'd" plain of Salisbury which bids

> The lark to leave her bower, and on her trembling wing,
> In climbing up tow'rd heaven, her high-pitch'd hymns to sing
> Unto the springing day; when, 'gainst the sun's arise,
> The early dawning strews the goodly eastern skies
> With roses every where.

In the seventh Song he quaintly calls upon Malvern, "king of hills", to deliver a defence of mountain-scenery:

Malvern does this, and in an *apologia* which extends over some
seventy verses, vigorously but not very poetically, asserts his
superiority to what he calls the "flatter kind" of valleys,
fields and groves; in the ninth Song the mountains of Wales
call forth from the poet a second tribute of praise.

The somewhat jejune conception of the marriage of
two rivers which Spenser had formed in his account of the
Thames and Medway (*Faerie Queene*, IV. 2), is imitated by
Drayton, and carried to excessive length in his account of
the marriage of the Thame and Isis, whose offspring is the
Thames (Song XV.). Drayton also follows Spenser — and
Chaucer before him — in introducing tedious flower and tree-
lists in his work, but his description, in Song XIII, of the
birds which inhabit the forest of Arden, though not rising
wholly above the inventory level, shows that he was, like
Chaucer, a true lover of birds. The picture of early morning
in Arden, which preludes this description of the birds, is
aglow with colour and animation:

> When Phœbus lifts his head out of the winter's wave,
> No sooner doth the earth her flowery bosom brave,
> At such time as the year brings on the pleasant spring,
> But hunts-up to the morn the feather'd sylvans sing:
> And in the lower grove, as on the rising knole,
> Upon the highest spray of every mounting pole,
> Those quiristers are perch'd with many a speckled breast.
> Then from her burnish'd gate the goodly glitt'ring east
> Gilds every lofty top, which late the humorous night
> Bespangled had with pearl, to please the morning's sight;
> On which the mirthful quires, with their clear open throats,
> Unto the joyful morn so strain their warbling notes,
> That hills and vallies ring, and even the echoing air
> Seems all compos'd of sounds about them every where.

In Song XIV. Drayton enters upon that familiar controversy as to the respective attractions of town and country
life which Barclay had introduced to English poetry in his
Eclogue of the *Citizen and Uplandishman* a century before.
Drayton, it need scarcely be said, is whole-heartedly on the
side of the country, and in the following verses anticipates
the famous "God made the country and man made the town"
of William Cowper:

> Fools gaze at painted courts, to the country let me go,
> To climb the easy hill, then walk the valley low;
> No gold-embossed roofs to me are like the woods;
> No bed like to the grass, no liquor like the floods:
> A city's but a sink, gay houses gawdy graves,
> The muses have free leave to starve or live in caves.

Thus, wandering leisurely from county to county, Drayton slowly advances in his work, till at last he reaches the counties of Westmoreland and Cumberland. With a brief description of the mountains of the Lake District, the full glory of which a greater than Drayton was destined to reveal, he brings to an end the "strange Herculean toyle" which had occupied him for so many years.

Samuel Daniel[1]) (1562—1619), who takes his place with Drayton as one of the chief Elizabethan poets of the second magnitude, need not delay us long. Only on rare occasions does he introduce Nature into his poetry, and when it appears, its purpose is usually that of furnishing a simile. In his *History of the Civil Wars* such similes are frequent. The pictures which they introduce are for the most part commonplace; the conflicts of animals or the flow of a river is depicted, but there is scarcely ever any trace of original and first-hand observation. Perhaps the best of them is the comparison which he draws betwen the aged Talbot, dying in the thick of the fray with his spoils around him, and the oak which in its fall bears down other trees with it:

> Then, like a sturdy oak, that having long
> Against the wars of fiercest winds made head,
> When, with some forced tempestuous rage more strong,
> His down-borne top comes over-mastered,
> All the near-bordering trees he stood among
> Crushed with his weighty fall lie ruined:
> So lay his spoils, all round about him slain,
> To adorn his death, that could not die in vain.
> > *History of the Civil Wars,* VI. 95.

In one of his short lyrics, which he calls *An Ode*[2]), there is an exquisite picture of the gladness of spring, which Daniel, in accordance with the accepted tradition of the

---

[1]) *Works,* ed. Grosart, 5 vols. 1885.
[2]) Grosart, Vol. I. p. 259.

Renascence love-lyrists, contrasts with the sadness and despair which harbour in his own breast. The springtide scene
is made up of familiar features, but these are expressed with
that choiceness of manner in which Daniel surpassed almost
all his contemporaries:

> Now each creature joys the other,
>   Passing happy days and hours;
> One bird reports unto another,
>   In the fall of silver showers;
> Whilst the earth, our common mother,
>   Hath her bosom decked with flowers.
>
> Whilst the greatest torch of heaven
>   With bright rays warms Flora's lap,
> Making nights and days both even,
>   Cheering plants with fresher sap:
> My field, of flowers quite bereven,
>   Wants refresh of better hap.
>
> Echo, daughter of the air,
>   Babbling guest of rocks and hills,
> Knows the name of my fierce fair,
>   And sounds the accents of my ills.
> Each thing pities my despair,
>   Whilst that she her lover kills.

Richard Barnfield (1574—1627) rarely shows creative
power in his poetry; except in his famous *Ode,* "As it fell
upon a day", he is at most a clever imitator — sometimes
of Virgil, but more often of Spenser — and like most imitators,
he falls a prey to the foibles of his masters, while missing
their chief points of excellence. He is a professed lover of
the country, but though he lived the life of a country gentleman, his pictures of rural life and rural scenery are by no
means original. The pastoral convention appears in *The
Affectionate Shepherd*[1]), and again in *The Shepherd's Content,*
in its most pronounced form, and the latter poem is singularly
lacking in all that pertains to a healthy, faithful conception
of the country-side. In the former poem Barnfield introduces
the usual catalogue of flowers, and describes the rise and
the setting of the sun in the vapid language of classical
mythology:

---

[1]) Bullen, *Longer Elizabethan Poems,* p. 151.

> By this, the Night (with darkness over-spread)
> Had drawn the curtains of her coal-black bed:
> And Cynthia muffling her face with a cloud,
> (Lest all the world of her should be too proud)
> Had taken conge of the sable Night,
> That wanting her, cannot be half so bright.

His *Ode*[1]), already referred to, is endued with a delicacy of fancy and reflection which are not met with elsewhere in his poems. Its opening verses, familiar as they are, may be quoted here as the truest Elizabethan echo of the Chaucerian delight in a May morning:

> As it fell upon a day
> In the merry month of May,
> Sitting in a pleasant shade
> Which a grove of myrtles made,
> Beasts did leap, and birds did sing,
> Trees did grow, and plants did spring;
> Everything did banish moan,
> Save the nyghtingale alone:
> She, poor bird, as all forlorn,
> Lean'd her breast up-till a thorn,
> And there sung the dolefull'st ditty,
> That to hear it was great pity.

Nicholas Breton[2]) (1545?—1626?), if a confession made by him in his *Toys of an Idle Head* is to be believed, was one who preferred reading about Nature to the exercise of his own powers of observation. In spite of this, he shows a keen and intelligent appreciation of the simpler pleasures of a country life, and in his *Passionate Shepherd* he paints that life very felicitously:

> Who can live in heart so glad
> As the merrie countrie lad?
> Who upon a faire greene baulk
> May at pleasures sit and walk?
> And amid the azure skies
> See the morning sun arise?
> While he hears in every spring
> How the birdes do chirp and sing:
> Or before the hounds in cry
> See the hares go stealing by.

---

[1]) Bullen's *Longer Elizabethan Poems*, p. 266.
[2]) Works, ed. Grosart.

Or along the shallow brook,
Angling with a baited hook,
See the fishes leap and play,
In a blessed sunny day:

Or to hear the partridge call,
Till she have her covey all.
Or to see the subtle fox,
How the villain plies the box:
After feeding on his prey,
How he closely sneaks away,
Through the hedge and down the furrow,
Till he gets into his burrow;
Then the bee to gather honey,
And the little black-hair'd coney
On a bank for sunny place
With her fore-feet wash her face:
Are not these worth thousands moe
Than the courts of kings do know?

There is no suggestion of book-learning in this passage: the poet is face to face with the country-side, which he loves for its own sake and adorns with no Arcadian glozing. These verses might indeed have served as a model for Milton's *L'Allegro,* had a model been needed.

The poems of Sir John Davies[1]) (1569—1626) belong to the early years of his life when he was still a gay and rather quarrelsome young Templar, and before political and forensic honours fell to his lot. His philosophical *Nosce Teipsum,* on which his reputation chiefly rests, does not concern us in this place, but his *Orchestra* and his *Hymns of Astræa* reveal incidentally a penetrative insight into Nature and some originality of thought. The curious defence of the Terpsichorean art in his *Orchestra* has a good deal more than mere quaintness to recommend it to the modern reader. Davies' attempt to prove that all natural phenomena are ever busily engaged in dancing leads to some spirited descriptions, the charm of which is not wholly destroyed by the strained fancifulness of the general idea. Among these dancers of Nature are the sun, the moon, the air and the sea:

For lo! the sea, that fleets about the land,
And like a girdle clips her solid waist,
Music and measure both doth understand:

---

[1]) *Works,* ed. Grosart (The Fuller Worthies' Library) 1869.

> For his great crystal eye is always cast
> Up to the moon, and on her fixed fast :
>   And as she danceth in her pallid sphere,
>   So danceth he about the centre here.

> Sometimes his proud green waves, in order set,
> One after other flow unto the shore,
> Which when they have with many kisses wet,
> They ebb away in order as before;
> And to make known his courtly love the more,
>   He oft doth lay aside his three-fork'd mace,
>   And with his arms the tim'rous earth embrace.
>   *Orchestra* [1]), XLIX, L.

The flowers, likewise, are made to dance, and the stanza in which their motion is described reveals a glimpse of that imaginative power which gives to the natural world a conscious existence:

> See how those flowers, that have sweet beauty too,
> (The only jewels that the earth doth wear,
> When the young sun in bravery her doth woo,)
> As oft as they the whistling wind do hear,
> Do wave their tender bodies here and there;
>   And though their dance no perfect measure is,
>   Yet often times their music makes them kiss.
>   Ibid, LV.

The *Hymns of Astræa* [2]), which appear to be merely clever and courtly acrostics on the words 'Elisabetha Regina', are in reality a good deal more, for though all the Hymns set forth the glory of the queen, many of them are addressed to the fair things of Nature. There are Hymns "To the Lark", "To the Nightingale", "To the Month of May" and "To the Month of September", and the author unites in them the artistic finish of the art-lyric with the spontaneity and directness of the popular song. The Hymn "To the Lark" anticipates the best work of Blake in its chastened simplicity and joyance:

> Early, cheerful, mounting lark,
> Light's gentle usher, morning's clerk,
>   In merry notes delighting;
> Stint awhile thy song, and hark,
>   And learn my new inditing.

---

[1]) Published by Bullen in *Some Longer Elizabethan Poems* (An English Garner) p. 5.

[2]) *Ibid.* p. 111.

Bear up this hymn, to heaven it bear,
E'en up to heaven, and sing it there,
    To heaven each morning bear it:
Have it set to some sweet sphere,
    And let the angels hear it.

This ascription of poems to natural objects, though common enough in the romantic poetry of the last hundred years, is extremely rare in the Elizabethan age, and this fact gives a peculiar charm to these lyrics of Sir John Davies. Similar in character to the Hymn "To the Lark" is that "To the Rose", upon which the poet lavishes fancies no less graceful and courtly:

Eye of the garden, queen of flowers,
Love's cup, wherein he nectar pours,
    Ingendered first of nectar;
Sweet nurse-child of the spring's young hours,
    And beauty's fair character.

Best jewel that the earth doth wear,
E'en when the brave young sun draws near,
    To her hot love pretending;
Himself likewise, like form doth bear,
    At rising and descending.

John Donne[1] (1573—1631), the intrepid originality of whose poetry is becoming more and more recognised by students of literature, was only in a minor degree the avowed poet of Nature. The true province of his poetry was human passion. But the originality of manner which characterises all his work appears also in his occasional references to the natural world. Where he introduces landscape-scenes into his poems, he invariably turns his back upon the artificialities of pastoralism, and eschews the hackneyed mythological colouring by means of which poets sought to replace the direct study of Nature. Thus in his poem, *The Sun-Rising*, he substitutes for the stale conceits of Phœbus, Aurora and Tithonus the following racy picture, the very effrontery of which is pleasing after what we have been accustomed to:

Busy old Fool, unruly sun,
Why dost thou thus
Through windows and through curtains call on us?
Must to thy motions lovers' seasons run?

---

[1] *Poems,* ed. Grosart (The Fuller Worthies' Library) 1872.

Saucy pedantic wretch, go, chide
Late school-boys and sour prentices;
Go tell court-huntsmen that the king will ride;
Call country-ants to harvest offices;
Love, all alike, no season knows nor clime,
Nor hours, days, months, which are the rage of time.

The same freshness and glad *abandon* characterise his song of praise to Bishop Valentine in the *Epithalamion* written in honour of the marriage of the Princess Elizabeth to the Count Palatine of the Rhine. Here he is on Chaucerian ground, but his fancy roams none the less freely:

Hail, Bishop Valentine! whose day this is,
All the air is thy diocese,
And all the chirping choristers
And other birds are thy parishioners:
Thou marryest every year
The lyric lark and the grave whispering dove,
The sparrow that neglects his life for love,
The household bird with the red stomacher;
Thou mak'st the blackbird speed as soon
As doth the goldfinch or the halcyon;
The husband cock looks out, and straight is sped,
And meets his wife which brings her feather-bed.
This day more cheerily than ever shine,
This day, which might inflame thyself, old Valentine.

The little poem called *The Blossom* reveals another side of Donne's poetic genius. Here there is a quiet reflectiveness and a sense of the deep meaning which lies hidden in the simple things of Nature which is almost Wordsworthian:

Little think'st thou, poor flower,
Whom I have watch'd six or seven days,
And seen thy birth, and seen what every hour
Gave to thy growth, thee to this height to raise,
And now dost laugh and triumph on this bough —
Little think'st thou
That it will freeze anon, and that I shall
To morrow find thee fall'n or not at all.

Verses such as these may well call forth a sense of regret that Donne did not on more frequent occasions direct his rare imaginative powers to the interpretation of Nature.

Chapter XIV.

THE PRE-SHAKESPEAREAN DRAMA.

The drama is a form of literature which, by its very nature, is almost exclusively concerned with human character and action, or, more exactly, with human character as asserted in action; all else is of secondary importance. External Nature, if introduced at all, must be placed in strict subordination to humanity; landscapes must not be painted for their own sakes, but only to serve as background to human action, or, in one way or another, be brought into contact with the life and affairs of men. In this respect the romantic drama is placed under greater restraint than the classical. The lyricism of Greek tragedy, and the important place occupied by the choral ode in its structure, gave the tragedian frequent opportunity for introducing a poetic address to the powers of Nature, or even a description of some well-known scene of natural beauty. Of such a character is Prometheus' invocation of "the divine ether and swift-winged breezes", the earth, the sun and "the infinite laughter of the waves" in the play of Æschylus, or Sophocles' lyric description of the nightingale groves of "gleaming Colonos" in the *Œdipus Coloneus*. References to Nature, comparable with these of the Greek tragedians are, of course, not wholly absent from the romantic drama of the Elizabethans, but the structural character of that drama made their introduction less easy and less pertinent.

The biblical plays in which the English drama takes its rise are exclusively concerned with the story which they have to tell, or with the moral to be derived from it: in a popular cycle like the *Towneley* or *Wakefield Plays* even the moral aspect is often sacrificed to a racy handling of the plot. The Old English poems on biblical themes, such as the *Genesis, Exodus, Daniel* and Cynewulf's *Christ,* show with what readiness landscape description was introduced into narrative poetry at a time when its presence there was regarded as essential. But the authors of the biblical plays, writing in a different age, and having a different purpose before them, pass lightly over such scenes as the creation of the world, the passage of the Red Sea, or the sorrow of Nature at the death of Christ. The creation story is told in the most business-like way in all the play-cycles with the exception of that of York. The author of the York-plays — which are recognised as being the oldest of all the extant cycles (*circ.* 1430) — extends the story of the creation over two plays, and endavours to amplify somewhat the biblical account of the six days' work. Thus the divine command, "Let the earth bring forth grass, the herb yielding seed, and the fruit tree yielding fruit after his kind, whose seed is in itself, upon the earth", is expanded in the following manner:

> Þe erthe sall fostyr and furthe bryng,
> > buxsumly as I wyle byde,
> Erbys and also othyr thyng,
> > well for to wax and worthe to wede;
> Treys also þar-on sall spryng,
> > with braunchis and with bowis on-brede,
> With flouris fayr on heght to hyng,
> > and fruth also to fylle and fede.
> And þane I will þat þay
> > of hem selfe have þe sede,
> And mater þat þay may
> > be lastande furth in lede.
>
> And all þer materis es in mynde,
> > for to be made of mekyl might,
> And to be kest in dyveris kynde
> > so for to bere sere burguns bright.
> And when þer frutys is fully fynde,
> > and fayrest semande unto syght,
> Þane þe wedris wete and wynde
> > oway I will it wende full wyght,
> And of þere sede full sone,
> > new rotys sall ryse up right.

Þe third day þus is done,
Þire dedis er dewly dyght.
The Creation to the Fifth Day[1]) *ll.* 33—44.

The poet does not depart very far from his text, but it is clear that he has allowed a certain play of the imagination in his treatment of the story, and also that he has a sense of the beauty of Nature.

The Mystery of the Flood was chiefly prized by the authors of biblical plays as furnishing comic relief in the story of the shrewish obstinacy of Uxor Noe : there is very little reference to the rise and fall of the waters, though the Towneley dramatist gives us a charming conversation between Noah and his wife on the subject of the dove, sent from the ark when the waters have abated :

Noe.   The dowfe is more gentill, her trust 1 untew,
       Like unto the turtill, for she is ay trew.
Uxor.   Hence bot a littill she commys, lew! lew!
       She bryngys in her bill some novels new;
            Behald !
         It is of an olif tre
        A branch, thynkys me.
       Noe. It is soth, perde,
         Right so is it cald.
Doufe, byrd full blist, fayre myght the befall!
Thou art trew for to trist as ston in the wall;
Full well I it wist, thou wold com to thi hall;
Uxor. A trew tokyn ist we shall be savyd all. [2])

Neither the Sacrifice of Isaac, the Departure from Egypt, nor any of the other Old Testament Mysteries claims our attention, but the greater fulness of treatment meted out to the story of the birth, passion and death of Christ sometimes made an opening for the interpretation of Nature. The famous Second Shepherds' Play of the Towneley cycle brings us very near to English shepherd life in the fourteenth century, but though the atmosphere of the Yorkshire uplands is all about the play, and local colour is not absent, there is no direct landscape painting. Local colour, which is amusingly out of

---

[1]) *York-Plays,* ed. Lucy T. Smith, 1885.
[2]) *Towneley Plays,* ed. G. England (Early English Text Society Extra Series, LXXI).

place in a biblical play is still more strongly marked in the
Shepherds' Play of the Chester cycle, where one of the
shepherds speaks as follows :

> I have walked in woodes ful wylde,
> Under bushes my bower to build,
> From fierce storms my sheep to shield,
>   My semely wethers to save.
>
> From comelie Conway unto Clyde
> Under hilles them to hyde.
> A better shepherd on no side
>   No earthlie man may have.

The Offering of the Magi in the Towneley Plays introduces a conversation between the three kings as to the
meaning of the star in the east, in the course of which the
beauty and radiance of the star is dilated upon. The same
play in the York cycle opens with a speech of Herod,
hurled forth in the true "Ercles vein" which Bottom the
weaver loved, in which the king vaunts that even the
elements are subject to him. The winds, clouds and planets
are all his vassals, and when he likes, —

> The rakke of þe rede skye full rappely I ridde,
> Thondres full thrallye by thousandes I thrawe.

Once only in the biblical plays do we approach within
reasonable distance of that sympathetic interpretation of
Nature which characterises many of the plays of Shakespeare.
This is in the story of the Resurrection as told in the York
cycle. Anna is conversing with Pilate, Caiaphas and the
centurion concerning the death of Christ, and the dramatist,
expanding St Matthew's account of the convulsion of Nature
in the hour of death, makes the centurion give a spirited
account of what happened:

> All elementis, both olde and ȝing,
> In ther maneres þai made mornyng,
>   In ilke a stede;
> And knewe be countenaunce þat þer kyng
>   Was done to dede.
>
> Þe sonne for woo he waxed all wanne,
> Þe mone and sterres of schynyng blanne,
> Þe erthe tremeled, and also manne
>   be-gan to speke ;

Þe stones þat never was stered or þanne
gune a-sondir breke.

If there is little reference to Nature in the biblical
Mysteries, there is still less in most of the Morality plays and
Interludes, the themes of which offered little scope for
landscape painting. The lyric element in these plays slightly
exceeds that of the Mysteries and once or twice these lyrics
introduce the country and country life. Thus in *Lusty
Juventus*[1], one of the latest of the series (circ. 1547),
Juventus, Fellowship, Hypocrisy and Abominable Living join
in a song in which the old theme of the pleasures of youth
and the beauty of May is pleasingly set forth:

> Do not the flowers spring fresh and gay,
> Pleasant and sweet in the month of May?
> And when their time cometh, they fade away;
> > *Report me to you, report me to you.*
>
> Be not the trees in winter bare?
> Like unto their kind, such they are;
> And when they spring, their fruits declare.
> > *Report me to you, report me to you.*
>
> What should youth do with the fruits of age,
> But live in pleasure in his passage?
> For when age cometh, his lusts will suage:
> > *Report me to you, report me to you.*

The *Interlude of the Four Elements*[2], printed in 1519, is
a curious piece of work, introducing learned dissertations on
such topics as the situation of the four elements, the cause
of rain, snow, wind and thunder, and of the ebb and flow
of the sea. But although the speeches of Natura Naturata
and Studious Desire on these matters are intimately concerned
with the physical interpretation of Nature, they have alas!
nothing to do with its poetic interpretation, and we may
safely follow the self-cancelling advice of the author in his
preface, and "leave out much of the sad matter" in such a
study as this.

As the romantic drama grew shapely through its contact
with Latin plays, and advanced along the two paths of tragedy

---

[1] Printed in Dodsley's *Old English Plays*, ed. Hazlitt, Vol. II.
[2] Dodsley, Vol. I.

and comedy, the dramatist's fondness for setting his plot
against a background of scenic description also developed.
Classical study led to the introduction of mythological renderings
of such phenomena as nightfall or sunrise, by means of which
the dramatist kept his audience informed of the time of day at
which any particular action takes place. Thus the play of
Gorboduc[1]) commences with a picture of dawn succeeding night:

> *Viden.* The silent night that brings the quiet pawse
> From painfull travailes to the wearie daye,
> Prolonges my carefull thoughts, and makes me blame
> The slow Aurore that so, for love or shame,
> Doth longe delaye to shew her blushing face;
> And now the daie renewes my griefull plainte.

In the field of comedy *Gammer Gurton's Needle*[2]) is an
important play for our present purpose. The play introduces
no descriptions of landscape, but its author, William Stevenson,
makes a notable advance in choosing a story of English rustic
life as the subject of his plot. It is true that the famous
Shepherds' Play of the Wakefield cycle anticipates *Gammer
Gurton's Needle* in this direction, but whereas that play stands
alone, the work of Stevenson paves the way for those delightful scenes of country life which Greene has given us in
Friar Bacon and Friar Bungay, and Shakespeare in *As You
Like It* and *A Winter's Tale*.

The plays of Lyly,[3]) with the exception of *The Woman in
the Moon*, are in prose, and concern us only in as far as relates
to their lyrics. Of these the song which Tryco sings in the fifth
act of *Alexander and Campaspe* brings us nearest to Nature:

> What bird so sings yet so dos wayle?
> O 'tis the ravish'd nightingale.
> "Jug, jug, jug, jug, tereu," she cryes;
> And still her woes at midnight rise.
> Brave prick song, who is't now we heare?
> None but the larke so shrill and cleare.
> How at heaven's gate she claps her wings,
> The morne not waking till shee sings!
> Heark, heark, with what a pretty throat
> Poor Robin-Redbreast tunes his note!

---

[1]) *Sackville's Works*, ed. R. W. Sackville-West, 1859.
[2]) Dodsley's *Old English Plays*, Vol. III.
[3]) *Complete Works*, ed. Warwick Bond, 1902.

> Heark how the jolly cuckoes sing
> "Cuckoe", to welcome in the spring;
> "Cuckoe", to welcome in the spring.

The honour is sometimes claimed for Lyly of having first introduced lyric verse into the drama. This is not strictly true, for songs appear at rare intervals both in the biblical plays and the Moralities[1]); but it was Lyly who first made such dramatic songs general. It is a fitting symbol of the moulding and refining influence of Lyly on Shakespeare that this song of Trycho should find an echo in the matchless "Hark, hark! the lark at heaven's gate sings" of Imogen.

Coming in the next place to the band of University playwrights — Greene, Peele, Marlowe and Kyd — who stand between Lyly and Shakespeare, we find the dramatic interpretation of Nature extending its borders on every side. The romantic idealism of Greene and Peele finds a channel in the painting of scenes of country life, while in Marlowe and Kyd Nature is brought into very close relation with human emotion and human strivings. The open-air freshness which we meet with in the plays of Robert Greene[2]) (1560?—1592), and which contrasts so forcibly with the squalour of his life, is most noticeable in the Fressingfield scenes of *Friar Bacon and Friar Bungay*. Here there is little deliberate landscape painting, and, accordingly, little which lends itself to quotation, but Greene creates an atmosphere the wholesomeness and charm of which will last for all time. Moreover, while he has cast upon the person of his Margaret an idealising glow, he has avoided the artificiality of pastoral convention. Margaret, though she talks glibly of Phœbe and Semele, Paris and Œnone, is a true daughter of the farm, and rightly describes herself and her companion Joan as "country sluts of merry Fressingfield". Prince Edward finds her otherwise employed than the heroines of the courtly pastorals:

---

[1]) For instance, "The Good Gossips' Song" in the Noah Mystery of the Chester cycle, and the song from *Lusty Juventus*, given above.
[2]) *The Works of Greene and Peele*, ed. Dyce, 1858.

> Into the milk-house went I with the maid,
> And there amongst the cream-bowls she did shine
> As Pallas 'mongst her princely huswifery:
> She turn'd her smock over her lily arms,
> And div'd them into milk to run her cheese;
> But, whiter than the milk, her crystal skin,
> Checked with lines of azure, made her blush
> That art or nature durst bring for compare.

In thus lighting up English country life with the radiance of his own idealism, Greene was doing high service for dramatic literature. *Gammer Gurton's Needle* had painted in realistic fashion the humours of English farm life, but it was Greene who first saw, and made his spectators see, the poetry of that life.

Greene's other plays present little of importance for our purpose here; he is generally disinclined to introduce descriptions of scenery, but the occasional Nature-similes, scattered through his plays, disclose his prompt discernment of natural beauty. The following, from *A Looking-Glass for London*, which Greene wrote in collaboration with Lodge, is as delicate as anything in Shakespeare:

> Sleep like the smiling purity of heaven,
> When mildest wind is loth to blend the peace;
> Blest may you be, like to the flow'ring sheaves,
> That play with gentle winds in summertime.

George Peele (1558?—1597), while inferior to Greene as a revealer of the grace and charm of English country life, is a much more deliberate painter of scenery. Dramatic effect is indeed often sacrificed by Peele in order to introduce some piece of description which shall set forth the riches of his fancy and his love for gorgeous colouring. The speech of Flora in the first scene of *The Arraignment of Paris* may serve as a good illustration of his manner:

> Not Iris, in her pride and bravery,
> Adorns her arch with such variety;
> Nor doth the milk-white way, in frosty night,
> Appear so fair and beautiful in sight,
> As do these fields and groves and sweetest bowers,
> Bestrewed and decked with parti-coloured flowers.
> Along the bubbling brooks and silver glide
> That at the bottom do in silence slide,

> The water-flowers and lilies on the banks,
> Like blazing comets, burgeon all in ranks;
> Under the hawthorn and the poplar-tree,
> Where sacred Phœbe may delight to be,
> The primrose, and the purple hyacinth,
> The dainty violet, and the wholesome minth,
> The double daisy and the cowslip, queen
> Of summer flowers, do overpeer the green;
> And round about the valley as ye pass,
> Ye may ne see for peeping flowers the grass:
> That well the mighty Juno, and the rest,
> May boldly think to be a welcome guest
> On Ida hills, when to approve the king,
> The Queen of Flowers prepares a second spring. I., 1.

Here the light play of Peele's fancy is at its best: what might have been a mere catalogue is raised to the level of true poetry by the shaping hand of a great word-artist and a great colorist.

The thirst for beauty which the Renascence had so potently stimulated was as keenly felt by Peele as by any poet of his generation. In his *David and Bethsabe* he handles a theme which might have formed the subject of one of the early Mystery-plays. But how different is Peele's treatment of the story from that which would have been possible to any of the Mystery-writers! He wantons in the sensuous beauty which certain situations of the plot presented to him, and festoons such scenes with landscape description of exotic colour and fragrance. Bethsabe's address to the Zephyr, overheard by the amorous David, is a case in point:

> Come, gentle Zephyr, tricked with those perfumes
> That erst in Eden sweetened Adam's love,
> And stroke my bosom with thy silken fan:
> This shade, sun-proof, is yet no proof for thee;
> Thy body smoother than this waveless spring,
> And purer than the substance of the same,
> Can creep through that his lances cannot pierce;
> Thou, and thy sister, soft and sacred air,
> Goddess of life and governess of health,
> Keep every fountain fresh and arbour sweet;
> No brazen gate her passage can repulse,
> Nor busy thicket bar thy subtle breath;
> Then deck thee with thy loose delightsome robes,

> And on thy wings bring delicate perfumes,
> To play the wanton with us through the leaves.

The spirit of the Renascence, with its unquenchable thirst for beauty, breathes in these lines, as in so much of Peele's work.

Thomas Nash (1567—1601), besides assisting Marlowe in his *Dido, Queen of Carthage,* was the sole author of the comedy, *Summer's Last Will and Testament*[1]) (acted 1593), which celebrates Henry VIII.'s famous jester. In playful reference to his hero's name, Nash introduces the four seasons amongst his characters, and the song which is sung by Ver, as he enters with his train, "overlaid with suits of green moss, representing short grass", is one of the most beautiful spring-songs in Elizabethan poetry, and should serve to keep Nash's memory fresh, when his novels and pamphlets are long forgotten:

> Spring, the sweet spring, is the year's pleasant king,
> Then blooms each thing, then maids dance in a ring,
> Cold doth not sting, the pretty birds do sing,
> Cuckoo, jug, jug, pu-we, to-wit, to-whoo.

> The palm and may make country houses gay,
> Lambs frisk and play, the shepherds pipe all day,
> And hear we aye birds tune this merry lay,
> Cuckoo, jug, jug, pu-we, to-wit, to-whoo.

> The fields breathe sweet, the daisies kiss our feet,
> Young lovers meet, old wives a-sunning sit;
> In every street these tunes our ears do greet,
> Cuckoo, jug, jug, pu-we, to-wit, to-whoo.
>   Spring, the sweet spring.

Christopher Marlowe (1564—1593)[2]) surpasses all his predecessors in the domain of Nature-poetry as in so much else. The exuberant wealth of his genius, expressing itself in luxuriance of fancy and pomp of words, gives a heightened effect to all his landscape scenes.' He rarely indulges in mere scenic description, but anticipates Shakespeare in his recognition of a bond of sympathy between Nature and humanity. Thus in his earliest work, *Tamburlaine,* the hero, stirred to the depths of his soul by the death of Zenocrate, exclaims :—

---

1) Dodsley, Vol. VIII.
2) *The Works of Christopher Marlowe,* ed. Dyce, 1850.

Black is the beauty of the brightest day;
The golden ball of heaven's eternal fire,
That danced with glory on the silver waves,
Now wants the fuel that inflam'd his beams;
And all with faintness, and for foul disgrace,
He binds his temples with a frowning cloud,
Ready to darken earth with endless night.
Zenocrate, that gave him light and life,
Whose eyes shot fire from their ivory brows,
And temper'd every soul with lively heat,
Now by the malice of the angry skies,
Whose jealousy admits no second mate,
Draws in the comfort of her latest breath,
All dazzled with the hellish mists of death.

*　*　*

Apollo, Cynthia, and the ceaseless lamps
That gently look'd upon this loathsome earth,
Shine downwards now no more, but deck the heavens
To entertain divine Zenocrate:
The crystal springs, whose taste illuminates
Refined eyes with an eternal sight,
Like tried silver run through Paradise
To entertain divine Zenocrate.

Part II., Act II., Scene IV.

Amid all the bluster and fanfaronnade of this declamation there is heard the accent of a genius of rarest quality and of limitless daring. Tamburlaine, in his lordly imperiousness, feels that Nature itself is subject to his will, and must mourn with him in his hour of grief. The same thought finds still more grandiloquent utterance in the closing scene of this play, when death at last assails Tamburlaine himself:

Theridamas. Weep, heavens, and vanish into liquid tears!
Fall, stars that govern his nativity,
And summon all the shining lamps of heaven
To cast their bootless fires to the earth,
And shed their feeble influence in the air;
Muffle your beauties with eternal clouds;
For Hell and Darkness pitch their pitchy tents,
And Death, with armies of Cimmerian spirits,
Gives battle 'gainst the heart of Tamburlaine!
Now, in defiance of that wonted love
Your sacred virtues pour'd upon his throne,
And made his state an honour to the heavens,
These cowards invisibly assail his soul,

> And threaten conquest on our sovereign;
> But if he die, your glories are disgrac'd,
> Earth droops, and says that hell in heaven is plac'd!

This attitude towards the natural world, though it may be expressed by the general term sympathetic, is quite different from the sympathetic interpretation of Shakespeare's plays. In them Nature is made to reflect the emotions of men, storm on land or sea synchronising with the storm of inward conflicts, while calm abroad corresponds to calm within the human breast. Here something else is aimed at. The interpretation is sympathetic in so far as Nature is recognised as having an influence upon humanity; what is new and peculiarly Marlowesque is the idea that Nature can be made obedient to the will of man.

On the rare occasions on which Marlowe introduces pure description into his plays, he appears as the corrival of Peele, and even of Spenser, in his command over the sensuous beauty of Nature. The nurse's description of her orchard and garden in *Dido* is all colour and fragrance:

> I have an orchard that hath store of plums,
> Brown almonds, services, ripe figs and dates,
> Dewberries, apples, yellow oranges;
> A garden where are bee-hives full of honey,
> Musk-roses, and a thousand sort of flowers;
> And in the midst doth run a silver stream,
> Where thou shalt see the red-gill'd fishes leap,
> White swans, and many lovely water-fowls.
> Now speak, Ascanius, will you go or no?
>
> *Dido*, Act IV.

Marlowe's genius was so essentially poetic that it comes at times into conflict with his sense of dramatic fitness. Barabas, the Jew of Malta, is one of the most truculent characters in the whole range of Elizabethan tragedy, yet Marlowe makes him express his delight on recovering his money-bags from the hand of Abigail in verses of the most delicate beauty:

> Now, Phœbus, ope the eye-lids of the day,
> And, for the raven, wake the morning lark,
> That I may hover with her in the air,
> Singing o'er these, as she does o'er her young.
>
> *Jew of Malta*, Act II.

Thomas Kyd[1]) (1557—1595) reveals in his plays a considerable insight into Nature, and has some intuition also of a sense of sympathy between Nature and man. He is fond of indicating the change from day to night or night to day, and bedecks his descriptions of such changes with classical allusions, though at the same time he also falls back upon his own insight into Nature. Thus in the third Act of his *Cornelia*, his heroine describes with considerable detail the coming of the dawn:

Cornelia: The cheerful cock, (the sad night's comforter)
　　　　Waiting upon the rising of the sun,
　　　　Doth sing to see how Cyntia shrinks her horn,
　　　　While Clytia takes her progress to the east;
　　　　Where, wringing wet with drops of silver dew,
　　　　Her wonted tears of love she doth renew.
　　　　The wand'ring swallow, with her broken song,
　　　　The country-wench unto her work awakes;
　　　　While Cytherea, sighing, walks to seek
　　　　Her murder'd love transform'd into a rose.

In the same play he introduces a suggestive simile of Alpine scenery:

　　　　As on the Alps the sharp Nor-North-east winds,
　　　　Shaking a pine-tree with their greatest power,
　　　　One while the top doth almost touch the earth,
　　　　And then it rises with a counterbuff.
　　　　So did the armies press and charge each other,
　　　　With selfsame courage, worth and weapons, too.
　　　　　　　　　　　　　　　　　　　　　　Act V.

In his *Spanish Tragedy* he follows the example of Marlowe, and represents Nature as obeying the will of man. He expresses this idea with that vehemence which the next generation of dramatists singled out for persistent ridicule, but which is just as characteristic of Marlowe as of Kyd:

Hieronymo. The blust'ring winds, conspiring with my words,
　　　　At my lament have moved the leafless trees,
　　　　Disrob'd the meadows of their flow'red green,
　　　　Made mountains marsh with springtide of my tears,
　　　　And broken through the brazen gates of hell.
　　　　　　　　　　　　　　　　　　　　　　III. vii.

---

[1]) *Works,* ed. Boas, 1901.

Chapter XV.

SHAKESPEARE.

In the plays of Skakespeare the wheel comes full circle. In his interpretation of Nature, as in so much else, Shakespeare has broken down all the barriers which obscured the poetic vision of his predecessors, and has made all Nature his. He lays his spell upon all the manifestations of the natural world, recognises beauty or suggestiveness in them all, and finds everywhere analogies to the life of humanity. The delight of Chaucer or Spenser in the sensuous beauty of Nature is his, but so also is Cynewulf's or the Gawayne-poet's appreciation of the grandiose. He sees poetry in the storm which sweeps "with eyeless rage" across the northern moorland in *King Lear* no less than in the soft moonlight of an Italian night in Portia's garden at Belmont. The sentimental attitude towards Nature of the Elizabethan sonneteers is everywhere reflected in his poems, while, even in so early a work as *Venus and Adonis*, we see how this sentimentalism becomes caught up into that more transcendent sphere of poetry in which faith in the sympathetic interaction of Nature and humanity becomes implicit:

No flower was nigh, no grass, herb, leaf or weed,
But stole his blood and seem'd with him to bleed.
This solemn sympathy poor Venus noteth.   1055—57.

In his *Tamburlaine*, we see Marlowe groping after this sense of sympathy between Nature and man, and when he discerns it, making it subservient to that will-worship which is the be-all and end-all of Marlowesque tragedy: but what is but dimly, and in part falsely, conceived by Marlowe, is by Shakespeare firmly grasped, and consecrated to poetic service.

The limitations imposed upon the poetic interpretation of Nature by the drama hamper Shakespeare to a less extent than they did his predecessors. He encounters those limitations with limitations of another kind, and makes the shortcomings of the Elizabethan carpenter and stage-decorator the occasion for some of his most exquisite scenic description. A single illustration will make this point clear. In *Macbeth*, when Duncan and his attendants approach Macbeth's castle, Shakespeare saw the need of bringing the situation and aspect of the castle clearly before the minds of the spectators. The stage decoration was incapable of doing this; hence the noble verses which usher in the scene:

Duncan. This castle hath a pleasant seat; the air
Nimbly and sweetly recommends itself
Unto our gentle senses.

Banquo.   This guest of summer,
The temple-haunting martlet, does approve
By his loved mansionry that the heaven's breath
Smells wooingly here: no jutty, frieze,
Buttress, nor coign of vantage, but this bird
Hath made his pendent bed and procreant cradle :
Where they most breed and haunt, I have observed,
The air is delicate.
                                    Macbeth I. vi. 1—10.

These verses of description serve a double purpose. Placed as they are on the lips of the two men so soon to be murdered — the one within the castle, the other in its precincts — they carry with them a force of tragic irony. The delicate air and idyllic calm which the sight of the castle suggests to Duncan and Banquo are in mocking contrast to the deeds of murder so soon to be committed there. Besides this, these verses bring before the spectator's mind the character of the situation. They do this, not by means of an elaborate description of the castle with its moat and ramparts, gates and portcullises, but by singling out one detail in the land-scape — the house-martin building its nest under the shelter of the buttresses — which gives a key to the whole, and by stimulating the spectator's imagination, enables him to realise the whole scene and the prevailing mood of the landscape.

In dealing with Shakespeare's interpretation of Nature,
it is convenient to accept the usual classification of his works
into Poems, Comedies, Histories and Tragedies, and at the
same time to follow, as closely as possible, the order of
composition. A final class will contain those romantic dramas
which belong to the closing years of his dramatic career.

The Poems.

Shakespeare's poems belong to an early period of his
life, and to a time at which he may be expected to be under
the influence of earlier masters, and ready to bow the knee
to accepted conventions. Such is, however, only to a very
slight extent the case with his interpretation of Nature.

In *Venus and Adonis* he handled a classical myth, yet
the poem is singularly free from the the tawdry mythological fancies — the endless references to Phœbus, Titan,
Aurora and Zephyrus, — which are so frequently met with
in poems of this character. The sanity of Shakespeare's taste
enabled him to avoid this easily besetting sin of courtly
poetry. In other directions the influence of classical poetry,
though apparent, is never oppressive. Ovid is more or less
followed in the story of the metamorphosis of Adonis into
a flower, and occasionally Shakespeare indulges in a certain
Ovidian lusciousness of description; but this appears less in
the painting of Nature than in the love-plaints of the amorous
goddess. *Venus and Adonis* contains very little pure description of natural scenery. Scarcely any attempt is made
to paint the scene where Venus first meets her rose-cheeked
boy, or that in which she finds him dead. But that Shakespeare could describe with the most complete individualisation
is apparent from the detailed picture of Adonis' steed, (*Venus
and Adonis, vv.* 295—306). This description is a magnificent
tour de force, but much of it is scarcely poetry. It would
do credit to a horse-fancier, but is not quite worthy of
Shakespeare. It was a method of description, too, which he
never repeated; his subsequent method was to introduce, in

the place of a bewilderingly exhaustive enumeration
the features in a picture, a wise selection of the salient
points.

The description of the boar is a distinct advance on
that of the steed : here there is less detail and more poetry :

> On his bow-back he hath a battle set
> Of bristly pikes, that ever threat his foes ;
> His eyes, like glow-worms, shine when he doth fret ;
> His snout digs sepulchres where'er he goes ;
> Being moved, he strikes whate'er is in his way,
> And whom he strikes his crooked tushes slay.
>
> His brawny sides, with hairy bristles armed,
> Are better proof than thy spear's point can enter ;
> His short thick neck cannot be easily harmed ;
> Being ireful, on the lion he will venture ;
> The thorny brambles and embracing bushes,
> As fearful of him, part ; through whom he rushes.
>
> vv. 619—630.

In addition to such purely descriptive passages as these,
the poem is full of similes and comparisons drawn from
natural life, and revealing a very piercing observation of
Nature. There is the simile of the mountain snow melting
before the midday sun (v. 750), and of the snail,

> Whose tender horns being hit,
> Shrinks backward in his shelly cave with pain.
>
> vv. 1033—1034.

The earthquake, shaking earth's foundations, is described
(v. 1046), as also the adder "wreathed up in fatal folds"
(v. 880), and the "dive-dapper" or little grebe, "peering through
a wave" (v. 86.). With the exception of the passage already
quoted (p. 216), there is very little trace in *Venus and Adonis*
of a sympathetic interpretation of Nature. It is true that
Shakespeare describes how the bushes endeavour to retard
Venus in her pursuit, and how birds, beasts and fishes delight
in the beauty of Adonis, but this is merely Ovidian fancy,
reproduced by Shakespeare, but scarcely felt by him.

In *The Rape of Lucrece* Nature is less before Shakespeare's mind than in *Venus and Adonis*. Where description
occurs, it assumes the highly rhetorical character which is
so firmly stamped upon the whole course of the poem. Thus

Lucrece's address to "comfort-killing Night" is sheer rhetoric, running riotously through a waste of verbiage. Nature-similes, and analogies which do not extend to fully developed similes, are fairly frequent, while compared with *Venus and Adonis*, there is an advance in the use of metaphor. Of the many similes, perhaps the most striking is that of the incoming tide:

> As through an arch the violent roaring tide
> Outruns the eye that doth behold his haste,
> Yet in the eddy boundeth in his pride
> Back to the strait that forced him on so fast,
> In rage sent out, recall'd in rage, being past:
> Even so his sighs, his sorrows, make a saw,
> To push grief on and back the same grief draw.
>
> *vv.* 1667—1673.

In some of the comparisons there is a strong suggestion of the far-fetched imagery which characterises both the euphuistic writings of Shakespeare's contemporaries and also the fantastic poems of the Caroline period. Of such a nature is the following:

> Ay me! the bark peel'd from the lofty pine,
> His leaves will wither and his sap decay:
> So must my soul, her bark being peel'd away.
>
> *vv.* 1167—1169.

But *The Rape of Lucrece* gives promise of that deep sense of sympathy between man and Nature which Shakespeare brought out so forcibly in his dramas. On the fatal night, Nature is brought into accord with the crime to be committed, just as in *King Lear* the tempest on the heath accords with the tempest in Lear's own soul, and enhances the tragic effect of the main issue. In *Lucrece*, this idea is only faintly suggested, but it is nevertheless there:

> Now stole upon the time the dead of night,
> When heavy sleep had closed up mortal eyes:
> No comfortable star did lend his light,
> No noise but owls' and wolves' death-boding cries,
> Now serves the season that they may surprise
> The silly lambs: pure thoughts are dead and still,
> While lust and murder wakes to stain and kill.
>
> *vv.* 162—168.

The *Sonnets*, written when Shakespeare's experience of life was greater, and his genius more matured, are extremely rich in references to external Nature. The narrow compass of the sonnet forbade detailed description, but in the similes and metaphors, scattered in rich profusion among these poems, there is abundant illustration of the beauty and suggestiveness which Shakespeare discovered in the world which lay around him. How splended is the comparison in Sonnet LXXIII. of the autumn of human life to the autumn of Nature! —

> That time of year thou mayst in me behold,
> When yellow leaves, or few, or none, do hang
> Upon those boughs, which shake against the cold,
> Bare ruin'd choirs, where late the sweet birds sang.

Another, and almost equally masterly picture of autumn occurs in Sonnet XII: —

> When lofty trees I see barren of leaves,
> Which erst from heat did canopy the herd,
> And summer's green all girded up in sheaves,
> Borne on the bier with white and bristly beard,
> Then of thy beauty do I question make,
> That thou among the wastes of time must go,
> Since sweets and beauties do themselves forsake,
> And die as fast as they see others grow.

In Sonnet VII., contrary to the habit of his later years, Shakespeare elaborates to its farthest limits the simile between the life of man and the daily course of the sun, the whole sonnet being concerned with the setting forth of this analogy :

> Lo, in the orient, when the gracious light
> Lifts up his burning head, each under eye
> Doth homage to his new-appearing sight,
> Serving with looks his sacred majesty ;
> And having climb'd the steep-up heavenly hill,
> Resembling strong youth in his middle age,
> Yet mortal looks adore his beauty still,
> Attending on his golden pilgrimage ;
> But when from highmost pitch, with weary car,
> Like feeble age, he reeleth from the day,
> The eyes, 'fore duteous, now converted are
> From his low tract, and look another way :
> > So thou, thyself out-going in thy noon,
> > Unlook'd on diest, unless thou get a son.

The sonnets reveal Shakespeare as a very close observer
and masterly portrayer of the sky and of all atmospheric
phenomena. His description of the sun's course through the
heavens has just been quoted; in Sonnet XXXIII. he paints
with supreme power the beauty of a clear sunrise followed
by a cloudy day. The scene is introduced in order to
illustrate the change which has taken place in his relations
with his friend : —

> Full many a glorious morning have I seen
> Flatter the mountain-tops with sovereign eye,
> Kissing with golden face the meadows green,
> Gilding pale streams with heavenly alchemy;
> Anon permit the basest clouds to ride
> With ugly rack on his celestial face,
> And from the forlorn world his visage hide,
> Stealing unseen to west with this disgrace :
> Even so my sun one early morn did shine
> With all-triumphant splendour on my brow;
> But, out, alack ! he was but one hour mine,
> The region cloud hath mask'd him from me now.

Shakespeare's love for detailed simile at this period of
his career is seen in the reference to the rose and canker-
bloom in Sonnet LIV.; certain flowers are again and again
pressed into the service of the sonnets, and in each case
they are introduced to point an anology to human concerns.
Thus in Sonnet XCVIII., Shakespeare refers to the flowers
of "proud-pied April, dress'd in all his trim", and in the
succeeding sonnet he fancifully accuses the flowers of having
drawn their beauty and fragrance from his friend :

> The forward violet thus did I chide :
> Sweet thief, whence didst thou steal thy sweet that smells,
> If not from my love's breath? The purple pride
> Which on thy soft cheek for complexion dwells
> In my love's veins thou hast too grossly dyed.
> The lily I condemned for thy hand,
> And buds of marjoram had stol'n thy hair;
> The roses fearfully on thorns did stand,
> One blushing shame, another white despair.

The Comedies.

Shakespeare's comedies vary very much both in the
degree and in the manner in which references to Nature

appear. In *The Comedy of Errors* there is scarcely a single reference to the associations of the country, whereas such open-air comedies as *A Midsummer Night's Dream* and *As You Like It* are full of the most delicate landscape painting. Yet even in *The Comedy of Errors* the reader is made to feel Shakespeare's extraordinary insight into Nature, when he meets with such a verse as, —

> In sap-consuming winter's drizzled snow.
>
> V. i. 310.

The songs of Spring and Winter at the close of *Love's Labour's Lost* introduce a landscape scene somewhat different from those already noticed. The two parallel pictures are marked by simple homeliness, and breathe the atmosphere of the English farm-yard. Human life is absent from neither, the characters introduced harmonising in every way with the scenes amid which they are placed.

The detailed elaboration of a landscape scene, which has been noticed in connection with Shakespeare's poems, appears also in his early comedies. In *The Two Gentlemen of Verona* the course of a river is described with that love for fine phrasing and rich sensuous beauty which we associate with Keats, but which is equally characteristic of Shakespeare in his early work :

> The current that with gentle murmur glides,
> Thou know'st, being stopp'd, impatiently doth rage :
> But when his fair course is not hindered,
> He makes sweet music with the enamell'd stones,
> Giving a gentle kiss to every sedge
> He overtaketh in his pilgrimage;
> And so by many winding nooks he strays,
> With willing sport, to the wild ocean.
>
> II, vii. 25—32.

It was the rare beauty of such descriptions as this which appealed so powerfully to Shakespeare's contemporaries, and won for him the epithets of "honey-tongued" and" mellifluous".

The famous moonlight-scene at the close of *The Merchant of Venice* furnishes a striking instance of Shakespeare's sympathetic interpretation of Nature. After the storm and stress of the trial-scene, comes the idyllic calm of the evening at Belmont. The moonlight sleeping upon the bank, the sweet wind gently kissing the trees, and the myriad stars which, like "patines of bright gold", inlay the floor of heaven, are singled out as illustrating the exquisite beauty of this Italian night. By this time Shakespeare had learnt to paint his landscape in accordance with a principle of wise eclecticism, rather than by an accumulation of minute details. The most striking features are singled out, and by virtue of these the whole picture is clearly imaged in the reader's mind.

The delicate workmanship, airy grace and arch humour of *A Midsummer Night's Dream* have been recognised by every Shakespearean student. In this play the dramatist, claiming as his own the delightful fairy-lore of rural England, has placed his fairies amid scenery of the most beautiful character. Elizabethan literature is rich in the spoils of popular fairy-lore. Oberon, king of fairyland, came into England with Lord Berners's rendering of the French prose-romance, *Huon de Bordeaux* in 1534, and subsequent editions of this work in 1570 and 1601 point to its popularity during the Elizabethan age. Shakespeare's appreciation of fairy-lore is revealed not only in *A Midsummer Night's Dream,* but also in the familiar description of Queen Mab in *Romeo and Juliet*; while outside of Shakespeare, there is the dainty portrayal of fairy life given by Drayton in his *Nymphidia,* and by Herrick in certain poems of his *Hesperides,* to mention only the greatest of the Elizabethan poets who felt and expressed the poetic graces which lurk hidden in this lore.

The plot of *A Midsummer Night's Dream* is laid in Attica, but in reality the scenery is English — the scenery of the English midland counties where Shakespeare's early years were spent. Detailed descriptions of landscape are here even more frequent than is usually the case in these plays. In Act II, Scene 1., occurs Titania's description of a rainy season, the picture being set forth with great fulness of detail:

> Therefore the winds, piping to us in vain,
> As in revenge, have suck'd up from the sea
> Contagious fogs; which falling in the land,

Have every pelting river made so proud,
That they have overborne their continents:
The ox hath therefore stretch'd his yoke in vain,
The ploughman lost his sweat; and the green corn
Hath rotted ere his youth attain'd a beard:
The fold stands empty in the drowned field,
And crows are fatted with the murrion flock:

*   *   *

And thorough this distemperature we see
The seasons alter: hoary-headed frosts
Fall in the fresh lap of the crimson rose,
And on old Hiems' thin and icy crown
An odorous chaplet of sweet summer buds
Is, as in mockery, set; the spring, the summer,
The chiding autumn, angry winter, change
Their wonted liveries; and the mazed world,
By their increase, now knows not which is which.
II. 1. 88—114.

This picture of a deluged land is painted with astonishing force: the range is wider than that of the landscapes of Shakespeare's poems, and the selection of details is extremely apt. In sweetness of verse, however, though not in extent of range, it is surpassed by the oft-quoted speech of Oberon later in the same scene.

I know a bank where the wild thyme blows,
Where oxlips and the nodding violet grows;
Quite over-canopied with luscious woodbine
With sweet musk-roses, and with eglantine.
II. 1. 249—252.

Theseus' description of his Spartan hounds in Act IV. Scene 1 becomes especially interesting when placed in comparison with the description of the horse in *Venus and Adonis*, for the advance in poetic strength is incalculable:

Their heads are hung
With ears that sweep away the morning dew:
Crook-knee'd and dew-lapp'd like Thessalian bulls;
Slow in pursuit, but match'd in mouth like bells
Each under each.
IV. 1. 117—121.

This does not yield a single point to the other picture on the score of exactness of observation, but here the details, instead of being baldly enumerated, are adorned with the richest brocade of poetic diction. Besides pure description, *A Midsummer Night's Dream* is extremely rich in similes drawn from Nature. The exquisite comparison of Hermia and Helena to a "double cherry seeming parted" is too familiar for quotation; no less apposite is the simile introduced to illustrate the flight of the "rude mechanicals" when Bottom appears in their midst wearing the ass's head:

> As wild geese that the creeping fowler eye,
> Or russet-pated choughs, many in sort,
> Rising and cawing at the gun's report,
> Sever themselves and madly sweep the sky,
> So, at his sight, away his fellows fly.
>
> III. ii. 20—24.

That Shakespeare was a naturalist of no mean order has been forcibly shown by Mr. J. E. Harting in his work, *The Ornithology of Shakespeare*, and the above simile, taken with many others, illustrates how close was his observation of the habits and movements of birds.

It is generally acknowledged that much of the charm of Swift's *Gulliver's Travels* lies in the author's very fine sense of proportion in dealing with his giants and pygmies; the same consistency of diminution appears in the Elizabethan descriptions of fairy-life, in which Shakespeare set a fashion that was afterwards followed by Drayton, Herrick and others. The commissions of Titania to the attendant fairies in *A Midsummer Night's Dream* are characterised by this exquisite sense of proportion, as well as by a delicacy and gossamer lightness, born of the daintiest fancy:

> Feed him with apricocks and dewberries,
> With purple grapes, green figs and mulberries:
> The honey-bags steal from the humble-bees,
> And for night-tapers crop their waxen thighs,
> And light them at the fiery glow-worm's eyes,
> To have my love to bed and to arise;
> And pluck the wings from painted butterflies,
> To fan the moonbeams from his sleeping eyes.
>
> III. 1. 169—176.

In *As You Like It* Shakespeare returns once more to the free life of the forest. In founding this play upon Lodge's pastoral romance, he shows his attitude towards the Arcadianism of the Renascence pastoral. In this play Shakespeare ridicules, indeed, what Crabbe has called the "mechanic echoes of the Mantuan song". The matter-of-fact love-making of Touchstone and Audrey is introduced as a wholesome corrective to the amorous fancies of Silvius and Phœbe, who, in their turn, echo the love-sick complaints of the shepherds and shepherdesses of Lodge's pastoral. The exiled duke and his band of courtiers accept their enforced retirement to the woodlands with cheerful contentment, and endeavour to find 'sweet uses' in rural seclusion as in adversity. The duke is ready to attune his ear to the voice of Nature, and to find tongues in trees, books in the running brooks and sermons in stones ; but when opportunity comes, he is glad to leave this forest life and return to the city and the court. *As You Like It* furnishes us in fact with a fairly clear insight into Shakespeare's attitude towards the pastoral ideal. That ideal appealed to him in as far as it meant an appreciation of rural life and rural scenery ; but when it tried to make him shut his eyes upon the true aspects of the country, and when it created for itself a fictitious world of nymphs and swains placed amid unnatural surroundings, he covered it with ridicule. He seemed to feel, too, that even what was best in the pastoral ideal was only partially desirable, or desirable only for certain seasons of relaxation after the stress of city life. The exiled duke quits the forest of Arden for the turmoil of the city and the intrigues of the court: in like manner Shakespeare quits the idyllic calm and pastoral seclusion of *As You Like It* for the storm and stress of Roman life in the days of Cæsar and Brutus, or the fetid atmosphere of the court at Elsinore.

The Histories.

In the historical dramas the all-absorbing interest of political struggles would seem to be out of harmony with the study of the natural world and the painting of landscape. This is true as far as pure description is concerned, but the

15*

historical dramas are rich in similes and metaphors, which
exhibit keen insight into the appearance and working of
the things of Nature. In the earlier Histories, too, pure description is by no means absent. Thus in *2 Henry VI.*, there
is a singularly bold and figurative piece of description, conceived in a rather Marlowesque manner, but in every way
worthy of Shakespeare's literary prowess:

> The gaudy, blabbing and remorseful day
> Is crept into the bosom of the sea;
> And now loud-howling wolves arouse the jades
> That drag the tragic melancholy night;
> Who, with their drowzy, slow and flagging wings,
> Clip dead men's graves and from their misty jaws
> Breathe foul contagious darkness in the air.
>
> IV. 1. 1—7.

This description, although occurring in one of the earliest
of Shakespeare's plays, betrays at no point the hand of the
novice. It stands out in bold defiance of the purple and
gold sunset scenes of the conventional Elizabethan school
of poetry. How widely it differs, too, from the idyllic stillness of the nightfall in the closing scene of *The Merchant
of Venice*! The two descriptions, so different in character,
are yet in full accord with the respective situations. In the
comedy, all is repose and calm after storm: in the history,
we are in the midst of a fierce sea-fight, to the horrors of
which this picture of approaching night materially contributes.

In the same play there is introduced, incidentally, a
fine picture of the sea in the hour of tempest. Margaret of
Anjou is speaking, and describing her voyage across the
Channel:

> The splitting rocks cower'd in the sinking sands,
> And would not dash me, with their splitting sides.
>
> III. ii. 97—98.

A sea-storm is again introduced in *2 Henry IV.*, where
it forms a part of the king's famous soliloquy on sleep:

> Wilt thou upon the high and giddy mast
> Seal up the shipboy's eyes, and rock his brains
> In cradle of the rude imperious surge,
> And in the visitation of the winds,

> Who take the ruffian billows by the top,
> Curling their monstrous heads and hanging them
> With deafening clamour in the slippery clouds,
> That, with the hurly, death itself awakes?
>
> III. 1. 18—25.

One other purely descriptive passage may be noticed in connection with the Histories; in *Henry V.* Shakespeare makes the Duke of Burgundy draw a picture of the fields, gardens and vineyards of France, in which the course of the war has forced vegetation to run wild:

> Her vine, the merry cheerer of the heart,
> Unpruned dies; her hedges even-pleach'd,
> Like prisoners wildly overgrown with hair,
> Put forth disorder'd twigs; her fallow leas
> The darnel, hemlock and rank fumitory
> Doth root upon, while that the coulter rusts
> That should deracinate such savagery;
> The even mead, that erst brought sweetly forth
> The freckled cowslip, burnet and green clover,
> Wanting the scythe, all uncorrected, rank,
> Conceives by idleness and nothing teems
> But hateful docks, rough thistles, kecksies, burs,
> Losing both beauty and utility.
>
> V. ii. 41—53.

Similes and comparisons are very frequent in the Histories, and are drawn from the most varied aspects of the great domain of Nature. Occasionally, in his desire for full illustration, Shakespeare passes from one simile to another; thus, in *3 Henry VI.*, the king, describing the changes which take place in the course of the fight, compares the conflict with two natural phenomena:

> This battle fares like to the morning's war,
> When dying clouds contend with growing light,
> What time the shepherd, blowing of his nails,
> Can neither call it perfect day nor night.
> Now sways it this way, like a mighty sea
> Forced by the tide to combat with the wind;
> Now sways it that way, like the self-same seas
> Forced to retire by fury of the wind:
> Sometime the flood prevails, and then the wind.
>
> II. v. 1—9.

In the same play occurs the masterly comparison which Warwick draws between himself in his hour of ruin and the cedar felled by the axé:

> Thus yields the cedar to the axe's edge,
> Whose arms gave shelter to the princely eagle,
> Under whose shade the ramping lion slept,
> Whose top-branch overpeer'd Jove's spreading tree,
> And kept low shrubs from winter's powerful wind.
>
> V. ii. 11—15.

Equally luminous and imaginative are the shorter similes scattered broadcast through the pages of the Histories. Thus in *1 Henry IV.*, the king, referring to the unfortunate Richard, says, —

> So when he had occasion to be seen,
> He was but as the cuckoo is in June,
> Heard, not regarded.
>
> III. ii. 75.

No less pointed is the comparison in *Henry V.* of the precipice overhanging the sea with the brow overhanging the eye:

> Let the brow o'erwhelm it
> As fearfully as doth a galled rock
> O'erhang and jutty his confounded base;
> Swill'd with the wild and wasteful ocean.
>
> III. 1. 13.

Of greater moment than either pure description of landscape, or similes drawn from the natural world, is the sympathetic interpretation of Nature. The Histories are less expressive of this than the Tragedies, but passages may be found in them in which this idea rises to the surface. This implies on Shakespeare's part the recognition of certain clearly marked moods of Nature, and it is in this most especially that his treatment of Nature shows so immense an advance upon that of earlier or contemporary poets. We trace the recognition of this sympathy under its simplest form in the last utterance of the saintly king, Henry VI. Addressing Gloucester, he says, —

> The owl shrieked at thy bird, — an evil sign;
> The night-crow cried, aboding luckless time;

Dogs howled, and hideous tempest shook down trees;
The raven rook'd her on the chimney's top,
And chattering pies in dismal discords sung.
3 *Henry VI.*, V. 6. 44—48.

In the play of *Richard III.*, when this same Gloucester is drawing near to his death on the field of Bosworth, Shakespeare again conceives of Nature as being brought into association with human concerns. The time is an hour after sunrise, but the sun, as Richard avers, "disdains to shine":

The sun will not be seen to-day:
The sky doth frown and lour upon our army.
I would these dewy tears were from the ground.
V. iii. 283.

These verses, regarded by themselves, may seem to be merely the expression of a popular superstition; but when they are read in the light of other passages in Shakespeare's plays, they reveal the dramatist's sense of a sympathy between the outward manifestations of Nature and the life and destiny of men. The Tragedies are eloquent of Shakespeare's faith in this agency of Nature, but before considering them, let us consider the force of those verses with which the fifth act of *I Henry IV.* begins:

King. How bloodily the sun begins to peer
　　　Above yon busky hill! the day looks pale
　　　At his distemperature.
Prince.　　　　　　　The southern wind
　　　Doth play the trumpet to his purposes,
　　　And by his hollow whistling in the leaves
　　　Foretells a tempest and a blustering day.
King. Then with the losers let it sympathise.
　　　For nothing can seem foul to those that win.
V. i. 1—7.

This indication of the climatic conditions under which the fateful battle of Shrewsbury was fought serve the same purpose as the reference to the "temple-haunting martlet" in *Macbeth*, of which notice has already been taken: in the absence of stage-carpentry, they appeal to the inward eye of the spectator and body forth the forms of things unseen. But above all this, they reveal in clearest fashion that sense

of the sympathetic agency of Nature to which reference has
already been made, and of which more will be said later,
inasmuch as it is the most prominent feature in Shakespeare's
interpretation of Nature.

The Tragedies.

In dealing with the treatment of Nature in Shakespeare's
tragedies, it is well to distinguish between those composed
at the outset of his dramatic career — *Titus Andronicus,*
and *Romeo and Juliet* — and the great sequence of tragedies
which belong to the first decade of the seventeenth century. In
the former, Nature is introduced largely by means of pure
description; in the latter, objective landscape painting gives
place to that sympathetic interpretation, by virtue of which
the forces of the natural world are brought into sympathy
with, or antagonism to, the lives of men.

Titus Andronicus is peculiarly rich in natural description.
It contains detailed landscape painting, the mood of which is
now joyous and idyllic, now sombre and desolate. In Act II.
Scene iii., Tamora, addressing Aaron, paints the following
picture in language of surpassing beauty: —

> The birds chant melody on every bush;
> The snake lies rolled in the cheerful sun;
> The green leaves quiver with the cooling wind,
> And make a chequer'd shadow on the ground:
> Under their sweet shade, Aaron, let us sit,
> And, whilst the babbling echo mocks the hounds,
> Replying shrilly to the well-tuned horns,
> As if a double hunt were heard at once,
> Let us sit down and mark their yellowing noise;
>
> *   *   *
>
> Whiles hounds and horns and sweet melodious birds
> Be unto us as is a nurse's song
> Of lullaby to bring her babe asleep.

II. iii. 12—29.

In direct contrast to this picture is that which follows
immediately upon it in the same scene, and of which the
painter is again Tamora : —

A barren, detested vale, you see it is ;
The trees, though summer, yet forlorn and lean,
O'ercome with moss and baleful mistletoe :
Here never shines the sun; here nothing breeds,
Unless the nightly owl or fatal raven.

                                                II. iii. 93—97.

The exquisite Italian landscape of *Romeo and Juliet*, withits serene moonlight nights and golden dawns, is familiar to every student of Shakespeare. We are at all points reminded of the dramatist's early work in the descriptive passages of this play. Again and again there appears a certain fondness for the fanciful imagery of the classic nature-myth, in which the poets of the Renascence found especial delight. Thus in the opening scene, Montague, speaking of his son Romeo, says —

But all so soon as the all-cheering sun
Should in the farthest east begin to draw
The shady curtains from Aurora's bed,
Away from light steals home my heavy son.

                                                I. i. 133.

Similarly, in Juliet's famous soliloquy in Act III., Scene ii.: —

Gallop apace, you fiery-footed steeds,
Towards Phœbus' lodging; such a waggoner
As Phaëthon would whip you to the west,
And bring in cloudy night immediately.   III. ii. 1.

The same fondness for personification appears in the reference to "well-apparell'd April", which is described as treading "on the heel of limping winter", and again, though with more freedom of manner, in the more detailed picture of the wind in Act I. Scene iv.: —

And more inconstant than the wind, who wooes
Even now the frozen bosom of the north,
And, being anger'd, puffs away from thence,
Turning his face to the dew-dropping south.

                                                I. iv. 100.

There is less detailed description in *Romeo and Juliet* than in *Titus Andronicus*, but many exquisite pictures are introduced in outline. Such, for instance, is Romeo's allusion to the moon:

> Lady, by yonder blessed moon I swear,
> That tips with silver all the fruit-tree tops;

II. ii. 108.

or the simile used to describe the entranced Juliet: —

> Death lies on her like an untimely frost
> Upon the sweetest flower of all the field.

IV. v. 28.

The opening verses of the Friar's speech in Act II. Scene iii., while singularly original in idea, show at the same time Shakespeare's youthful delight in mythical allusions: —

> The grey-eyed morn smiles on the frowning night,
> Chequering the eastern clouds with streaks of light,
> And flecked darkness like a drunkard reels
> From forth day's path and Titan's fiery wheels.

But surpassing all in radiant imagery is the famous dawn-song of the lovers, with its references to the lark and the nightingale: —

> It was the lark, the herald of the morn,
> No nightingale: look, love, what envious streaks
> Do lace the severing clouds in yonder east:
> Night's candles are burnt out, and jocund day
> Stands tiptoe on the misty mountain tops:
> I must be gone and live, or stay and die.

III. v. 6—11.

In the series of tragedies written after 1600, there is, as was noticed above, far less description. This applies not only to the purely objective painting of landscape, but also to the landscape scenes which are introduced in simile. In these later plays, similes frequently yield place to metaphors, or, if introduced at all, they are strikingly terse. Thus the familiar comparison in *Julius Cæsar* of the rise and fall in men's fortunes to the flow and ebb of the tide is expressed in metaphor and not in simile. Here the metaphor is pressed to its farthest limits, but elsewhere we find it reduced to the compass of a single word. All this is in keeping with the changes which took place in Shakespeare's poetic style. The ceaseless rush of ideas in the more mature dramas was so great, that it made the careful elaboration of these ideas in exact and detailed language an absolute impossibility.

The tragedies are the arena of the stormiest passions of human nature; everything is in a state of disorder and unrest. To emphasize this, Shakespeare has recourse to the forces of Nature, and in the stormy crises of human life, he introduces the storms which course over land and sea. Thus in *Julius Cæsar* he paints the lurid scene of the thunderstorm which precedes the murder of Cæsar. Casca, describing it, declares: —

> I have seen tempests, when the scolding winds
> Have rived the knotty oaks, and I have seen
> The ambitious ocean swell and rage and foam,
> To be exalted with the threatening clouds;
> But never till to-night, never till now,
> Did I go through a tempest dropping fire.
>
> I. iii. 6.

The storm in *King Lear* is still more impressive, and is brought into still closer relation with human action, and with the tempest which rages in the breast of the aged king. In *Julius Cæsar*, the thunderstorm is introduced rather as a portent of evil than as an evil in itself, for Cæsar is not himself exposed to its inclemency. In the pitiless windstorm which sweeps over a wintry moorland in *King Lear,* thunder plays a part, but what is most impressive is the fury of the winds and the drenching rain. Here, too, the storm is not a portent of future evil, but a directly hostile force, which aggravates the torments of him who is driven to madness by the inhuman cruelty of his two daughters. Lear is aware of this, and in the stormy elements he sees —

> Servile ministers,
> That have with two pernicious daughters join'd
> Your high-engender'd battles 'gainst a head
> So old and white as this. O! O! 'tis foul!
>
> III. ii. 20.

In *Macbeth* storm reigns supreme. Thunder and lightning are the fitting accompaniments of the witches whenever they make their appearance, while, as in *Julius Cæsar*, murder is portended by a night of elemental fury:

> *Lennox.* The night has been unruly: where we lay,
> Our chimneys were blown down, and, as they say,

Lamentings heard i' the air, strange screams of death,
And prophesying with accents terrible
Of dire combustion and confused events
New hatch'd to the woful time: the obscure bird
Clamour'd the livelong night: some say, the earth
Was feverous and did shake.   II. iii. 50—57.

The sea-tempest of *Othello,* while it has an equally direct
bearing upon the main action, is introduced somewhat differently.
It does not occur at the time of the murder of Desdemona,
but on the occasion of the voyage to Cyprus. Placed thus,
its purpose is still the same, namely, to presage the strife and
tragic gloom which are to follow. There lurks irony in the
halcyon calm which greets Duncan on his arrival at Macbeth's
castle, but here Nature is harshly sincere. Shakespeare does
not waste words over the description: the picture is outlined
with a few incisive strokes, each one of which is full of
meaning, while the magnificent hyperbole in which the storm
is described enhances the feeling of terror which the scene
evokes:

Sec. Gentleman. For do but stand upon the foaming shore,
    The chidden billow seems to pelt the clouds;
    The wind-shaked surge, with high and monstrous mane,
    Seems to cast water on the burning bear,
    And quench the guards of the ever-fixed pole:
    I never did like molestation view
    On the enchafed flood.   II. i. 11—17.

There is extremely little painting of natural scenery in
Hamlet, whether it be introduced objectively, in simile, or
with the purpose of making the forces of Nature bear upon
human life. Yet the atmosphere of the play is brought before
the mind of the reader as surely as in *Macbeth.* He breathes
everywhere the "nipping and eager air" of a northern
clime, where everything is as far as possible removed from
the translucent loveliness of the Italian scenery of *Romeo
and Juliet.* It is, too, in accordance with the settled gloom
of this tragedy, that several of the most impressive scenes
are enacted by night. The ghost of the murdered king walks
at midnight; at cock-crow, when "the glow-worm 'gins to pale
his ineffectual fire", it is warned to depart; and when —

the morn, in russet mantle clad,
Walks o'er the dew of yon high eastern hill, —

it has vanished entirely. The crisis of the play, when an opportunity is given Hamlet of slaying Claudius at his prayers, also takes place at midnight, and it is evident that the saturnine humour of the Danish prince finds a sense of grim pleasure in the suggestions of the midnight season:

'Tis now the very witching time of night,
When churchyards yawn, and hell itself breathes out
Contagion to this world: now could I drink hot blood,
And do such bitter business as the day
Would quake to look on.   III. ii. 371.

The Romances.

In his last plays Shakespeare brings his readers back once more to those gentler aspects of Nature which had been prominent in the comedies, but which, in the long succession of tragedies, had yielded place to storm and turmoil. In these last plays, as in *As You Like It*, the scene of action is often removed from the sophisticated life of courts and cities to the genial influences of the country. Stormy winds and raging seas are found in *Pericles* and *The Tempest*, but these are exchanged for calm and sunshine long before the end is reached. These plays are also very rich in lyrics, many of which, like the breath of Sir Thomas Overbury's fair and happy milkmaid, "scent all the year long of June, like a new-made haycock". Of such a character is Autolycus's song in the *Winter's Tale*, "When daffodils begin to peer"; the exquisite "Hark, hark! the lark at heaven's gate sings" of *Cymbeline;* and the songs of Ariel and Iris in *The Tempest*.

In *Cymbeline*, much of the action is laid among the montainous districts of South Wales, where the king's sons appear as primitive Nature-worshippers, living in utter ignorance of the civilised life of courts, and yet developing into perfect manhood. In these last plays it would seem as though Shakespeare endeavoured to illustrate the idea, which at a later period was uppermost in the mind of Rousseau, that the truest form of princely education is that which can be obtained

through absolute retirement from the court, and through
contact with simple country life and the genial influences
of Nature. Such is the training of Perdita and Miranda, and
of the two sons of Cymbeline. In Guiderius and Arviragus
there is found strong manliness wedded to tenderness, while
the purity and moral strength of their characters stand out
in bold relief when these young princes are placed side by
side with the court-bred Cloten. This firmly rooted idea of
the dignity of a country life, as well as of the educative value
of such a life, lived far away from court influences and in
direct communion with Nature, was doubtless brought home
to Shakespeare by his own experience. The country had
spoken eloquently to him through the whole period of his
London life, and now the busy turmoil of the city and the
actor's career was soon to be superseded by the idyllic repose of the last years in the old Stratford home.

It is hardly necessary, at the close of this chapter, to
say anything more concerning Shakespeare's interpretation
of Nature. It would not be difficult to prove that he was
the greatest naturalist of his time, but in view of his greatness in other and higher spheres, it would scarcely be pro-
fitable. It is not only the fidelity and penetration of his
insight into Nature which appeal to the reader, but also his
recognition of the poetry of the natural world. It is difficult
to overestimate the element of romantic beauty which his
landscape painting contributes to such comedies as *A Midsummer Night's Dream* or *As You Like It*, or to the snatches
of matchless song which are found throughout his works.
The rural associations of Shakespeare's boyhood live on in
the dramas of his maturity, and contribute as much to their
poetic charm as any of the associations gathered by him in
later life. Yet the greatness of Shakespeare's interpretation
of Nature lies not so much in the objective delineation of
landscape as in the recognition of the sympathy which exists
between Nature and man. Chaucer, Spenser, and others of
lesser fame had mastered something of the art of painting
a landscape in words, but Shakespeare alone knew what
subtle interplay subsisted between the varying moods of

Nature and the varying moods of man. To enhance the idyllic repose which men and women experience, after a great strain has been removed from them, by placing them in the midst of a scene of serene moonlight beauty; or again, to intensify the tempestuousness of the aged Lear's passion by exposing him to the wild fury of the storm on the heath — this was the high art of Shakespeare, and in this the greatness of his interpretation of Nature mainly consists.

INDEX.